JAN 17 78

'88 - 242104

Bill

AFFLUENCE AND ANXIETY, 1945-PRESENT

Demo

AFFLUENCE and ANXIETY

1945
PRESENT

CARL N. DEGLER
Stanford University

David M. Potter, Carl N. Degler, Editors
American History Series

Scott, Foresman and Company

To my mother

FOREWORD   This book is the seventh title in a series of eight (to be offered alternatively in two large volumes) that will encompass the history of the United States from the first explorations and settlements to the present. Together the series will constitute in general coverage and time span the kind of work that students usually employ as a textbook for a college survey course in American history. Both this book and the series as a whole, however, are intended to be different from the material covered in the usual survey text.

Customarily, a textbook is largely filled with a chronological account of the "essential" facts of the past. Facts and chronology are, it is true, the building stones of historical knowledge, and familiarity with both is essential, but they do not provide the structure of the past by themselves. Rather, it is the framework of an era that the student must grasp if he is to retain and make sense out of the myriad facts that any book—text or other—throws in his path. By framework, however, we are not suggesting a skeleton or outline but the unity or essential thrust of the period—in short, its meaning.

Emphasis falls throughout upon explanation of the past. Why did events turn out as they did? What significance did these developments have for subsequent American history? What importance do they have for the present? How does the American experience compare with that of other countries in similar circumstances? How and why did American attitudes and values alter during the period in question?

The organization and some of the less important facts that are to be found in more conventional textbooks are absent from these pages. It is the conviction of the author and the editors of the series that understanding the relationship among events is more important than just memorizing customarily agreed-upon facts. Therefore, some facts have been omitted simply because they do not contribute to an understanding of the structure of the period.

This book has been written for American college students; that is, readers who have some acquaintance with the history of the United States. While the usual effort has been made to clarify and define obscure or unfamiliar terms and persons, a certain basic familiarity with the subject has been taken for granted. No student who has passed successfully through an American high school need worry about his ability to comprehend what appears within these covers, but it is hoped that his understanding of the direction and the causes behind the movements of American history will be enhanced by reading this book.

David M. Potter
Carl N. Degler

PREFACE

For a historian to attempt to write a short interpretative history of the last quarter century is a risky business at best. Few specialized studies have yet been written on which he can base his generalizations. Moreover, the events are still so fresh in mind that they cannot easily be separated from the events of yesterday. Indeed, the fact that the author actually lived through the period makes it difficult for him to achieve that detachment which traditionally strengthens the historian as he seeks to re-create the essential past out of the infinite number of facts of the past. And if writing recent history is risky, to attempt to discern meaning is doubly so; yet this book attempts to do just that. Like other volumes in the series, it seeks to provide in short compass some understanding of the period it covers—in this instance the quarter century since 1945—by organizing the myriad events of those years around a few central themes. Those themes, in this instance, are the great prosperity within the United States and the threat of world war from without.

Since this book is intended primarily, though hopefully not exclusively, for college students, much of the history it contains is as unknown to its readers directly as events of the nineteenth century. For that reason essential factual information has been provided in some detail. At the same time, it is equally important that the reader not be inundated with facts and events. Consequently, the book provides an understanding of the direction and thrust of the period, rather than a recital of people and events.

Aside from seeing the events of the period as manifestations of affluence and anxiety, the book takes two approaches that are worth emphasizing here at the outset. One of the revolutionary changes occurring after 1945 was the involvement of the United States with the rest of the world as never before in its history. As a result, this book allots as large a place to foreign affairs as to domestic history. Chapters on international affairs alternate with those on domestic matters. No longer is it possible to tuck away foreign affairs into a chapter at the end, as is often done in books on earlier periods of American history. In this book the Asian revolution of the 1940's is properly as much a part of United States history as the election of Harry Truman.

The second approach that differentiates this book is the effort made in Chapter Five to view recent American cultural, intellectual and social history as expressions of the two great influences of the years since 1945. Not everything in the wide spectrum of cultural achievement can be included, but it is hoped that there is enough to allow the reader to gain not only an adequate factual knowledge of the social and cultural developments but also an integrated understanding of the relationship between them and the political and economic history.

Undoubtedly some of the interpretations or meanings that I see now in the last quarter century will prove to be wrong or, more likely, simply irrelevant when viewed from a greater perspective, say, twenty-five years from now. But all history changes as our perspectives and insights alter. Meanwhile, this brief attempt at seeing the central thrust of our times may provide some temporary guidelines to understanding.

I would like here to acknowledge my gratitude to those who have helped me in bringing this volume to completion. First, I gratefully recognize once again my deep indebtedness to my colleague and fellow editor in this series, David M. Potter, who has given most generously of his time and incisive counsel. Another colleague in this series, Thomas C. Cochran, has read the manuscript with care and insight, providing not only valuable comments but what is perhaps more important—disagreement with some of my interpretations. His influence on the final product may be less than he would have liked, but it is clearly discernible, and I, and the reader, are indebted to him. I am also genuinely grateful for the cooperation and care taken by my editors, present and former, at Scott, Foresman: Nancy Abel, Donna Ellefson, and William A. Frohlich. They saved me from both errors of fact and infelicities of style. I am also indebted, as always, to Catherine Grady Degler for her close and critical reading of the manuscript and her encouragement at crucial moments. To Mildred Tubby, who always managed to produce a clean and accurate copy within a remarkably short span of time, I owe more than thanks. To the Lucy Maynard Fund of Vassar College I am indebted for financial help in meeting the costs of typing. Stephanie Saunders earned my gratitude for her painstaking effort in checking the bibliographies. Despite the care and help provided by all of these people, I have undoubtedly committed errors of fact and interpretation; for these I am, of course, solely responsible.

Carl N. Degler

CONTENTS

AFFLUENCE AND ANXIETY, 1945-PRESENT

CHAPTER ONE

ADJUSTING TO A NEW ERA, 1945-1953

*I*N THE YEARS immediately after the Second World War, Americans were taken doubly by surprise. Having been highly successful in their global war effort, they confidently believed that the question of peace or war had been settled for the forseeable future. Had they not worked hard at home and fought bravely abroad to secure peace? Had they not committed themselves unprecedentedly and with almost complete unanimity to a new international organization designed to maintain that peace? Americans were no less certain about their domestic future, though here their optimism gave place to foreboding. They could not shake off the memory of the long, dispiriting Depression from which the nation had emerged only upon the onset of war. Most Americans, of both high and low station, were sure that the prosperity of the war years would not survive the slower economic pace of peace. Accordingly, they braced themselves for another depression.

As events turned out, they were wrong on both counts. In international affairs the nation was almost immediately plunged into a protracted period of agonizing decision-making amid constant danger of war while on the domestic front the prosperity born and nurtured in the hothouse of war took firm root and flourished. Never before in American history had the country been free of a major depression for as long as two decades. For these reasons the 20 years after World War II were, in truth, a period of affluence and anxiety.

The Breakup of the Grand Alliance

The Death of F.D.R. On April 12, 1945, as the Allied armies were knifing into the very vitals of what Hitler had called his "thousand-year Reich," Franklin Roosevelt died of a cerebral hemorrhage in his summer White House at Warm Springs, Georgia. For weeks his friends and intimates had been worried by the devastating physical effects of the severe burdens under which he was laboring, but his death surprised as well as saddened the entire Allied world. It not only saddened but stunned Harry S. Truman, who was now to assume the suddenly vacated office.

Four days after he was catapulted into office, the new President sat down and wrote a revealing letter to his mother and sister, telling them of his first few hours as President and of the demanding tasks that now confronted him. He had gotten an inkling that something was wrong in the afternoon of April 12, for as he entered the office of his old friend Speaker Sam Rayburn, he was told that Steve Early, the President's confidential secretary wanted to talk with him. Early told him to come to the White House "as quickly and as *quietly*" as possible. Truman literally ran all the way to his office in the Senate to tell his staff that he had been summoned to the White House and that no one was to be told about it. At the White House he was ushered quickly upstairs to Mrs. Roosevelt's study, where she put her arm around his shoulder and said, "Harry, the President is dead." Truman was staggered as never before in his life. "I had hurried to the White House to see the President," he wrote, "and when I arrived, I found I was the President." His most trying task, he went on, was addressing Congress three days later. It went off well, he thought, even though he still felt "almost as scared as I was Thursday when Mrs. R. told me what had happened. Maybe it will come out all right."

Seeds of Suspicion. Truman came to the intricate problems of international relations uninformed and unprepared. Since his inauguration as Vice-President over two months earlier, he had seen Roosevelt only twice in private, and at neither of these times nor in Cabinet meetings, Truman later recalled, had he been informed or consulted about the weighty foreign policy decisions then being taken or contemplated.

Already, the Grand Alliance which had won the war against Hitler was entering upon its dissolution. For several weeks before the death of F.D.R., Prime Minister Winston S. Churchill had been warning Roosevelt of the differences between the Soviet and Western conceptions of the Polish settlement agreed to at Yalta. As early as March, for example, Churchill was convinced that Stalin would not honor the agreement made at Yalta to permit all political factions to be represented in the new Polish government. Although Roosevelt opposed Churchill's suggestion that a strong protest be lodged with Stalin, on April 1, F.D.R. firmly informed the Russian dictator that the Yalta agreement on Poland could not be ignored by the Soviets. Roosevelt was firm in this instance, but basically he was determined, as he once said, to get along with the U.S.S.R. in the postwar period regardless of the difficulties. He was convinced that an enduring peace depended upon Western and Soviet amity. Churchill, on the other hand, was more narrowly nationalistic and European in his diplomacy; he thought in terms of spheres of influence and power politics. Consequently, he appeared more realistic than F.D.R. who, like the President he served under during World War I, emphasized international organization and trusted in the liberal belief that all nations want peace and order in the world. Roosevelt was convinced that he could cajole and charm the Russian dictator out of his admittedly xenophobic suspicions and that the basic interests of the West and the Soviet Union were the same. Since Roosevelt did not outlive the war, it is impossible to know whether he would have changed his mind about the long-term possibilities of amity with the Soviet state.

More important than speculations about Roosevelt's attitudes after 1945, however, is the question whether a different American policy than that which was followed could have avoided the Cold War, which, in fact did follow hard upon the cessation of the war against Hitler. In recent years several commentators and scholars like D. F. Fleming and William Appleman Williams have argued that the roots of the Cold War lay more in the actions of the United States than in those of the Soviet Union. Certainly it is true, as we shall see, that even before the war ended, some American leaders were fearful of the new power of the Soviet Union and deeply distrusted its Communist ideology. It is equally certain, as we shall also have occasion to notice, that there were acts of the United States that provided a basis for Russian anxieties about the intentions of the United States. Yet on balance the historical record, as we now have it, does not support the revisionists' basic contention that Russian actions were essentially defensive against the expressed hostility of the United States. Or, to put the matter another way, if Russian behavior were merely defensive, this defense was at the expense of the Germans in the Russian zone, and the peoples of eastern Europe and was a threat to the independence of the western European peoples. For, Communist ideology aside for the moment, the great fact of the postwar world was that Russian power had tipped the traditional balance of power in Europe, thereby threatening the continent and the world.

In any event, the new President, as events were soon to show, was more like Churchill than F.D.R. in dealing with the Soviet Union. In confronting what can only be described as Russian obstinance and arrogance, Truman's patience and flexibility were limited. The stiffness of his response to the Russians may well have arisen from his lack of self-confidence—a state of mind that never afflicted Roosevelt—in a job that clearly overawed him at first.

The First Signs of Rift. Even before F.D.R. died, Stalin had shown his displeasure over the refusal of the United States and Great Britain to accede to his demands for a pro-Russian Poland. Well aware of the importance Roosevelt attached to the United Nations as a part of the peace settlement, Stalin announced that Foreign Minister V. M. Molotov would be unable to attend the signing of the United Nations Charter in San Francisco in June 1945. Only after strong urging by the United States, and in deference to Roosevelt's memory, did Stalin finally agree to Molotov's attendance at the signing, but the petulant gesture had been made. The Americans, too, at this early stage, demonstrated their lack of sensitivity toward their wartime ally. On May 8, the day after the Germans surrendered, the Truman administration ordered all lend-lease shipments to the U.S.S.R. terminated, because the war was now over. The Russians were genuinely shocked; as recently as January 1945, Molotov had talked to American officials about the need for large-scale aid from the United States in order to restore his devastated country. Truman, concerned over the obviously deteriorating relations between the United States and Russia, at the end of May dispatched Harry Hopkins as special envoy to Moscow to talk with Stalin. As a result, lend-lease shipments were temporarily reinstated, but the unfriendly gesture—though apparently unintended as such—had been made. Historic Russian suspicions of outsiders, never very far beneath the surface anyway, as well as Communist suspicions of capitalist states, were aroused.

Suspicion, however, was not a Russian monopoly. Specific Soviet actions aside, American leaders were anxious about Russian intentions and ambitions in Europe even before the war ended. As early as April and May 1945, Secretary of the Navy James F. Forrestal and Ambassador to the U.S.S.R.

Averell Harriman were writing memoranda filled with misgivings and concern about the intrusion of a powerful Russia into the heart of Europe. Even Secretary of War Henry L. Stimson, who was inclined to grant the Russians the benefit of the doubt in the interest of working with them for a durable peace, was shocked by the repressive nature of Soviet rule as he saw it in action behind the Russian lines at Potsdam in July. He wondered whether any accommodation was possible with a regime so antithetical to Western democracy.

Indeed, it was at the Potsdam meeting of heads of government that the quite different conceptions of the future of Germany held by the Soviets and the West came out into the open—differences that would still not be resolved a generation later. Prior to the conference, the Russians had granted to the new Soviet-dominated Poland a slice of eastern Germany to make up for the territory which the U.S.S.R. had taken over from Poland in 1939. At Potsdam, Stalin insisted that this new German-Polish border along the Oder-Neisse rivers be accepted by the United States and Great Britain, declaring that no Germans remained in the territory. Neither the British nor Truman would accept this patent falsehood, and they argued that the principle of self-determination of peoples could not be so casually overthrown. The most the Western powers would concede was that the Oder-Neisse line could be temporarily accepted, with the final determination of the border to be left to the peace conference with Germany. They did acknowledge as final the claim of the U.S.S.R. to portions of East Prussia.

The interminable arguments over reparations also boiled down to a conflict over the future of Germany in Europe. At Yalta, Stalin had extracted agreement from the Western Allies that, in view of the devastation wrought by the German armies, the U.S.S.R. was entitled to reparations. At Potsdam, Stalin spoke up for a definite figure; he asked for $10 billion worth of German capital equipment. Well aware that the Russians were already taking whatever they could use at home from their occupation zone of Germany, the Western Allies were reluctant to commit themselves to the denuding of the rest of Germany, too. For days the three parties wrangled over reparations, with the Russians holding out for an absolute figure and the Americans insisting that a percentage of *surplus* equipment—i.e., equipment not needed for a peacetime German economy—should be made available for reparations. The Soviets obviously feared that if a percentage figure were used, the actual amount of reparations would depend upon how much German equipment was declared as surplus. The Americans and British, for their part, feared that, considering the battered state of the German economy, an absolute figure would reduce German economic capacity to such a low point that the United States and Great Britain would have to pour money into the country if Germany were ever to revive economically. The impasse was broken at the very end of the conference by the Russians' agreeing to accept 25 per cent of surplus German equipment in the western zones and whatever they could obtain from the eastern zone, which they occupied. Considering Stalin's suggestion at Yalta that 80 per cent of German industry be given as reparations, the final agreement was a real concession on his part.*

One further conclusion of the Potsdam meeting was that Germany should remain a political and economic unit, though temporarily divided into Russian, American, British, and French zones. A similar temporary division of Berlin was also made, though the city was located over a hundred miles inside the Soviet zone of Germany. The decision to seek a unified Germany was a triumph for the two extra-continental powers (Britain and the United States) which had least to fear from a revived Germany. France, though unrepresented at Potsdam, was as dissatisfied with the prospects of a united Germany as the U.S.S.R. For the first few years after the war, the French resisted any steps which seemed to further the Potsdam decision to unify Germany, even going so far as to veto the printing of common postage stamps for all four zones.

It was evident from Potsdam that the Soviets expected the Germans to underwrite the rehabilitation of the U.S.S.R.; the revival of the German economy was neither desired nor assisted by the Russians. The Americans and the British, on the other hand, by their insistence that reparations be taken only from surplus equipment, demonstrated that their principal concern was the rapid restoration of German economic life. These two opposing attitudes toward German recovery were but one manifestation of two quite different conceptions of Germany's place in Europe. In the conflict between these conceptions, as we shall see, lay the seeds of the Cold War.

The differences over the future of Germany, however, were only signs of a much broader divergence of interest between Russia and the West. There was the immense ideological difference between Communism as a totalitarian political system and the free societies of western Europe and the United States. At times in the minds of American leaders and certainly in the minds of the American public, this difference was understandably paramount. But there was also a historical difference, stemming from the special experience of Russia, irrespective of its Communist ideology. Throughout its history Russia, for all its great size, had been the object of foreign invaders; its long, open borders, devoid of natural defenses, were easily penetrated. From the east during the Middle Ages, for example, it had been overrun by the Mongols and occupied by them for two centuries; in more modern times it had been invaded from the west by Poland, Sweden, Napoleonic France, Imperial Germany, Poland again, and then Hitler's Germany. To the Czars, as to Stalin later, the great Russian defense had been space—retreat into the vastness of Russia itself during war and annexation or domination of surrounding territories when peace came. Thus, for all its vulnerability to outside

*It has been estimated that the Russians took about $12 billion in reparations from the eastern zone of Germany. To this total should be added a few factories in the western zones which were turned over to the Russians pursuant to the Potsdam agreement. All reparations to the Soviets from the western zones were halted permanently in the spring of 1946.

attack, Russia had been an expanding state ever since the sixteenth century. Through the centuries, its expansion into Europe had been held in check by equally powerful states like Poland, Austria, and Germany. With the destruction of German power in central Europe in 1945, Russian power flowed easily and, from Stalin's point of view, naturally into the vacuum. To the West, however, the thrust of Russia into the heart of Europe could appear only as a threat, not simply because of Russia's frankly hostile Communist ideology, but also because this thrust upset the historic balance of power on that continent. After all, Germany's overthrowing of that balance in 1939 had forged the Grand Alliance in the first place. As we shall see, it was the increasing signs of Russian—and Communist—expansion during 1946 and 1947, when no state in Europe was capable of resisting it, that kept a reluctant United States in Europe to restore the balance.

Further Strains on the Grand Alliance. During the remainder of 1945 and most of 1946, at the meetings of the U.N. and at the Council of Foreign Ministers (set up at Potsdam for the discussion of unfinished business), the differences between the Western Allies and the Soviet Union were a constant source of recrimination and ever-growing hostility. The Russians always seemed to be pushing for every advantage. One day they would demand a say in the operation of the industry in the Ruhr region of Germany; another day, control over former Italian colonies in North Africa; a third day, a part in the governing of conquered Japan.

In such a context, the Soviet refusal to honor its agreement to evacuate neighboring Iran seemed particularly ominous. During the war the Soviet Union and Great Britain, in order to keep the Germans from taking over the rich oil fields there, had divided the country between them, with the understanding that the troops of both parties would be withdrawn within six months after hostilities. March 2, 1946 was the end of the six months, but the Russian troops, instead of leaving (British troops had left on March 1), were actually working to set up a puppet regime in the north Iranian province of Azerbaijan. The United States vigorously protested this expansion of Russian power in violation of a recognized international agreement; Iran itself appealed to the U.N. The aroused opposition of world opinion finally forced the Soviets to withdraw their troops in late May.

Two months later, in early August, Russian pressure was felt by another Middle Eastern country bordering the Soviet Union. Turkey was asked to grant naval bases to its giant neighbor and to share its control over the Dardanelles. Small pieces of Turkish territory were also claimed. The Soviet Union appeared to be reassuming the old czarist ambition to control the exit from the Black Sea; to many knowing Western observers, historical Russian expansionism was on the march once again.

That same month, when two American transport planes were shot down over Communist Yugoslavia by Yugoslav fighter planes, Americans were thoroughly aroused over Communist truculence. Secretary of State James F.

Byrnes sent Marshal Tito, the dictator of Yugoslavia, an ultimatum to return the captured airmen or face an appeal to the U.N.; Tito complied.

By the early spring of 1946, Truman's suspicions and fears about Soviet intentions were publicly evident. In March he sat on the platform at Fulton, Missouri, while former Prime Minister Winston Churchill deplored "the iron curtain" which he said had "descended across the continent" from "Stettin in the Baltic to Trieste in the Adriatic. Behind that line lie all the capitals of the ancient states of central and eastern Europe" – under the increasing control of the Soviet Union. Churchill gave accurate voice to the worries of American leaders when he said, "Nobody knows what Soviet Russia and its Communist international organization intends to do in the immediate future, or what are the limits, if any, to their expansive and proselytizing tendencies." He called for a close alliance of the English-speaking peoples to combat Soviet expansionism.

At about the same time in the United Nations, the representatives of the Soviet Union turned down the American plan for international control of nuclear energy, largely because the plan would have required the Russians to acquiesce in the American monopoly at a time, as later events were to demonstrate, when Soviet scientists were feverishly working to perfect their own nuclear weapons. But once again, to American eyes, it seemed as if a generous gesture – that is, voluntarily giving up exclusive control over the tremendous power of nuclear fission – had been rebuffed by the secretive uncooperative Soviet state.

The German question, despite seemingly endless meetings of the Council of Foreign Ministers, remained unsettled and a constant source of Soviet-American mistrust. By the fall of 1946, Secretary of State James F. Byrnes, apparently convinced that the Soviet Union did not desire a settlement of the German question at all, moved to resolve the matter without the U.S.S.R. In a speech delivered before a group of German leaders in Stuttgart in September, he informed the Germans that it was the Russians who were preventing the emergence of a viable and united Germany. Then, in effect, he abandoned the drive for a united Germany by accepting its division in fact. Soon after, upon Byrnes' invitation, the British merged their zone with the American one; the French, still anxious over the implications of revived German power, did not merge their zone until 1949. But already, by the close of 1946, it was evident that a divided Germany was the explosive result of the inability of the West and the East to agree as to the place of Germany in postwar Europe.

The Beginning of the Cold War. Some historians have seen in Secretary Byrnes' speech at Stuttgart the beginning of what columnist Walter Lippman named the Cold War – that state of hostility between the superpowers which remained precariously poised just short of actual military engagement. With the Stuttgart speech and the decision to merge the western zones, a new era opened. From now on conquered Germany would be increasingly wooed by the West in the contest with the Soviets. Less than two years after the fall of

Berlin, the Grand Alliance was not only ruptured, but the Allies themselves seemed on the verge of war.

In looking back over that first year and a half of uneasy peace, it is hard to isolate the precise origins of the break. Certainly the pretensions of the Russians seem fantastic, and the very audacity of Stalin's numerous demands undoubtedly alarmed the Western leaders, who were not used to thinking of the Soviet Union as a European power and feared its dominance of Europe. Furthermore, they were deeply distrustful of Communist ideology and its potentiality for what Churchill called "proselytizing" and what a later day would call "subversion." During that year and a half the Russians demanded control of the Dardanelles, colonies in North Africa, territory from Turkey, the Italian city of Trieste for Communist Yugoslavia, oil concessions if not territory in Iran, huge reparations from western Germany, active participation in the industrial Ruhr region of western Germany, a large loan from the United States, and a share in the occupation of Japan. But it is important to recognize that almost none of these demands or threats bore the fruits the Soviets wanted. The U.S.S.R., it is true, did obtain reparations from eastern Germany, though precious little from the western part, and about $100 million from Italy and one third of the defunct German Navy; but all the other demands were resisted successfully by the West. Yet the very inability of the one-time Allies against Germany to look upon Europe and Russia's place in it with the same eyes made the Cold War a reality. The postwar adjustment abroad, then, was a cold war ever threatening to become hot. It was the primary source of American anxiety for the next 15 years.

Readjustment at Home

Harry S. Truman. As the great wartime alliance disintegrated and the problems of reconversion at home mounted, the man who headed the government of the United States seemed singularly ill-prepared for his momentous tasks. Born in 1884 in western Missouri, Harry Truman grew up on a farm, and, except for a few months in law school, he received no education beyond high school. A serious, even studious lad, he read much when a boy, if only because the glasses he wore seemed to preclude more active pastimes. As a young man he worked in a bank, ran the family farm for ten years, and upon the outbreak of war in 1917 entered the army as a captain in the artillery. After the war he tried his hand at running a haberdashery with an army buddy, only to have what promised to be a flourishing business go under in the little crash of 1921. For most of the 1920's and early 1930's, he was active in local politics in Jackson County, Missouri, where he supported the Kansas City political machine of Tom Pendergast. In 1934, with the permission of Pendergast, he ran successfully for the United States Senate. Truman was never well-to-do, and as late as 1940 he was too poor to be able to save his mother's home from foreclosure. As a senator Truman made a national reputation for himself by his diligent, honest, and important work during the war as head of a senatorial committee investigating the fulfillment of war contracts. Largely on the strength of the reputation he earned in that capacity, he received the nomination for Vice-President in 1944.

Personally, as he himself once said, "I look just like any other fifty people you meet in the street." Yet there was something more than ordinariness about him, as he was soon to demonstrate in the White House. Despite his limited background, he exhibited while President a remarkable talent for making quick, unambiguous, and generally sound decisions. His forthright, even naïve, outspokenness won him respect among his subordinates; his honesty and dignified sense of duty evoked the admiration of those who at first may have felt he was too unimpressive for the most awesome office in America. He could, it is true, be unduly irascible in public, and he was sometimes intensely loyal to those who were unworthy of such sentiment. Thus when he was Vice-President, he insisted upon attending the funeral of his corrupt former boss, Pendergast, despite the objections of his advisers, because he thought Pendergast had been a good friend.

His simple dignity and sense of humility in the big job at first won him the support of most Americans, who are always ready to sympathize with a man struggling to do his best against great difficulties. In the long run, however, he still had to prove himself. When, in the early months of his administration, the knotty problems he was called upon to unravel did not yield to easy solution, wits soon began poking fun at his inadequacies. "I wonder what Truman would do if he were alive?" was one of many jokes at his expense.

Although Truman retained the Roosevelt Cabinet for a while, he soon found his own men to take up the principal posts. The two most influential voices in his administration were those of James F. Byrnes of South Carolina, who became Secretary of State in June 1945, and Fred M. Vinson of Kentucky, who assumed the duties of Secretary of the Treasury that same summer. Henry A. Wallace, a holdover from the Roosevelt Cabinet, was compelled to resign as Secretary of Commerce in September 1946, after he had publicly criticized the foreign policy of the administration at the very time that Secretary Byrnes was in Europe carrying on particularly frustrating negotiations with the Russians. Wallace's sympathy for the Soviet Union would find further expression as the presidential candidate of the Progressive party during the campaign of 1948.

The Problems of Demobilization and Reconversion. Upon the surrender of the Japanese, the dismantling of the military might of the United States proceeded rapidly. On September 18, 1945, the President told the country that men were being returned to civilian life at the rate of 650 an hour, every hour of the day, every day of the week. By the first month of 1946, he promised, the rate would be up to 35,000 discharges a day. Although the rate reached the level that the President promised, Americans were still not satisfied. Early in January 1946 American soldiers rioted and demonstrated in

At military installations around the world in 1946, American GI's protested the delay in their return to civilian life. This one in Manila was one of the largest, but one of the more peaceful, demonstrations. *Photo: UPI*

Japan, France, India, Korea, and Germany, demanding an even faster rate of return home. Relatives at home were also putting pressure upon Congress and the White House toward the same end. Straining transportation and discharge facilities to the utmost, the government had released almost seven million men and women from the armed forces by April 1946. At the end of that year, the armed forces had been cut by more than 80 per cent from wartime strength.

The economic problems posed by the ending of the greatest war effort in American history were enormous. Factories that had been producing for the war now needed suddenly to be converted to peacetime production. The imminent cancellation of a large part of the $100 billion of annual wartime government expenditures presaged serious effects upon the economy. Within a month after Japan's surrender, $35 billion of war contracts were cancelled, and armament production was cut back 60 per cent. At war's end 10 million civilian workers were employed in war work, and another 12 million members of the labor force were in the armed services. As demobilization proceeded and war plants closed, millions of workers poured into the labor market seeking jobs. Within ten days of the Japanese capitulation, 2.7 million men and women were released from armament and other war production. In the light of these circumstances, it was quite realistic in the fall of 1945 to expect 10 to 12 million unemployed by the end of 1946. Indeed, as late as the end of 1946, 58 per cent of some 15,000 businessmen questioned confidentially by

Fortune magazine said that they thought a depression with large-scale unemployment would surely occur within a decade.

Yet at the same time that it looked as if the threat of depression was most pressing, other factors suggested that a runaway inflation was also possible. As a result of the war-born prosperity, property values, both urban and rural, had climbed over 40 per cent since 1939, and stock market prices were 80 per cent above the level of 1942. Such inflated values inevitably encouraged speculation and pushed up prices. Moreover, spending power, which had accumulated in the hands of consumers long unable to spend their money because of wartime shortages and controls, was tremendous. Liquid assets of individuals and corporations in 1944 totaled almost $200 billion; in 1920 at the end of the First World War, the figure had been only $45 billion. These inflationary pressures also acted, of course, as antidepression forces.

Another force acting to prevent a depression was the high level of government expenditures. In 1945 professional economists had confidently assumed that the annual federal budget after the war would not go above $25 billion. But, in point of fact, it never fell nearly that low. Indeed, it seldom went below $45 billion, and by the end of the 1950's the budgets were almost double that figure. For these reasons, despite the expectations of businessmen and economists alike, no postwar depression occurred.

The Eruption of Labor Unrest. During the war labor unions, which had taken a voluntary no-strike pledge for the duration of the conflict, generally lived up to their agreement, despite a 30 per cent rise in prices. Upon the conclusion of the war in Europe, however, workers became increasingly restless, and the number of strikes began to shoot upward. Once the war with Japan was over, the pressure for wage increases could no longer be contained. In the fall of 1945, a wave of strikes broke over the nation. Usually the demand was for a 30 per cent wage increase, by which workers sought to maintain wartime levels of income now that overtime pay was no longer likely. The rash of strikes spread alarmingly. In September over 4 million man-days were lost in strikes as compared with fewer than 1.5 million in April. In October the record of the previous month was more than doubled. The high point was reached in February 1946, when some 23 million man-days were lost because of strikes.

The President, though he conceded the justice of many of the demands for higher wages, was worried that the interruption of production would delay, if not endanger, a smooth transition to a peacetime economy. He exhorted both management and labor to seek peaceful solutions to their differences, but such appeals did nothing to halt the strikes or to induce employers to grant wage increases without strikes. Equally unsuccessful was the labor-management conference which the President hopefully called in November to discuss the insistent demands for wage increases.

Actually, the President sometimes seemed to encourage labor unrest. In a radio address to the nation at the end of October, for example, he pointed out

RECONVERTING THE ECONOMY

Three principal characteristics of the postwar economy were the increasing importance of 1) services, 2) government spending and employment, and 3) state and local government participation in the economy. Employment in both services and government has grown rapidly, more than doubling since 1945. Employment in manufacturing, however, has remained relatively stable. With consumer spending at an all-time high, spending by all levels of government reached 50 per cent of that total—a striking measure of the part government has played in sustaining the postwar prosperity. Although federal government spending dropped after the war, it has grown steadily since 1948. Even more impressive, however, has been the growth of state and local governmental spending. *Sources:* Bureau of Labor Statistics, *Employment and Earnings.* Bureau of the Census. Office of Business Economics, *Survey of Current Business.*

SHIFTING EMPLOYMENT

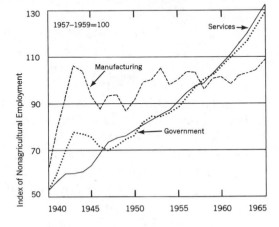

1957–1959=100

Services

Manufacturing

Government

Index of Nonagricultural Employment

1940　1945　1950　1955　1960　1965

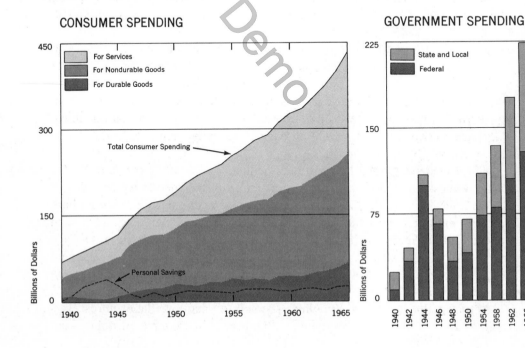

CONSUMER SPENDING

For Services
For Nondurable Goods
For Durable Goods

Total Consumer Spending

Personal Savings

Billions of Dollars

1940　1945　1950　1955　1960　1965

GOVERNMENT SPENDING

State and Local
Federal

Billions of Dollars

1940 1942 1944 1946 1948 1950 1954 1958 1962 1966

that, with the reduction in overtime pay, purchasing power might shrink by as much as $20 billion. As a consequence, he said, whenever company profits seemed to permit, higher wages were necessary in order "to sustain adequate purchasing power and to raise the national income." On the other hand in the same speech, he told employers that they must not expect any price increases, because inflation was also an ever present danger. The President, like the economy itself, seemed to be caught between the devil of inflation and the deep blue sea of depression.

The wave of strikes continued through most of 1946, with the number of workers out that year reaching 4.6 million, as compared with slightly less than 3.5 million in 1945. (Yet this postwar labor unrest was slighter than that after the First World War. The year 1919, the comparable postwar year after the First World War, witnessed over 4 million on strike, out of a considerably smaller total work force.) Although the number of men on strike diminished in 1947, the continuing rise in prices in subsequent years encouraged strikes. No sooner would an industry gain a wage increase than inflation would induce the unions to go out on strike again in an effort to keep up with prices. This pattern continued into the early fifties as inflation became the persistent tendency of the economy.

Returning to Economic Normalcy. As workers went out on strike in order to keep up with the rising cost of living, the government began to drop the economic controls which it had imposed during the war. The number of ration points on butter was reduced in July 1946. In August gasoline rationing was ended, and the death toll on the highways that month jumped 26 per cent over that for the same month in 1944. Shortly thereafter, new automobiles were taken off the ration list. In rapid fashion the other extreme wartime restrictions on the economy were removed, though price and wage controls remained. The nation was fast returning to its old ways. As after the First World War, what the people seemed to want was "normalcy."

One other sign of the desire for normalcy was the public clamor for tax relief. To win the war the government had spent $380 billion between 1940 and the close of 1945, about 40 per cent of which had been raised by taxes, a proportion unequaled in the history of American war financing. The administration, uncertain whether inflation or deflation would be the major problem of the postwar era, hesitated to alter the tax structure, but Congress and the nation were determined to cut taxes; to them the only question was how large the cut should be. When Secretary of the Treasury Vinson, responding to the public wish, recommended a small cut to Congress (it would have amounted to about $5 billion in 1946), he was greeted with open arms, for he was the first Secretary of the Treasury to propose a tax cut since the halcyon days of Andrew Mellon almost two decades earlier. The bill Congress wrote cut much deeper into revenues than Vinson had recommended. The Revenue Act of 1945, which the President signed in November, reduced individual and corporation taxes by $9 billion and, in an effort to stimulate business, repealed the wartime excess profits tax. All told, 12 million taxpayers, it was estimated, were removed from the tax rolls by the cut. It was not yet six months since the end of the war with Japan; normalcy was coming up fast.

Prices and Unions. Two big, unresolved issues harrassed the nation through most of 1946. One was prices and their control, and the other was the power of labor unions.

With the war over, price controls seemed to many much less justified than during the emergency. And it was true that with the incentive of war patriotism removed, many Americans refused to abide by government regulations on prices. The fight in Congress and in the press over price controls, which lasted through most of 1946, was certainly encouraged by political partisanship—but it was also more than that. It was, in reality, a continuation of the debate first begun in 1932 over the extent of the government's role in the economy. One group, largely composed of liberals, New Dealers, the administration, and northern, urban Democrats in Congress, insisted upon a continuation of government price controls in order to hold down prices for consumers until supply could catch up with demand. Their opponents, mainly businessmen and Republicans in and outside of Congress, contended that unless the incentive of price rises was restored—i.e., unless government controls were removed—supply would never be sufficiently stimulated to equal demand. The latter group, in short, wanted to leave the matter to private business and the market.

The history of the period gave some support to both sides. When in the summer of 1946 the President, by vetoing a price control law that was full of loopholes, allowed price controls to lapse entirely, prices rose 16 per cent within two weeks, just as the President had predicted. On the other hand, when controls were reinstated on meat, cattle raisers and packers kept their meat off the market, and the nation's consumers once more found it impossible legally to obtain a piece of good meat at a butcher shop. Illegal black market operations flourished; one survey showed that in the fall of 1946 more than 66 per cent of all meat sold was purchased from black market butchers. By late 1946 price controls were so strongly objected to and so ineffectually supported that, when the election returns in November showed a Republican victory, the administration abandoned virtually all controls over wages and prices.

The ending of controls, however, did not result immediately in either the elimination of shortages or the stabilization of prices. Shortages continued in a whole range of products, from butter and bacon to lumber and coal, from X-ray tubes, white shirts, and chewing gum to beer, washing machines, and toasters. The wartime earnings and savings of the American people, now suddenly released, gobbled up goods as they poured forth from the factories and salesrooms. Almost a year later in September 1947, prices were still breaking records, with butter selling for a dollar a pound and eggs for a dollar a dozen.

Rising prices did encourage a high rate of business activity. Department store sales in 1946 were 263 per cent above the 1936–1938 average, and obvious luxuries like phonograph records were being sold like penny candy; some seven million Decca records alone were sold in the first quarter of 1946. Reports even circulated that prosperous farmers in Nebraska and Oklahoma were buying light airplanes to travel to their widely separated farms. Employment was also up, along with prices. America was in the midst of a postwar boom of prodigious proportions. What surprised everybody was that it did not end in a grand bust.

The second pressing issue of 1946 was organized labor's power. Labor unions had grown greatly under the encouragement of New Deal labor legislation and wartime prosperity. But the power of national unions to disrupt the economy seriously did not become evident until several postwar strikes had taken place. During the steel, automobile, coal, and shipping strikes, all citizens, in one way or another, felt the great power labor could exert. (Actually, most of the strikes did not last long, since most of them were settled quickly with an 18.5 cent wage increase, following the pattern set by the General Motors strike in the winter of 1945–1946.) These big national strikes were provoking Congressional concern.

Congress was already considering a labor control bill introduced by Representative Francis Case of South Dakota, when the President, in early 1946, was compelled to deal with a national railroad stoppage. Some weeks before, in an effort to prevent the strike, Truman had ordered the government to assume operation of the railroads, but on May 23 the workers went out on strike anyway as planned. With all the railroads halted, the country was faced with the prospect of economic breakdown. Truman, choosing to see the strike as a blow against the government because of the nominal control it had been exercising over the roads, told the nation that "the crisis of Pearl Harbor was the result of action by a foreign enemy. The crisis tonight is caused by a group of men within our own country, who place their private interests above the welfare of the nation." The next day, in an atmosphere of mounting apprehension, he appeared before a joint session of Congress to ask for legislation that would permit him to draft all railroad workers into the Army. But even while he was speaking, the show of government power brought the strike to an end. Despite the ending of the strike, the House quickly passed Truman's labor draft by the overwhelming vote of 306 to 13. The Senate would not go along because conservative Republican Senator Robert A. Taft would have nothing to do with a measure which "offends not only the Constitution, but every basic principle for which the American Republic was established. Strikes cannot be prohibited without interfering with the basic freedom essential to our form of government."

Soon thereafter, however, Congress did pass the Case labor bill, but Truman vetoed it on the ground that its way of controlling nationwide strikes was basically antilabor and therefore conducive to further strife. His veto was sustained by the House. Yet the growing demand for some federal controls over labor unions did not die. It became a major issue in the 1946 Congressional elections, and more successful efforts to curb union power would be mounted in the next Congress.

Looking Backward and Forward. Despite the boom, the country could not yet forget the Depression, as the Employment Act of February 1946 made evident. Originally planned during the war years as a measure that would have committed the federal government to maintain full employment, the bill was pared down considerably as it passed through Congress. The provisions for mandatory government expenditures in times of depression were removed. Instead, a council of economic advisers was created to inform the President on economic matters, and the President was required to submit to Congress an annual report on the state of the economy. Despite the lack of any antidepression machinery in the act, the measure constituted a revolution in American political and social thought since the days of Herbert Hoover. It was now officially recognized that the government bore responsibility for checking on, if not maintaining, full employment. Never again would massive unemployment be viewed as beyond the legitimate power and action of the federal government. In that sense the Employment Act of 1946 was the last of the depression-born New Deal measures. Thereafter economic reform measures would be sparked by the recognition that affluence was characteristic of the American economy. This new approach would be most evident in the antipoverty measures of the Kennedy and Johnson administrations, when the principal justification for such measures was that an affluent society could not countenance poverty even among a minority of its citizens.

In marked contrast to the backward-glancing Employment Act, was the Atomic Energy Act of the same year. It looked to the future—an anxious future dark with the fearsome mushroom cloud. After much debate in Congress, the law placed exclusive control and development of nuclear energy in the hands of a civilian Atomic Energy Commission. For the first time in the history of the technological revolution that had begun over two centuries earlier, an American government assumed full responsibility for the regulation and development of a scientific innovation. The act also lodged in the President alone the power to decide on the use of nuclear weapons in war.

The Election of 1946. If Harry Truman and his administration, in carrying through the principles of the New Deal, thought of themselves as following the wishes of the people, the first postwar Congressional election soon showed how mistaken they were. In November 1946 a Republican Congress was returned for the first time since the election of 1928. The Republicans, capitalizing on the pervasive dissatisfaction with rising prices and strikes and the anxieties aroused by the Cold War, campaigned with the simple and effective slogan "Had enough?" The response of the voters was to award the Republicans a solid majority of 57 in the House and a small one of 6 in the Senate. Democratic losses were not only substantial, but some of the old stalwarts of the New Deal, like Senator Joseph Guffey of Pennsylvania, went down in defeat. Furthermore, 45 of the 128 House members who had voted to sustain Truman's veto of the antilabor Case bill failed to retain their seats. Despondent Democratic Senator William Fulbright even publicly suggested that Truman resign in favor of a Republican so that the country would be spared the handicap of a divided government.

Truman Versus the Eightieth Congress

Congressional Republicans. The new Congress, which convened in January 1947, rightly interpreted its election as a mandate to enact a substantial tax cut, to free business from government interference, and to pass legislation regulating the labor unions. The political outlook of the Republican party and its leaders in Congress was decidedly conservative. Many of its members had been waiting a long time to be in a position to reverse the social and economic trends set in motion by Franklin Roosevelt's New Deal. The intellectual as well as the political leader of the Republicans in Congress was Robert A. Taft, the senior senator from Ohio. The son of a former President, Taft had twice been brushed aside by his party in presidential nominating conventions, but he was still hopeful. Although in the context of the post-New Deal years Taft was generally denominated a conservative, a more accurate description would be nineteenth-century liberal. His single-handed killing of Truman's very popular move to draft striking railroad workers stemmed from his firm belief that the individual should be free from governmental regimentation. He did, however, support federal housing legislation and federal aid to education, on the grounds that a free society needs to care for the education and environment of its children. (Many years later President Eisenhower, often regarded as a more liberal Republican than Taft, admitted that he was not prepared to support such uses of federal power.) Taft's independence of mind was also evident in the blunt and impolitic statements he made, such as his advice in 1946 that those complaining of high food prices should "eat less." As chairman of the Senate Labor Committee, Taft was responsible for writing the labor legislation the country seemed to be waiting for.

The Taft-Hartley Act. Interest in a labor control bill was strong from the outset of the Eightieth Congress. On the very first day, 17 labor bills were dropped into the House hopper. Indeed, as the passage of the Smith-Connelly War Labor Disputes Act in 1943 and the Case bill in 1946 showed, Congressional sentiment for greater control over labor had been growing for some time. Moreover, the President himself, despite his favorable stance toward labor and his veto of the Case bill, encouraged Congress in his State of the Union message to consider some kind of labor-management legislation.

The labor bill that Fred Hartley of New Jersey introduced and that was passed in the House by an overwhelming vote was extremely restrictive of labor unions. The Democrats in Congress were, furthermore, incensed at the speed with which the bill was rushed through the Republican House. The Senate, however, under the guidance of the careful and principled Taft, was more deliberate, and its bill became, in effect, the final version. Working closely with southern Democrats, many of whom agreed with him on the need for curbs on labor unions, Taft succeeded in writing a bill that would be able to withstand a presidential veto and yet do the job its authors set for it.

As it was finally enacted, the Labor-Management Relations Act of 1947 listed a number of unfair labor practices of unions, much as the Wagner Act of 1935 had listed unfair labor practices of employers. Indeed, it was evident from the act that one of the authors' intentions was to equalize the advantages that labor had secured under the New Deal. Hence the act outlawed secondary boycotts (boycotts against an employer by a nonstriking union to help a striking union), the closed shop, (one which hired only union members) the checkoff (the collection of union dues by employers from pay envelopes), certain kinds of jurisdictional strikes, and featherbedding, (pay without performance of commensurate work). To cope with national emergency strikes, the President was empowered, regardless of the Norris-LaGuardia Anti-Injunction Act of 1932, to seek a court injunction and to proclaim a "cooling-off" period of up to 80 days. If the dispute was not settled at the end of that period, the last offer of the employer must be presented to a vote of the union members before the strike could be resumed.

In this last-offer provision, as in the requirement that all union leaders must legally attest that they were not Communists, the act revealed its authors' distrust of labor leaders. "The vote for the Taft-Hartley bill," Representative Hartley wrote later, "was not a vote against unions. It was a vote against the tactics of the *leaders* of union labor" and a "vote for the rank and file within the labor movement." The distrust that many businessmen felt for the New Deal's prolabor Wagner Act was also reflected in the provision creating the office of the General Counsel, separate from the National Labor Relations Board itself. In this way the Taft-Hartley Act gave credence to the charge of many employers that the Board under the Wagner Act acted as both prosecutor and judge.

In general it might be said that whereas the Wagner Act had placed the power of government behind the organizing of labor, the Taft-Hartley Act now shifted the emphasis to concern and protection for the man who did not want to join a union. Only in that sense was the act anti-union, for it did nothing to change the Wagner Act's basic assumption that labor unions and collective bargaining were desirable. The supporters of the bill, Hartley wrote, saw it as "the first step toward an official discouragement" of a trend which had "permitted and encouraged" labor "to grow into a monster supergovernment."

Leaders of labor and liberals in general opposed the bill during its passage through Congress, calling it a "slave labor" bill. In view of the large majorities that passed the bill originally, Truman had reason to fear that his veto might be overridden. Nonetheless, he sent the measure back to Congress with a stinging veto message, concluding "that the bill is a clear threat to the successful working of our democratic society." The House and then the Senate quickly passed the bill over his veto.

Despite the unremitting opposition of labor unions and Democratic presidential candidates and Presidents ever since, the Taft-Hartley Act has remained on the books without substantial change. The act seems to be in accord with what the American people wanted to see after a decade of prolabor legislation under the New Deal. The Taft-Hartley Act is unique in being the only piece of legislation in over 20 years that seriously altered a policy instituted by the New Deal.

The Drive for Tax Relief. Even before the conservative Republican Congress got around to labor legislation, it turned eagerly to tax reduction. H.R. 1, the first bill in the House that session, provided for a flat 20 per cent cut for all taxpayers with net incomes below $302,400. Liberal Democrats as well as administration leaders scornfully denounced such a windfall for the big taxpayer. The bill came "right out of the Andrew Mellon primer of special privilege," asserted one southern Democrat. When the Senate received the bill, it scaled down somewhat the cuts for the high income brackets, but the President vetoed the measure nonetheless, branding it as "the wrong kind of tax reduction, at the wrong time." In view of the inflationary pressures in the economy, he contended, the surplus should be used to pay off the debt rather than to cut taxes. Moreover, he pointed out, by offering a flat percentage cut for all income brackets, the bill, in effect, was offering more relief to high income recipients than to low. Truman's veto was only the second veto of a tax reduction bill in the nation's history. (Roosevelt's in 1944 was the first.) It was narrowly sustained in the House by two votes.

The Republicans, nevertheless, continued to push for a tax cut. In July, Truman vetoed a measure almost identical with the first one, but a third such bill, passed in December 1947, became law over his third veto. By that time, though, even the President was supporting a tax cut plan of his own because of the substantial surplus for the fiscal year 1947–1948. As a result, his opposition seemed less disinterested and convincing than earlier. The Revenue Act of 1948, when it became law that April, cut rates on all personal income taxes to the extent of some $6.5 billion. No changes were made in income tax rates for corporations.

The National Security Act. In domestic affairs the one other notable achievement of the Eightieth Congress was the attempt to unify the national defense establishment. For some time the executive had been trying to move in the direction of putting the Navy, Army, and Air Force under a single head. In February 1947 the administration sent a bill to Congress providing for the creation of a single Department of Defense. Immediately, the three services began to object to various features of this measure that seemed to place them at a disadvantage. As a result of their resistance, the act, as passed on July 25, provided for less centralized control than Truman's original bill, but it did set up a Department of Defense, composed of the three services under a single civilian head. A Joint Chiefs of Staff, composed of representatives from each of the services, was also created. Most important, the act placed procurement, research, and intelligence in the three services under central boards or agencies in an effort to eliminate duplication of effort. A National Security Council, including the Vice-President, the Director of Defense Mobilization, the Secretaries of State and of Defense, and the President, was created to coordinate foreign and defense policies. The first Secretary of Defense, James F. Forrestal, Roosevelt's and Truman's diligent and earnest Secretary of the Navy, was appointed on September 17, 1947.

The Democrats Stay In

If Harry Truman thought himself unworthy of, and unprepared for, the Presidency when he took office, by 1948 he was eager to show the country that he had learned much in the interim. Many of his party, though, especially the liberal New Deal wing, were not so pleased with him, and some even sought, unsuccessfully, to interest General Dwight D. Eisenhower, whose political affiliations were then unknown, in the Democratic nomination. Many other Democrats opposed Truman's nomination simply because they thought he could not win. But the President had the votes at the convention and was nominated on the first ballot, with Alben W. Barkley of Kentucky as his running mate. In his acceptance speech to the convention, Truman showed his mettle as a politician, announcing that he would call a special session of Congress that summer to challenge the Republican leadership to pass his program. When the Congress met and, as might have been anticipated, refused to do as Truman directed, the President was provided with a convenient whipping boy for the duration of the campaign.

Despite this advantage, Truman ran under severe handicaps. At the Democratic convention the party had been split by the insistence of northern urban liberals that a strong plank on behalf of civil rights for Negroes be put into the platform in accordance with the President's own strong message on the subject earlier in the year. Two days after the Democratic convention, a convention of States Rights Democrats, meeting in Birmingham, Alabama, nominated Strom Thurmond of South Carolina as its candidate. With strong support in Alabama, Mississippi, South Carolina, and Louisiana, the "Dixiecrats," as they were soon named, threatened to take away from Truman many traditionally Democratic votes in the South. Extreme left-wing liberals, Communists, and those Americans in general who thought the Truman foreign policy toward the Soviet Union was too intransigent found an advocate in Henry A. Wallace, Truman's former Secretary of Commerce, who now became the presidential candidate of the newly organized Progressive

During the campaign of 1948, Harry Truman traveled around the country by train, making frequent informal whistle-stop talks. Since 1960 candidates have relied entirely upon air travel and TV appearances to bring them into "personal" contact with the voters. *Photo: UPI*

party. Wallace campaigned on a platform of social reform and a conciliatory policy toward the Soviet Union, generally opposing all measures the United States had taken in foreign affairs since 1945.

The Great Surprise. After the resurgence of Republican strength in 1946, the return of the Republicans to the White House seemed assured, and Truman's personal and political liabilities only reinforced that assurance. Following an ineffectual attempt to nominate General Eisenhower, the Republicans turned again to Thomas E. Dewey, governor of New York, and the candidate of the party in 1944. Earl Warren, the popular governor of California was named as the vice-presidential candidate. Sure of his victory, desirous of arousing hostility from no one, and contemptuous of the man in the White House, Dewey spoke mainly of the need for national unity and attacked none of the reforms of the Democratic New Deal, though they were essentially Truman's platform. If intellectuals and radio and television commentators sometimes criticized Dewey's platitudinous and fireless campaign, they nevertheless conceded, along with the public opinion pollsters, that his election was certain.

Only Harry Truman, it seemed, was not convinced. Taking a cue from the enthusiastic response to a speech he delivered extemporaneously in April, the President embarked upon a highly informal speaking tour across the country, stopping his campaign train at any place a crowd could be gathered. At each stop he would launch into a freewheeling, impromptu attack on the Republicans, disdaining the aloof, statesmanlike delivery of Dewey. Again and again he castigated "that no-good" Eightieth Congress, blaming the legislation it enacted, such as the Taft-Hartley Act, or its failure to pass his own program, for the ills of the nation. The enthusiastic response of the crowds he entertained in this lively fashion spurred him on to further extravagant denunciations of Republicans at the next stop. "Those fellows," he shouted, referring to the Republicans, "are just a bunch of old mossbacks . . . gluttons of privilege . . . all set to do a hatchet job on the New Deal." Often he employed the timeworn rhetoric of class prejudice. "I warn you," he told one crowd, "if you let the Republicans get control of the government, you will be making America an economic colony of Wall Street." Even foreign policy was discussed in a homely fashion. In Oregon he told his audience, "I like old Uncle Joe Stalin. Joe is a decent fellow but he is the prisoner of the Politburo. The people who run the government won't let him be as decent as he would like to be." By the close of the campaign, a good part of the country had been given a one-man personal appearance show by the President of the United States. By his own count, Truman traveled some 32,000 miles and delivered 356 speeches, or about 10 a day, far exceeding the effort of his confident and younger opponent.

Election night in 1948 was at first mystifying and then electrifying. It was not completely unexpected that Truman should lead in the early returns, since his strength lay in the cities, which reported first. But as the night wore on, his initial lead was never lost, and sometimes it even grew. By the next morning the final vote was not yet in, but it was evident that Harry Truman would still be President. Great newspapers like the *Chicago Tribune* and respected commentators like H. V. Kaltenborn were hard to convince, but, just before noon of the next day, Dewey conceded that what Truman had said all along was going to happen had, in fact, happened. Even for those who had not voted for Truman, it was exhilarating and refreshing to have the voters turn the tables on the experts; Harry Truman never let the poll-takers forget their embarrassment of that night.

If on election day Truman's victory seemed a political miracle, a closer look brought forth some more plausible explanations. For one thing, the election was really very close: out of a popular vote of 50 million, Truman led Dewey by only 2 million. For another, Americans had not forgotten the Depression or the New Deal. It was evident that by associating himself with the social legislation of the New Deal, Truman drew the votes of those who had supported Roosevelt. In some respects he did better. By harping on the fall in farm prices and promising farmers the continuation of price supports, Truman recaptured the farm vote which Roosevelt had been unable to hold in 1940 and 1944. By taking the farm states of Iowa, Wisconsin, Ohio, Wyoming, and Colorado, all of which had been lost by F.D.R. in the two previous elections, Truman snatched victory from seemingly sure defeat. Moreover,

THE ELECTION OF 1948

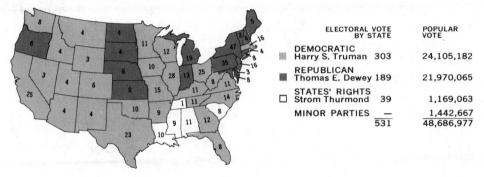

	ELECTORAL VOTE BY STATE	POPULAR VOTE
DEMOCRATIC Harry S. Truman	303	24,105,182
REPUBLICAN Thomas E. Dewey	189	21,970,065
STATES' RIGHTS Strom Thurmond	39	1,169,063
MINOR PARTIES	—	1,442,667
	531	48,686,977

with the war over, the Midwestern German vote, which had been drifting away from Roosevelt ever since 1940, returned to the Democrats. Finally, although the defection of the Dixiecrats cost Truman 39 electoral votes and four states in the Deep South, it simultaneously guaranteed him the urban Negro vote in the crucial industrial states of the North. That a Democrat should win the presidency even when the South was split was new evidence of the substantial gains the Democratic party had made in the nation since 1932; it had clearly replaced the Republicans as the dominant party in the country. Wallace's appeal, once thought to be fatal to Truman's chances for retaining the liberal vote, turned out to be slight and unimportant, though it may have helped to give New York to Dewey.

The Fair Deal. In his inaugural address Truman spoke of his program as the Fair Deal, defining it as an extension and codification, as it were, of the more famous New Deal. His program called for civil rights legislation, particularly a fair employment practices act to prohibit racial discrimination in jobs and an antilynching bill. He also urged upon Congress a national health program, aid for public education, and support for the construction of low-income housing. True to his pledge in the campaign, he advocated the repeal of the Taft-Hartley Act, but without success, despite his reiteration of the recommendation. His Secretary of Agriculture, Charles Brannan, a dynamic Coloradan, who was one of the few Cabinet officers to support Truman's candidacy actively in 1948, advanced a radical solution to the problem of farm surpluses, but also without success. The Brannan plan would have subsidized farmers while permitting farm prices to fall to natural, unsupported levels in order to allow food costs for urban consumers to drop. (A form of this plan was instituted under Lyndon B. Johnson almost 20 years later.)

Although Truman returned to the White House with a Democratic Congress, his program was only partly enacted. There were always enough conservative Democrats, usually from the South, to join with the Republicans to beat down his bills. The conservatives of both parties were sufficiently strong to prevent, for example, the passage of any civil rights measures during the whole four years. It would require the Negro revolution of the 1950's to bring home to both the Democratic party and the nation how overdue such legislation was.

Truman did, however, succeed in obtaining a housing act in 1949, thanks to the collaboration of Senator Robert Taft, the Republican leader; moreover, the minimum wage was raised to 75 cents an hour to compensate for the continuing inflation. In 1950 the Social Security Act was significantly broadened in its coverage for the first time since enactment 15 years before. Some ten million persons, largely self-employed people hitherto not covered by the act, were now included in its provisions. (Farmers, agricultural workers, and domestic servants still remained outside the social security system.) Some reorganization of the executive branch was also undertaken after Herbert Hoover, upon the request of the President, submitted a report suggesting ways to increase the efficiency of the government. Most of the changes that Truman recommended, pursuant to the Hoover Report, were accepted by Congress.

During 1949, for the first time since the 1930's, the economy slid into a slump, with some four million unemployed by early summer. The recession was of short duration, for by the fall an upturn was already in sight; the massive unemployment, which was so feared after the experience of the 1930's, never materialized. Despite the recession, however, prices continued to rise.

Mink Coats and Deep Freezers. After 1949 Truman was increasingly plagued by revelations of corruption in his administration. The Republicans endeavored to inflate some of the accounts that were coming out of Congressional investigations in 1949 and 1950 into Democratic Teapot Dome scandals, but the examples of corruption were more often petty, isolated acts than indications of widespread, if hidden, malfeasance. More than petty or isolated, however, were the forced resignations of 4 collectors and 31 other officials in the Bureau of Internal Revenue because of irregularities in the conduct of their offices. Occasionally the scent of corruption came close to home, as when Colonel Harry Vaughn, the President's friend and personal aide, was shown to have accepted a deep freezer from a man having business with the government. In 1951 the Democratic National Chairman himself resigned after being charged by a Congressional inquiry with "selling" influence. Although no serious scandals were ever found, the sporadic acts of corruption gave some substance to Republican charges that the Democrats were becoming careless as a result of being too long in control of the executive branch of the government.

Fair Deal and New Deal. As Harry Truman himself acknowledged, the Fair Deal was an attempt to extend the principles of Franklin Roosevelt's New Deal into a new era. It appealed to the same social groups—industrial workers, ethnic minorities, and farmers—who had been the mainstay of the early Roosevelt coalition. Moreover, like the New Deal, it relied upon the federal government for the achievement of its ends, thus continuing the trend toward centralization begun at the opening of the century with Theodore Roosevelt. On the other hand, in some respects it went beyond the New Deal, as in the field of civil rights, where Truman assumed a more courageous and forthright position than Roosevelt ever had. It might also be said that Truman's vigorous support of organized labor was equally in marked contrast to Roosevelt's more cautious, even at times patronizing, approach.

The men around Truman, though, were several cuts below those who, like Harold Ickes, Harry Hopkins, Rexford Tugwell, Tom Corcoran, and Thurmond Arnold, helped make the New Deal one of the most intellectually exciting political movements in all American history. (Only the Kennedy administration would rival it.) The only member of Truman's immediate political family (below the Cabinet level) who even approached the caliber of the New Dealers was Clark Clifford, one of Truman's White House aides. Clifford was a young, personable, and talented lawyer from St. Louis who masterminded the campaign of 1948. Clifford went back to private practice in January 1950. In the mid-1960's he would reappear as an adviser to Lyndon B. Johnson, and in 1968 he became Johnson's Secretary of Defense.

The Revolution in Foreign Policy, 1947–1948

At the same time that the Truman administration was wrestling with the complicated problems of a domestic adjustment to peacetime, it was called upon to confront a dangerously deteriorating situation in Europe and in the world balance of power. The administration's response to this fact constituted nothing less than a revolution in American foreign policy. Although the roots of that revolution ran back to 1945 and 1946 when difficulties with the Russians had first become apparent, it was catapulted into public view by more immediate events during the early months of 1947.

The European Economic Crisis of 1947. While the United States fruitlessly sought to settle the political state of Europe through peace treaties and conferences, the economy of western Europe labored to recover from the war. Production limped and restoration lagged. Even loans from America did not seem to help, for the $3.75 billion loan made to Britain in 1946 was already fast running out. Intended to last the British for four years, the funds instead would be exhausted in a year and a half. Of all the countries of western Europe, Britain, aside from Germany, was probably the worst off, because it was so heavily dependent upon imports. Some 42 per cent of British food and raw materials came from dollar-area countries, yet only 14 per cent of British exports went to those same areas. As a consequence, Britain was running a constant deficit in dollars as it endeavored to keep its people alive. This dollar gap existed to some degree in all the countries of western Europe, for all of them depended upon American imports for a significant portion of their food and equipment.

The struggle of the British people to survive attracted world attention in January 1947, when the worst blizzard since 1894 swept down upon the island, adding new misery to old. Hundreds of villages and towns were completely isolated as telephone and telegraph lines broke and roads became choked by snow and ice. The digging of coal was halted because either the miners could not get to the mines or trucks and trains could not move to haul away what coal was brought up. Without fuel, railroads and factories gradually came to a standstill. The production of electricity fell off, and for a number of weeks the British government reimposed the blackout in an effort to conserve fuel and power. It took four months for production to regain the level of December 1946. One authority estimated that $800 million of precious exports, which could never be made up, were lost because of the blizzard.

That savage winter hurt all the countries of western Europe. Starvation stalked the streets in dozens of villages and cities. In France the winter destroyed 3.5 million acres of winter wheat—a blow that came on top of the shortages caused by the drought during the previous summer.

The winter by itself, of course, did not cause the economic plight of Europe; the economic sickness was deeper than that. But the devastating effects of the weather brought the economic malaise of Europe to the attention of the dullest observer.

The Truman Doctrine. The most immediate result of the economic crisis was the decision by the British government to abandon its efforts to support the government of Greece in its war against Communist-supported guerrillas. Toward the end of February 1947, the British government quietly informed the United States that, as of April 1 of that year, the traditional British interests in Greece and Turkey were to be abandoned in the face of diminishing dollar reserves.

Almost immediately President Truman and Secretary of State George C. Marshall, who had succeeded James F. Byrnes in January 1947, called Congressional leaders to a secret meeting in the White House to discuss the British action. Marshall and Undersecretary of State Dean Acheson briefed the Congressional leaders of both parties on the gravity of the situation in the Middle East should British power be withdrawn. Even the best informed congressmen had had no inkling of how close the British government was to abandoning its traditional role as a stabilizing influence in the eastern Mediterranean. After Truman told the meeting that he thought the United States should take up the British position in the strategic area by offering aid to Greece and Turkey, Republican Senator Arthur H. Vandenberg, chairman of the important Foreign Relations Committee, remarked, "Mr. President, if that's what you want, there's only one way to get it. That is to make a personal appearance before Congress and scare hell out of the country."

On March 12 Truman did as Vandenberg advised. He appeared before a joint session of Congress to ask for $400 million in immediate economic and military aid for Greece and Turkey. "We shall not realize our objectives" of peace and order in the world, he told Congress and the American people, "unless we are willing to help free institutions and their national integrity against aggressive movements that seek to impose upon them totalitarian regimes. This is no more than a frank recognition that totalitarian regimes imposed on free peoples, by direct or indirect aggression, undermine the foundations of international peace and hence the security of the United States." The speech, received with great solemnity by Congress, aroused much discussion throughout the country. Vociferous and often strident opposition came from conservatives and left-wing liberals in an unusual and uneasy display of agreement. Everybody recognized that the policy meant a sharp departure from the whole history of American foreign relations. The United States, for the first time in peace, was being asked to commit its military (though that was deliberately underplayed in the President's message) and economic strength to the defense of countries outside the Western Hemisphere. Congress placed its sanction upon this historic turn in policy when the Senate in April, and then the House in May, voted the emergency funds asked for by the President.

In his eagerness to win Congressional and popular approval for the new policy, President Truman virtually ignored the United Nations, mainly on the grounds that the U.N. was in no position to offer aid and, perhaps more important, because the Soviet veto might well have prevented any action at all. Senator Vandenberg and others outside government, though, could not accept a policy that seemed to by-pass the United Nations. Public opinion polls, for instance, reported that a majority of the American people were displeased with Truman's ignoring the U.N. The administration rectified what Vandenberg referred to as its "colossal blunder" by accepting the Senator's amendment to the aid bill. Vandenberg's amendment provided that American aid to Greece and Turkey would be terminated if and when the U.N.—freed by prior agreement from the threat of an American veto—should vote that it deemed such aid unnecessary or undesirable.

The Crisis Deepens. Even as Congress debated the emergency aid to Greece and Turkey, it was clear to knowing people that the plight of Europe was so serious that the less than half a billion dollars which the President asked for in behalf of Greece and Turkey was no more than a palliative. Walter Lippmann, the noted newspaper commentator, for example, on April 5 warned that only massive aid, along the lines of the old lend-lease arrangements, would be able to stem the ominous decline of the European economy. When Secretary Marshall returned from an exhausting and fruitless foreign ministers' conference in Moscow in late April, he told the country: "The recovery of Europe has been far slower than had been expected. Disintegrating forces are becoming evident. The patient is sinking while the doctors deliberate." The very next day he asked George F. Kennan, an expert on Russia and the head of the Policy Planning Section of the State Department, to draw up recommendations for preventing the economic collapse of Europe.* In May, as disturbing reports of actual starvation came from Europe, the United States rushed grain to Germany, where individual rations had sunk as low as 800 calories per day.

While Kennan and his staff worked behind the walls of the State Department on a plan for European aid, Marshall prepared to broach his revolutionary idea to the people of the United States and to the world. He presented his plan, which ever after has been called by his name, in a short commencement address at Harvard University on June 5, 1947. Abandoning the strong ideological tone of anti-Communism that suffused the Truman Doctrine, Marshall based his offer on considerations of human need. "Our policy," he said, "is not directed against any country or doctrine, but against hunger, poverty, desperation and chaos." But whatever assistance is given, he emphasized, must "not be on a piecemeal basis as various crises develop. Any assistance that this Government may render in the future should provide a cure rather than a mere palliative." He was also careful to make it clear that he was not excluding the Soviet Union and the states of eastern Europe from the offer.

Within hours after Marshall had finished speaking, Foreign Minister Ernest Bevin of Great Britain, contrary to his own recollections two years later, was already reading the address, a copy of which had been sent directly to him. Bevin, as he remarked later, "seized the offer with both hands." Within 22 days after Marshall concluded his address, the representatives of most of the countries of western and central Europe were assembling in Paris to discuss the carrying out of his idea.

The Marshall Plan. As worked out by the administration, the offer that Marshall extended to Europe in June turned out to be a bold experiment in containing Communism by eliminating the poverty and misery on which it fed. The heart of the experiment was an American grant of $17 billion to European countries, spread over a period of four years, with $6.8 billion of that figure to be expended in the 15 months following April 1, 1948. The figures had been arrived at by the administration as a result of discussions with, and studies of, the 16 participating nations, all of which were located west of the iron curtain. (The U.S.S.R., after some hesitation, had finally refused to have anything to do with the offer and required its satellites and its neighbors like Czechoslovakia, which was interested, to stay away from the discussions.)

The very boldness of the administration's bill, not to mention its expense, made it suspect among many people in the United States. Senator Vandenberg, who became an ardent champion of the plan in the Republican-controlled Senate, had to fight hard to overcome the suspicion in Congress. In present-

*Kennan had been thinking about the problem of Russian expansionism for some time. His conclusions became the primary justification for what was later called the policy of containment. Kennan argued that if Russian expansionist tendencies were firmly resisted, developments inside the Soviet Union would, in time, reduce the pressure for expansion, thus rendering the Communists more cooperative in international affairs. His first public statement on containment—earlier ones circulated privately in the government—appeared anonymously in the magazine *Foreign Affairs* in July 1947. Later, the same statement appeared in his book *American Diplomacy, 1900–1950* (Chicago, 1951).

ing the bill to the Senate in December 1947, he called it "a calculated risk" to "help stop World War III before it starts." Within the purview of this plan, he told his colleagues, "are 270,000,000 people of the stock which has largely made America. . . . This vast friendly segment of the earth must not collapse. The iron curtain must not come to the rims [*sic*] of the Atlantic either by aggression or by default." Tirelessly, he defended the plan against the charge, usually from his conservative, economy-minded Republican colleagues, that it was a gigantic "international WPA," "a bold Socialist blueprint," or a plain waste of American money.

While Congress was holding hearings on the European aid bill that fall, Europe was sinking deeper into the economic abyss. The British, in a desperate effort to reduce imports, cut each person's meat ration to 20 cents worth *per week*. In September, President Truman urged Americans not to waste any food, for Europe needed all that could be spared. A few days later he urged Congress to consider immediate stop-gap aid of $580 million to prevent starvation in Europe in the coming winter. In October he called upon Americans to observe meatless Tuesdays and eggless Thursdays in an effort to conserve grain for Europe. (Cattle and poultry were heavy consumers of grain.) At his request liquor distillers agreed to a 60-day shutdown in a further effort to save grain.

The Consummation of the Revolution. If the effects of the winter of 1946–1947 left some Americans still unconvinced of the need to help Europe, they could not remain so in the face of the unremitting pressure of the Communists. In February 1948 Communist workers' groups suddenly took over the government of Czechoslovakia. Thus the country in central Europe, whose government most Americans considered closest to their own form of democracy, slipped behind the iron curtain. Nor was it any comfort to know that the largest political parties in France and Italy were Communist, that these parties slavishly supported the foreign policy of the Soviet Union, and that they were influential in the labor unions. Soon after the Czech coup the administration received word from the usually calm American commander in Berlin that he had reason to believe that a Russian attack upon western Europe was imminent. As a result on March 17, the President spoke before Congress and to the country via radio, pointedly identifying the U.S.S.R. as the "one nation" obstructing peace and threatening the non-Communist world. He urged Congress not to put off enacting the European Recovery bill, universal military training, and a temporary reinstatement of the draft. Soviet pressure continued to mount. On March 21 and April 1, the Russians placed restrictions on troops and supplies going across their zone of Germany to Allied stations in Berlin. The Berlin blockade did not start in earnest for another two months, but already the intimations were being felt. On April 2 Congress passed the European Recovery bill, granting the President about 90 per cent of the funds he had asked for the first year but refusing to commit itself for any longer period.

The Significance of the European Recovery Program. In speaking about the Marshall Plan in later years, American statesmen sometimes portrayed it as a remarkably unsordid act, welling up from the deep generosity of the American people. As we have seen, however, that description does not really fit the facts. Americans conceived and carried out the ERP primarily because it promised to promote the security of the United States. Yet it is true that the European Recovery Program was more than simply a means of containing Russian Communism. It was an adventurous act on the part of the American people to deal vigorously, at substantial cost to themselves, with a large and complicated problem. The $12.5 billion that was given to the 16 participating countries between April 1948 and June 1951 was more than a means of putting the western European economy on its feet; it was part of a deliberate design to bring the economy of western Europe up to date and to encourage the introduction of new machines, new methods, and new approaches. Only through such a fundamental overhauling, it was decided, could production reach a level adequate to maintain the inhabitants of western Europe at a decent standard of living.

Probably at no other time, except during the war years, has American influence been so directly and deeply felt in Europe as it was in the years of the ERP. American experts and advisers swarmed across 16 countries,

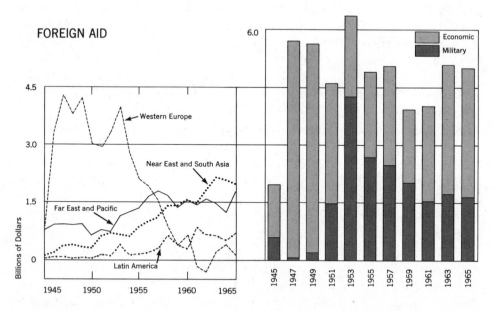

American foreign aid has shifted from economic aid to Western Europe to a mixture of economic and military aid, almost none of which goes to Western Europe. Most U.S. aid in 1965 went to Asia. Aid to Latin America, although still a small percentage of the total, has grown steadily, especially after the Alliance for Progress was formed. After the Korean War began, military aid grew rapidly, until it was well over 50 per cent of the total in 1953. Since that date, however, reliance on military aid has steadily declined. *Source:* Office of Business Economics. Data show net assistance.

advising here, helping with new techniques there, cajoling reluctant European businessmen and labor leaders in still a third place, always in pursuit of that elusive productivity, which for Europe meant the difference between a low subsistence economy and one that could provide a healthy and satisfying life for all classes of society. Gradually the effect became apparent. By 1951 production had increased in all the countries with the average growth amounting to some 37 per cent in three years. Eventually, though such a goal was not included in the original plan, the ERP propelled western Europe in the direction of economic integration and unification and away from tariff walls, blocked currencies, and nationalistic self-sufficiency. Americans, always convinced of the value of their tariff-free states as a gigantic national market, could not help but think that a similar political and economic framework would work the same wonders in Europe. By the time the original Marshall Plan was coming to an end, the European Steel and Coal Community and the Common Market, both destined to come into being in the late 1950's, were already foreshadowed by the habits and practices of economic cooperation fostered among the 16 nations by the ERP.

After the invasion of South Korea by Communist North Korean troops in June 1950, the ERP rather suddenly shifted from a strictly economic recovery program, in which no funds were to be used for military expenditures, to an adjunct of the military defense of the West. Thereafter, projects were undertaken with military objectives uppermost, and the revolutionary scheme to rehabilitate and renovate the economy of Europe was abandoned, only half-finished. But before it was dropped, the example of a great nation's undertaking to lend its treasure and its brains to assist the ancient continent from which it had been born had been displayed for all the world to see. Regardless of the undoubted benefit that the United States reaped from the Marshall Plan, the program still stands as one of the world's most remarkable examples of an enlightened foreign policy in action. Upon the rehabilitation of Europe, after all, rested the success of the foreign policy of the United States for the next decade, from the North Atlantic Treaty Organization to the successful defense of the Republic of Korea.

Point Four. In his inaugural address in January 1949, President Truman added another dimension to the American commitment to work for the improvement of the world's economy. As the fourth point in his address, he announced that the United States would undertake "a bold new program for making the benefits of our scientific and industrial progress available for the improvement and growth of underdeveloped areas." In subsequent years American technicians spread around the globe, assisting primitive farmers to become less so, introducing better means of disease prevention and cure, and generally helping to bring the labor-saving and life-saving technology of the West to the unproductive economies of Asia, Africa, and South America.

An Unprecedented Commitment. The capstone to the arch of Truman's policy of containment of Russian Communism was the North Atlantic Treaty

Organization. Early in 1948, as Russian pressure on Europe continued to mount, Great Britain, France, Belgium, Luxembourg, and the Netherlands joined together in a mutual defense pact. Later in the year, when these Brussels Pact countries, as they were called, asked the United States to associate itself with them, the Truman administration suggested that the number participating be increased. In the final agreement, 12 countries on both sides of the north Atlantic joined the alliance; the number was increased to 14 in 1952, when Turkey and Greece became members. In Article five of the treaty, all the signatories agreed "that an armed attack against one or more of them in Europe or North America shall be considered an attack against them all." But the kind of assistance expected of any signatory was only that which could be constitutionally provided—a clause demanded by the American constitutional requirement that only Congress may declare war.

The signing of the treaty at Washington on April 4, 1949, was an historic moment in the diplomatic history of the United States. For the first time during peace, the United States had obligated itself to come to the assistance of nations in Europe. This obligation was the strongest yet in the course of the diplomatic revolution that had begun only four years earlier with the ratification of the United Nations Charter. American attitudes had indeed come a long way since World War II when President Roosevelt had informed Stalin and Churchill that after the war was over, the American people would not permit United States forces to be stationed in Europe for more than two years at the most. The North Atlantic Treaty encountered little opposition in the

EUROPEAN DEFENSE ALLIANCES

- NATO members in Europe, 1949 (or by date of admission)
- Warsaw Pact members, 1955

Figures indicate millions of dollars of Marshall Plan aid.

Senate, passing with the vigorous help of Senator Vandenberg, by a vote of 82 to 13 on July 21, 1949. In early 1951 General Eisenhower was brought back from his retirement post as president of Columbia University to serve as Supreme Commander of the new 12-nation force. By 1953 NATO counted 60 ground divisions and 5000 planes at its disposal, as compared with the 16 divisions that could have been mustered in 1950 against an estimated 125 Russian divisions. There was still no equality of force between NATO and the Russians, but the new army of the Atlantic community would provide a warning that an attack was being mounted. The size of the Russian striking force that would be necessary now would have to be so large that it could not be organized without detection far in advance of the assault. There would thus be time for further defensive actions to be taken.

The Berlin Blockade. One of the reasons that the United States and western Europe established NATO, was the Russian threat to Berlin. Indeed, soon after the European Recovery Program went into effect, the simmering conflict between the United States and the Soviet Union over Germany boiled up to a new level of danger. Genuinely concerned over the economic plight of Europe, including Germany, the United States in early 1948 reformed the currency in the western zone of Germany as one of the measures for the rehabilitation of that devastated country. The Soviets, still fearful of, and hence opposed to, a united Germany that might be friendly to the West,

Three West Berliners stand atop the still uncleared ruins of their city watching one of the hundreds of U.S. airlift planes come in for a landing during the Berlin blockade in 1948–1949. Note the small size of the plane compared with today's transport planes. *Photo: Fenno Jacobs-Black Star*

saw in the American move a threat to the economy of its zone in eastern Germany, since the new currency would also circulate in West Berlin, which was well inside the Russian zone.

The Russian response to the currency reform was the closing of all rail, auto, and barge routes to West Berlin. The United States, Great Britain, and France were faced with the choice of going to war over the question of access to Berlin or of abandoning the change in the currency. Then another possibility was suggested: to supply Berlin by air, since the Western powers possessed their own airfields in Berlin. Thus began the gigantic airlift of more than 3000 tons of food, fuel, and raw materials each day, which the 2.5 million people living in the western zone of the city needed. To carry out such an assignment, an almost uninterrupted line of planes flew across the Soviet zone of Germany every day and night for over ten months. This prodigious feat of organization, courage, and stamina captured the imagination of the West, restored the sagging morale of the West Berliners, and saved the city. The Russians, perhaps recognizing that they were already pressing hard against the limits of Allied tolerance, did not use their military aircraft to disrupt the airlift. Not until May 1949, however, were the ground transportation facilities again open to the West. By then the airlift had clearly demonstrated the ability of the Allies to supply Berlin through the winter, when fuel for heating needed to be brought in, as well as in the summer.

The successful containment of Russian power in Europe did not end the pressure upon the West. As will be seen in the next chapter, just as new bulwarks were being thrown up in Europe, unexpected dangers were also rising in Asia. But even before the Communist threat was felt in Korea, the fear of Communism in the United States gave birth to a domestic witch hunt that surpassed even the excesses of the Red Scare at the end of the First World War.

The Great Fear, 1949–1954

In 1789, early in the French Revolution, a nameless fear seized the peasants of France. For months, afraid yet without knowing the source of that fear, they went on a rampage against the Old Regime, burning, looting, and killing those they suspected of opposing the revolution. Historians have called this emotional outbreak *La Grande Peur*. A similar, though less violent, outburst of irrational fear seemed to grip the American people during the five years between 1949 and 1954. Like the French peasants who feared that the landlords were launching counterrevolution, the American people in those years feared that international Communism was so powerful and so pervasive that its agents might strike anywhere, from within the country as well as from without. As long as the Great Fear persisted, suspicion corroded hitherto healthy and trustful relations among Americans. Friends became circumspect with one another; people feared to exercise their fundamental right to sign petitions to their government; teachers were compelled to swear that they were not Communists; United States senators trembled before one of their number who appointed himself the grand inquisitor of Communists; the State Department and other government agencies summarily fired all employees who had ever been even remotely connected with leftish causes; and the overseas information service of the United States was subjected to a humiliating investigation by two young men whose antics made their country the laughingstock of Europe.

The roots of the Great Fear are to be found in the deteriorating international situation in Europe during 1946 and 1947. Once it was recognized that in the developing contest between the Western world and the U.S.S.R., members of Communist parties would serve as spies and agents for the Soviets, the loyalty of Communists and Communist sympathizers in government became a subject of intense concern and inquiry. (To that extent, the Great Fear contained more objective justification than the Red Scare of 1919, when Bolshevik strength in international affairs was a figment of the imagination, not a reality.) As early as March 1947, President Truman ordered a check of all federal employees to find out whether any should be dismissed for Communist affiliation or sympathy. Later that year a permanent board was set up to evaluate any charges of disloyalty that were brought against government employees.

The federal loyalty program became a target for many liberals, because the loyalty of an employee was being ascertained by an examination of his past acts and affiliations—a procedure which might or might not be an accurate measure of his present loyalty. Moreover, it was also evident that merely unconventional or radical ideas, unrelated to any Communist affiliation, were often taken by the authorities as evidence of disloyalty. Although all persons concerned admitted that no one possessed a constitutional right to be employed by the government, the practice of dismissing a man from a job he had competently filled for many years simply on the basis of dubious charges against his loyalty endangered the liberties of an American citizen.

The Uncovering of Communist Spying. If the establishment of a loyalty program alerted the public to the dangers of Communist espionage, the revelations before Congressional committees and in open court of actual spying in behalf of the Soviet Union, provided evidence that justified the program in the eyes of a large number of Americans. In 1948, the same year that the government of Czechoslovakia was taken over by a minority of well-organized Communists, a witness told a Congressional committee that she had received classified information from government employees for transmission to the Soviet Union when she was a Russian agent before the war. Another former Communist and Russian agent, Whittaker Chambers, by then a respected senior editor of *Time* magazine, told the same committee that he, too, had received secret information from Communists employed in the State Department in the late 1930's.

In 1949, as the threat of Russian Communism abroad continued to grow, the search for Communist plots within America reached a new high. That was the year in which the Communists gained complete control of China, and the Soviet Union successfully exploded its first nuclear device, thus breaking the American monopoly. That was also the year of the trial of 11 leaders of the Communist party of the United States, charged by the government, under the Smith Act of 1940, with conspiracy to advocate the overthrow of the government by force and violence. The trial lasted over ten months, filled with bitter exchanges between the defense attorneys and the judge, and ended in the conviction of the accused. While the trial was going on, more revelations of Communist espionage continued to reach the front pages of the nation's newspapers.

By this time fear of Communists and their sympathizers was spreading beyond government. In June 1948 the University of California required each of its 4000 faculty members on pain of dismissal to swear that he was not a Communist. (A year later, 157 faculty members were fired for refusing to take the oath.) The National Education Association, the leading organization of teachers in the country, voted in July that Communist teachers should be barred from all schools. In September at Peekskill, New York, a pleasant country town just north of New York City, a bloody, hate-filled, anti-Communist riot broke out. Thousands of angry, fearful men and women stoned and manhandled a group of admirers of the Negro singer Paul Robeson because of his known sympathy with the Soviet Union. Some 145 people were hurt in the resulting melee.

The Hiss Case. Although Alger Hiss was not technically charged with spying or with being a former Communist, his trial for perjury in 1949 was certainly the most sensational of the several public examinations of Communists in government. It was also the most divisive. Part of the testimony of Whittaker Chambers when he appeared before the House Committee on Un-American Activities in 1948 concerned Alger Hiss, a State Department employee in the late 1930's and early 1940's, but by 1948, the president of the highly respected Carnegie Endowment for International Peace. Chambers testified that he had received from Hiss secret State Department documents for transmission to the Soviet Union. At first Hiss denied ever knowing Chambers, but later conceded that he knew Chambers slightly under another name. Under oath Hiss categorically denied ever passing secret documents to Chambers or anyone else. Although the formal charge brought against him was no more than perjury—the statute of limitations precluded any more serious charge—to most Americans the trial of Alger Hiss, which began in May 1949, was a trial for espionage, if not for treason.

The emotions stirred by Hiss' two trials—the jury could not agree in the first one—ran deep. Hiss, carefully groomed, well-educated, highly respected, and strongly supported in his first trial by eminent figures in public life, stood in sharp contrast to the unkempt Chambers, who, though by then prosperous,

In a dramatic moment in the Hiss case, Alger Hiss, standing at the right, is asked to identify Whittaker Chambers before the House Committee on Un-American Activities. Chambers is standing before the committee dias at the far left. *Photo: UPI*

testified candidly, almost embarrassingly, to his early dissolute, irresponsible life as a writer, Communist agent, and professional liar. To those people who had always suspected that the New Deal was soft on Communism, Alger Hiss—who had been a minor figure in the Roosevelt administration—seemed to be living proof that they had been right all along. Liberals who distrusted renegade Communists and disliked anyone who reported the activities and ideas of former friends to vindictive Congressional investigating committees refused to believe that Hiss could be guilty, even when he was convicted and sentenced to five years in prison. Hiss' innocence, despite the verdict of the jury, remained an article of faith among many liberals, even though during the trial Hiss was unable to counter some very damaging evidence brought against him. Efforts toward obtaining a new trial, though strenuously pushed, were fruitless.

Spies and the Bomb. Before 1950 most of the allegations and evidence of Communist infiltration of the government pertained to the years before the war. In 1950, however, the double-headed fear of domestic Communists and Russian military power came together in a new and frightening combination: the public learned that American Communists had helped steal the secrets of the nuclear bomb for the Soviet Union. The first report of such activities came from abroad in February 1950, when the British government announced the arrest of Klaus Fuchs, a German-born physicist who was then employed at the British government's nuclear energy establishment at Harwell and who, during the war, had worked at Los Alamos, New Mexico, on the development of the first nuclear bomb. Fuchs soon confessed to giving scientific information on the nuclear bomb to the Soviets. In May the Federal Bureau of Investigation, which had been responsible in the first place for alerting the British to Fuch's treachery, arrested an American Harry Gold as an accomplice of Fuchs. During the summer months, other Americans, including a married couple, Julius and Ethel Rosenberg, were arrested for having taken part in a conspiracy to obtain and pass secret information on the nuclear bomb to the Soviet Union. When brought to trial, all of them were found guilty; the Rosenbergs were executed in 1953 for their part in the conspiracy while the others received long prison terms.

To these sensational revelations, the Congress responded with the Internal Security Act of 1951, passing it over Truman's veto, in which he denounced the measure as a threat to the liberties of all Americans. The act required Communist and Communist-front organizations to register with the government and to identify as Communist all their official mail and literature, as well as placing other restrictions on the party. The most severe of all the provisions of the act, and the one that measured the extremity of Congressional concern, was the clause that authorized the government to place all Communists, citizens and aliens alike, in concentration camps whenever a national emergency should occur.

The Rise and Fall of McCarthy. The arrests and trials of Communists, along with the revelations of Communist espionage, continued during 1951 and 1952, but the most significant element furthering the Great Fear in these years and after was the rise to prominence of Senator Joseph R. McCarthy. Like Alger Hiss, the junior Senator from Wisconsin seemed to trigger off tremendous emotions in the American people. To many Americans he appeared for a number of years to be the most forthright and effective opponent of Communists in the nation. To those who suspected his motives and doubted his allegations of Communist infiltration of government, he seemed to be the greatest menace to democratic government in our history. From hindsight it appears that he was not quite either. McCarthy's anti-Communism was shallow and largely a handy vehicle for personal glory and reelection; his following, which at times was huge, posed no serious political threat, for it received no program from its leader, and apparently McCarthy had none. He was a product and a perpetuator of the Great Fear, but he could not survive it.

McCarthy gained prominence as an anti-Communist in 1950, when he announced in a speech at Wheeling, West Virginia, that 57 or more Communists were then working in the State Department. The Senate later cleared the department of the charge of harboring Communists, but McCarthy's allegations of Communists in government, though never any more soundly based than the first one, continued. In the atmosphere of the Great Fear, his power to intimidate government officials and private citizens grew alarmingly, aided, it should be said, by extreme anti-Communist Democrats as well as Republicans (McCarthy was a Republican). When, as a result of the Republican victory in 1952, McCarthy became chairman of the Senate committee on Government Operations, he gained a new and effective platform for his attacks. From this vantage point, he and his committee proceeded to investigate the State Department, the overseas information service, and any other aspect of government that interested them. He did not hesitate to encourage employees of the executive branch to reveal to him confidential information from their departments. Whole sections were turned inside out as the State Department tried vainly to satisfy McCarthy's standards of purity in matters of Communist infiltration. Inasmuch as McCarthy was the self-appointed authority on the subject, no organization could ever be clear of the charge if he did not consent to the clearance.

As the foregoing suggests, McCarthy was not partisan in his allegations; he attacked the administration of the Republican Eisenhower as vigorously as he had that of the Democratic Truman. Indeed, so powerful was he felt to be that, during the 1952 campaign, Eisenhower agreed to sit on the same platform with him and to delete from his speech passages praising General George Marshall, even though Eisenhower had deeply resented the attacks McCarthy had made earlier in the Senate upon General Marshall.

Imprisoned in the grip of the Great Fear, many Americans supported the Senator despite his failure to uncover any Communists in government or to strengthen the security of the United States. As late as January 1954, a Gallup poll reported that 50 per cent of the American people viewed McCarthy and his activities with favor. Few of his wild allegations seemed excessive in the anxious atmosphere of the Great Fear. When the Senator sent two young, untrained assistants to survey the United States information centers in the capitals of Europe, men on two continents gasped to think that such irresponsibility could be countenanced in a great democracy. Yet so substantial was the fear of McCarthy that responsible officials whom his investigators suspected of disloyalty were obligingly fired.

McCarthy's power to frighten, however, came to a surprisingly abrupt end in 1954. The turnabout began with a 35-day Senate investigation of the Senator's alleged attempts to interfere in the operation of the Army. During those hearings millions of Americans saw for themselves on their television screens the famous Communist hunter's unprincipled, wily tactics, which he now directed against the representatives of the United States Army. Many people now began to have second thoughts about McCarthy's integrity and intentions as a fighter against Communism. Even before the Army hearings were concluded, McCarthy became the subject of a hearing himself before a select committee of the Senate inquiring into his conduct as a senator. For years he had insulted and impugned the motives of his fellow senators. At the conclusion of the inquiry, the Senate condemned his conduct; 67 of his colleagues voted against him, though a mere 12 months before only Senator

William Fulbright of Arkansas had been willing to stand out against an appropriation for McCarthy's committee. Though he suffered no actual loss of senatorial privileges, McCarthy's influence and power did not survive his condemnation. He soon went into a physical decline, dying in 1957. The effects of his activities were not so quickly removed. As President Eisenhower wrote a decade later, "McCarthyism took its toll on many individuals and on the nation. No one was safe from charges recklessly made from inside the walls of congressional immunity. . . . Innocent people accused of Communist associations or party membership have not to this day been able to clear their names fully."

In 1954 the Russian menace to the security of the United States and Europe was as great as when the Great Fear first enveloped Americans, but by that date, as the end of McCarthyism showed, they no longer thought that the internal enemy was as dangerous as the foreign. As a consequence, they could turn their attention from a tortured, unending search for "traitors" in their midst, to the maintenance of vigilance abroad.

SUGGESTED READING

There are several single-volume books that cover the years between the end of World War II and 1960, but none does the job with a racier style and greater anecdotal richness than Eric Goldman, *Crucial Decade—and After** (1960).

The question of the origins of the Cold War has now spawned a literature of some size and contentiousness. William Appleman Williams, *The Tragedy of American Diplomacy** (revised ed., 1962), a general study of American foreign policy, and D. F. Fleming, *The Cold War and Its Origins, 1917–1960,* 2 vols., (1961) both see the United States as more guilty than innocent of the charge of provoking the U.S.S.R. before and after 1945. Gar Alperovitz, *Atomic Diplomacy** (1965) takes much the same position though emphasizing the effect of the atomic bomb on the development of U.S. policy toward Russia in 1945. The fullest and rather official view of the diplomacy of 1945–1946 is the authoritative Herbert Feis, *Between War and Peace: The Potsdam Conference** (1960). William H. McNeill, *America, Britain and Russia: Their Co-operation and Conflict, 1941–1946** (1953) is still one of the best short, critical surveys of these years, though it is now rather out of date. Martin F. Herz, *Beginnings of the Cold War* (1966) is thin on information, promising more than it delivers. It emphasizes Poland as the central issue between the U.S. and the U.S.S.R. Much more satisfactory, though strangely neglected, is the penetrating John Snell, *The War-Time Origins of the East-West Dilemma Over Germany* (1959).

There are already available a number of printed sources for the period. Harry S. Truman's *Memoirs,** 2 vols., (1955, 1956), while rather dull, is indispensable. Secretary of State James F. Byrnes has written of his activities during these crucial years in

---

*Available in a paperback edition

Speaking Frankly (1947). Walter Millis and E. S. Duffield, eds., *The Forrestal Diaries* (1951) provides important information on attitudes within the Truman administration; *The Private Papers of Senator Vandenberg,* edited by A. H. Vandenberg, Jr. (1952) offers insight into the private thoughts of a leading Republican senator of the time. Henry L. Stimson and McGeorge Bundy, *On Active Service in Peace and War* (1948) contains the recollections of the Secretary of War in the Roosevelt and Truman administrations.

There is no scholarly biography of Truman as yet, though Barton Bernstein is writing one. A sketchy, but useful volume on Truman before he became President is Frank McNaughton, *This Man Truman* (1945). Jonathan Daniels, *The Man of Independence* (1950) and Cabell Phillips, *The Truman Presidency* (1966) are by journalists who are favorably disposed toward their subject. Probably the closest thing to a scholarly survey of the Truman years is the excellent Barton J. Bernstein and Allen J. Matusow, eds., *The Truman Administration: A Documentary History* (1966).

On politics in general during Truman's administration, one of the most valuable and interesting is Samuel Lubell, *The Future of American Politics** (1952). Less valuable in retrospect, but helpful in getting the feel of the Truman years is Robert S. Allen and William V. Shannon, *The Truman Merry-Go-Round* (1950), an appraisal by journalists. H. A. Millis and Emily C. Brown, *From the Wagner Act to Taft-Hartley* (1950) puts the principal labor legislation of the Truman administration into historical perspective, from the point of view of labor. A defense of the law is made by one of its authors in Fred A. Hartley, *Our New National Labor Policy: The Taft-Hartley Act and the Next Steps* (1948). Randolph E. Paul, *Taxation in the United States* (1954) has some good analyses of Truman's fiscal policies.

The innovations in the Truman foreign policies are summarized in Carl N. Degler, "The Great Revolution in American Foreign Policy," *Virginia Quarterly Review,* XXXVIII (Summer, 1962) and presented in accurate detail by a participant in Joseph M. Jones, *The Fifteen Weeks** (1955). George F. Kennan, *Memoirs, 1925–1950* (1967) contains the elegantly written recollections of the author of the containment policy as seen from inside the State Department. He is usually critical of how the administration conducted foreign policy.

Probably the best study so far of McCarthy and the anti-Communist crusade is Richard H. Rovere, *Senator Joe McCarthy** (1959); Earl Latham, *The Communist Controversy in Washington* (1966), a scholarly study, emphasizes the hatred of the New Deal in explaining anti-Communism, rather than the threat from the Soviet Union. Alan Barth, *The Loyalty of Free Men* (1951) is a journalist's contemporary indictment of enforced conformity, loyalty oaths, and McCarthyism. A vigorous defense of Senator McCarthy is to be found in William F. Buckley, Jr., and L. Brent Bozell, *McCarthy and His Enemies** (1954). One of the major controversies of the period is treated with understanding in Alistair Cooke, *A Generation on Trial: U.S.A. v. Alger Hiss* (1950). Hostile to Hiss, but important for understanding the temper of the times, is the memoir by Hiss' opponent, Whittaker Chambers, *Witness* (1952). Owen Lattimore, *Ordeal by Slander* (1950) reveals from personal experience how McCarthy destroyed one expert on Asia.

CHAPTER TWO

THE EVOLUTION OF A FOREIGN POLICY FOR THE COLD WAR

W ARS HAVE A WAY of getting out of hand, of releasing forces and evoking reactions that surprise the participants. The Second World War was no exception. Americans suddenly discovered in 1948–1949 that as a result of the war against Hitler they had brought Russia into the center of Europe and had exchanged the threat of German for Russian power. To thinking men, this new development did not negate the once imperative reasons for the war against Germany, but it did show that even for the victors wars could have unexpected and undesirable consequences.

The Three-pronged Revolution in Asia

The Collapse of Colonialism. If the results of the war in Europe dropped new problems into the laps of Americans, in western Asia the results were bewildering. One of the ironies of the war was that the victors lost the most territory. The great colonial powers of Europe—Great Britain, France, and the Netherlands—which had ruled far-flung empires in Asia for as long as three centuries, found that the conclusion of hostilities in Europe also ended their authority in Asia.

The local movements against the colonial powers had begun before the war, of course, but the intrusion of the Japanese into southeast Asia gave a new impetus to the independence movements. As Asians the Japanese did their best to cultivate nationalist sentiment against the Western powers in the countries they overran, especially when, in 1944, it became evident that the Allied powers would soon reoccupy their colonies. The world had long known of the Indian movement for independence, but suddenly in 1944 and 1945 it learned also of similar movements in French Indochina, Malaya, Burma, Ceylon, and the Dutch East Indies. Thus when the western European powers returned to their former colonies, they found widespread popular unrest, loud demands for independence or autonomy, and sometimes, as in Indochina and the Dutch East Indies, armed rebellion against the mother country.

One by one the Europeans made the only possible response: they got out of Asia, some more gracefully than others. The United States, having promised the Filipinos their independence before the war, was ready first. Final independence was granted to the islands on July 4, 1946. The British, hard pressed by the losses of the war and now ruled by a Labour party government opposed to colonialism, recognized the direction in which the tides of change were running in Asia more quickly than did the Dutch and French. In February 1947 the British government announced its intention of granting independence by the following year to its valuable if unruly colony of India. Actually, bloody riots between Muslims and Hindus speeded up the process as well as split the Indian subcontinent into India and the newly created Muslim country of Pakistan. On August 15, 1947, both India and Pakistan became independent within the framework of the British Commonwealth of Nations. Less than six months later two other important British colonies, Ceylon and

Burma, gained their independence. In 1948 also, in western Asia, the British relinquished their authority in Jordan and Palestine, where they had been the dominant power since the First World War. The preparation of the Malay states for independence took somewhat longer, partly because the country was so disunited and partly because a fierce guerrilla war first had to be fought against Communist rebels. Nevertheless, in August 1957 Malaya became an independent state. Although Singapore, the once great bastion of British power in Asia, still flew the Union Jack, it, too, gained its independence in 1963. Thus, of the many areas once under British control in Asia, only the pinpoint of Hong Kong remained in 1965. All over Asia the sun was indeed setting on the British Empire.

Not all the European powers in Asia recognized the shape of the future. The Dutch, for example, though faced with a colonial rebellion when they returned to the East Indies, were not willing to grant it independence. For several years they fought strenuously against the nationalist forces, even though most of the world considered their cause lost and their ambition outmoded. In late 1949 they were compelled to agree to the complete transfer of power to the new nationalist government of the United States of Indonesia. Although in western Asia the French relinquished their control over Lebanon and Syria in 1946, in eastern Asia they resembled the Dutch, unable to accept the reality of the nationalist movements for independence. For almost a decade after 1945, the French struggled to suppress a continuous, large-scale military rebellion in Indochina. The most persistent of the nationalist elements was the Communist-led Vietminh, which had assumed authority from the Japanese in 1945. The climax of the long fight against the Vietminh came in 1954, when French resistance to this manifestation of the new Asian nationalism drew the United States into novel commitments in southeast Asia. These commitments and their consequences are more properly discussed later; here it is sufficient to note that in 1954 the French finally abandoned their 80-year-old sovereignty over Indochina.

The Nature of Anticolonialism. Historically, nationalism is a European phenomenon, originating and reaching its earliest flowering on that continent. But in expanding their power and their culture around the globe during the heyday of imperialism in the nineteenth century, the great colonial nations of Europe introduced nationalism to an Asia that barely knew either the idea or the word. Thus the whirlwind of nationalism that the colonial powers reaped in 1945 and after had actually been sown by the colonial powers themselves.

But if in that sense Asian nationalism was a product of the West, in a more fundamental sense it was anti-Western—a kind of revolt against Europe. The greatest fact in the minds of these former colonial peoples was their hatred of Western colonialism. For them there was nothing abstract about the term; its definition was drawn from decades and sometimes centuries of their own history. The countries they associated with that hated experience were the principal allies of the United States in Europe: Great Britain, France, Belgium, and the Netherlands. Efforts by the United States to counter this liability by portraying the Soviet Union as an imperialistic and colonial-minded power came to nought for a very good reason. American assertions about the imperialistic nature of Soviet policy may have been abstractly true, but in the minds of the new nations of Asia, the Soviet Union simply was not a colonial power in their sense of the word; the Communists had not held colonies in Asia and Africa. Since the Soviet Union and other Communist states were free of the taint of traditional colonialism, the emerging nations could—and did—deal with them as potential friends. Actually, however, most of the new nations, fearing to jeopardize their new independence by close association with either camp in the Cold War, preferred to be neutral in their international posture. But even that neutralist position caused difficulties. Under the Eisenhower administration, for example, Secretary of State John Foster Dulles severely criticized the policy of neutralism among the emerging nations. At one point he announced that neutralism, except under very special circumstances, was "an immoral and shortsighted conception." At other times he seemed to think of it as a way station on the way to Communist despotism.

In the 1950's the nationalist revolution in Asia, which was the great, new fact of international relations on that continent, spread to Africa as well. By that time, too, it was evident that to the urge for national independence had been added the drive for economic growth and an improved standard of living for the people. But national independence, the history of the postwar years makes clear, is much easier to achieve than is economic advancement. Virtually all of these new countries are, at best, peasant countries, devoid of capital, modern agricultural techniques, or an industrial base of any kind. Furthermore, almost all of them want to improve their economic status as rapidly as possible. They look to the wealthy countries, like those of western Europe, the United States, and the Soviet Union, for help. In this way the rise of the independent countries of Asia has had ramifications beyond the decline in power of the former mother countries, important as that is. It has also meant that Asia, Africa, and, to a certain extent, Latin America became areas in which the Western nations now competed against the Soviet Union and Communist China for the friendship of these new nations. In short, a whole new realm of Cold War competition was opened up as a result of the Asian revolution.

Yet winning the support of these new countries has not been—and will not be—easy for the United States. As a leader of the West, and a power with economic and financial connections ramifying throughout the world, the United States wants stability and order among the community of nations. But in the underdeveloped part of the globe, disorder and instability are the conditions of existence. During the 1950's and the early 1960's, the Russians, less dependent on and less involved in world trade and finance and essentially "outsiders," thought they could only gain from change. They welcomed economic breakdown and political instability in a way the United States could not. Americans may emotionally approve the nationalist ambitions of these emerging peoples and their hopes for economic betterment, but American interests are more likely to be hurt by upheaval and change than are the Communists'. The contrast in attitudes was most evident in the Congo crisis of 1961. The United States hurriedly sent in troops and supplies to restore order after the breakdown in government there, while the Communist states looked with favor and anticipation upon the upheaval. Since 1965, as will be seen in Chapter Four, the Russians have assumed a more traditional big-power attitude toward such upheavals, as evidenced by their mediation in the Indian-Pakistan border war. Since then, however, Communist China has taken the place of Russia as the primary outsider in the world and as the nation that feels it has more to gain than to lose from political instability and economic disorganization.

Effects of Anticolonialism in the U.N. One immediate consequence of the nationalist movements in Asia and Africa has been the alteration of the alignment of forces in the United Nations. As a result of the Cold War, the General Assembly has superseded the Security Council as the most important body of the United Nations. The Security Council, because the big powers' veto has inhibited action, has been gradually by-passed by the General Assembly, especially since 1950, when the United States, during the Korean War, succeeded in having the General Assembly assume the power to make recommendations to the member states when a threat to the peace arose. But if the General Assembly avoids the paralysis of the veto, it suffers from its equality of voting, regardless of the size of the state. Thus a vote by a small state like Costa Rica is equal to that of the Soviet Union or the United States. Such a procedure puts a premium upon numbers while ignoring the reality of power—always a dangerous practice in government. Between 1945 and 1965, 55 new countries from Asia and Africa, out of a membership of 116, gained admission to the United Nations. These nations, held together by their newness and their anticolonial origins, now constitute a formidable voting bloc. For most of these nations, the American resistance to Communist power in Asia or Europe is at best a secondary concern. It is their votes, for example, that have made it increasingly difficult for the American government to keep Communist China out of the United Nations; it is their votes that will finally force the United States to modify its policy on that score or face defeat.

The Transformation of Japan. The second prong of the revolution in Asia was the impact of the American occupation of Japan. Although ostensibly the representative of all the Allied powers that helped defeat Japan, the American commander in Japan, General Douglas MacArthur, was in fact the sole as well as the supreme authority during the occupation. Under his command the United States, besides stripping Japan of all its colonies, including Formosa and Korea, deliberately undertook to destroy the old Japan. A thoroughgoing and successful agrarian reform program redistributed the land to the peasantry, and a new constitution brought back parliamentary institutions. The constitution also reduced the emperor from a god to a mere symbol of national unity and removed the army from politics and government. Women were enfranchised for the first time and granted increased freedom in society. As Edwin C. Reischauer, an authority on Japanese history and ambassador to Japan under President Kennedy, wrote, "During the early postwar years in Japan, MacArthur played the role not only of the most radical American revolutionary of modern times but also one of the most successful." In accepting the revolution, the Japanese went so far, in their new constitution, as to repudiate, with the support of MacArthur, the waging of war or the maintenance of armed forces. Japan seemed on the way to complete abandonment of its militaristic tradition and its imperialistic ambitions in Asia.

When the Korean War broke out in 1950, however, the United States and its non-Communist allies in the war against Japan hastened to conclude peace with Japan, despite the objections of the Soviet Union. The treaty of peace was signed in September 1951, and in a separate agreement the United States was permitted to retain military bases in Japan. The United States also encouraged the Japanese to rebuild some of their dismantled military machine as a part of the defense against the rise of Communism in China. In the 1960's Japanese economic strength and prosperity made evident that it could not remain for long as a nonmilitary power. It was the wealthiest and economically strongest nation in Asia. But it was also evident that as a result of the war, the Japanese people had little wish for the role of a big power, much less for a revival of militarism.

The Rise of Chinese Communism. The third element in the Asian revolution was the conquest of China by the Communists. When the war ended in 1945, China was accorded the status of a great power by the United States and Great Britain. It received, for example, a seat as a permanent member of the Security Council of the United Nations. Most people assumed, now that the Japanese were defeated, that Generalissimo Chiang Kai-shek would establish himself as the head of the legitimate government of all China. Even Josef Stalin at the close of the war made a treaty recognizing the Generalissimo's government rather than that of the Communist leader Mao Tse-tung. The Chinese Communists with a sizeable army were stronger than many observers thought, partly because the Russians turned the Japanese equipment in Manchuria over to the Communists who refused to recognize Chiang as the head of China.

The United States, anxious to work out a peaceful settlement between Chiang and Mao, both of whom had fought against Japan, struggled through 1946 and 1947 to establish some basis for agreement. General George C. Marshall, at the suggestion of President Truman, traveled to China in 1946 in an effort to compose the differences between the two forces, but to no avail. Chiang, long an opponent of Communism, would not have Communists in his government, and the Communists, scenting success in the wind, would not disband their army. By the end of 1947, the two forces were engaged in open civil war, during which it became increasingly evident that Chiang did not enjoy the support of the masses of Chinese. His government, always dictatorial, was also blatantly corrupt and inefficient.

The Fall of Chiang Kai-shek. The progress of the Communists, whose forces were concentrated in the north, was at first slow and uneven, then swift and complete. By the end of 1948, they had captured all of Manchuria and were ready to challenge Chiang in China proper. Early in 1949 north China was in Communist hands, and the Generalissimo nominally resigned his offices in an effort to hold off further Communist penetration, but without effect. In September Mao Tse-tung announced the formation of the People's Republic of China, with its capital at ancient Peiping (now Peking) in the north. By the end of that year, the principal cities of south China were in Mao's hands, while Chiang Kai-shek and the remnant of his army fled to the island of Formosa some 100 miles off the southeast coast. The Soviet Union extended diplomatic recognition to the new regime in October, and in February 1950 a mutual assistance agreement and pact of alliance was signed in Moscow by the Soviet Union and the new Chinese People's Republic. With ratification in April, Communist power in Asia was consolidated, and the stage was set for its expansion.

The triumph of Communism in China came at precisely the time when the end of the Berlin blockade and the creation of NATO marked the diminution of the Russian Communist danger in western Europe. Thus a whole new area was opened to the Communist threat. In making the decision to render assistance to western Europe in 1947–1948, the United States had, in effect, elected to abide by whatever results Chiang, without massive aid from the United States, could achieve in Asia. In 1947–1949, as in the Second World War, Europe, with its highly skilled population and technically advanced society rightly came first on the American scale of priorities. The dependence upon Chiang, however, proved to be misplaced, for he could not stop the advance of the Chinese Communists. It was not accidental, therefore, that the next test of American foreign policy should come in Asia; there American power was weakest and its allies almost impotent. When the American representative, John Foster Dulles, came back from the foreign ministers' meeting in Paris in June 1949, he told Senator Vandenberg, "the Politburo knows that it has lost the Cold War in western Europe; . . . it's nervous about holding its European satellites; . . . it's preparing to concentrate largely on Asia." The prophecy soon proved remarkably accurate.

The Korean War

The Great Decision. On Saturday night June 24, 1950, President Truman was sitting in the library in his home in Independence, Missouri, when the telephone rang. It was the Secretary of State, Dean Acheson. "Mr. President," he said, "I have very serious news. The North Koreans have invaded South Korea." Truman, deeply shocked, replied that he would fly to Washington immediately, but Acheson, desirous of not alarming the country, requested that the President stay in Independence until the nature and extent of the invasion had been definitely ascertained. Meanwhile, Acheson secured the President's permission to call the Security Council of the United Nations into immediate session. The next day brought the news that the invasion was in deadly earnest; the President hastily left Independence for Washington for conferences with his military and diplomatic advisers. On the way to Washington, as he told the story later, he ran over in his mind the possible actions which the United States, already heavily committed in Europe, should take if, as seemed likely, the North Koreans refused to heed a cease-fire order from the Security Council. To Truman the invasion was a rerun of the old movie of Hitler's aggressions in the 1930's. "If this was allowed to go unchallenged," he wrote later, "it would mean a third world war, just as similar incidents had brought on the second world war." The President's advisers agreed that assistance must be given, and airdrops of supplies for the South Korean army were authorized that same Sunday. At the same time the President ordered the American Seventh Fleet in the western Pacific to take a position in the strait between the mainland and the island of Formosa in order to forestall a possible Chinese Communist invasion of Chiang Kai-shek's last stronghold. (This last decision, understandable in the context and excitement of the surprise attack by the Korean Communists, marked a sharp change in policy, which had far-ranging consequences. Up until then the United States had stayed out of military involvement in the Chinese civil war; thereafter it was a defender of Chiang's repudiated regime on Formosa and, by the same token, an avowed enemy of the Chinese Communists. The American action probably also influenced the Chinese Communists in making their decision to enter the Korean War later in the year.)

Limited aid to the South Koreans soon proved inadequate. On Monday, Syngman Rhee, the president of South Korea, appealed directly for United States intervention, as the surprisingly powerful North Korean army, sweeping everything before it, compelled Rhee's government to flee from its capital at Seoul. Truman, moving cautiously but resolutely, now ordered American air and naval forces to support the Republic of Korea forces, but with instructions not to attack targets north of the thirty-eighth parallel, the border between the two Koreas. The following day, June 27, the United Nations Security Council branded the North Koreans aggressors because they had refused to heed an earlier call for a cease-fire. It also called upon all the member states to aid the South Korean government. The administration, which had worked hard to secure the backing of the United Nations, immediately declared that the American forces were acting in behalf of the world organization, but added that the interposition of the Seventh Fleet was a United States and not a United Nations action.

On July 7 the Security Council recognized the United States as the leader of the U.N. forces, and President Truman named General Douglas MacArthur, already the American commander, the chief of the U.N. army. By this time, of course, the United States had found it necessary to commit ground troops to Korea, for it was evident that unless substantial ground support was forthcoming, the Communists would conquer the whole peninsula in a matter of days. President Truman authorized the first troops, at MacArthur's request, on June 30. At that time the United States counted not more than ten and a half infantry divisions and one armored division in its entire army.

The Background. From the beginning the Korean War was a strange business, certainly the least clearly defined war Americans had yet fought. The very border over which the aggression occurred was artificial, being but the arbitrary line at which Russian and American occupation troops agreed to meet in 1945. For years the line was the scene of numerous border clashes provoked by both sides, neither of which recognized the other as a legitimate government. Syngman Rhee, the head of the South Korean government, a Princeton graduate and a long-time Korean nationalist, was bent upon unifying his country, by force if necessary. So seriously did the American authorities view Rhee's intentions that they refused to supply his army with aggressive weapons like tanks and heavy artillery. The Russians took no such precautions permitting the North Koreans to build up a well-trained, well-equipped force, a fact that explained their spectacular early successes.

Furthermore, there is some reason for believing that the Russians and North Koreans did not expect the United States to intervene in the defense of Korea. In early 1949, at about the time the United States and Soviet occupation forces withdrew from both parts of Korea, General MacArthur, describing the Pacific Ocean as "an Anglo-Saxon lake" and defining the American defense perimeter in the western Pacific, omitted Korea. Less than a year later, Secretary of State Dean Acheson, addressing the National Press Club, again left Korea outside the United States defense line in the western Pacific. Almost pointedly he said that those countries outside the perimeter should, if they were attacked, look for aid from the United Nations. Did these statements encourage the North Korean attack? Many Republicans later on said they did; no one knows as yet.

The Russian boycott of the U.N. going on at that time as a protest against the denial of a seat to Communist China was another fact supporting the argument that they were surprised by American intervention. Thus when the resolution for United Nations intervention came before the Security Council, the Soviet delegate, Jacob Malik, was absent and could not veto it. Even though Trygve Lie, the Secretary-General, urged Malik to attend the meeting that was to vote on military intervention in Korea, Malik, much to the relief of the United States, refused to break his boycott. He did later, but by then his power to hamstring the U.N. operations in Korea was gone. The question remains: why did the Russians permit the U.N. to act in Korea?

The Entrance of the Chinese. To the Communists, to most Americans, and to the world, the month of August 1950 demonstrated how low American military power had sunk since 1945. The North Koreans had pushed the South Koreans and the whole American Eighth Army right down the peninsula into its tip around the port city of Pusan. Evacuation of the peninsula seemed imminent. Actually, the situation was not as bad as it appeared. As early as July 7, MacArthur had told the administration of his plan to recoup the situation as soon as United States forces in Korea had been built up. On September 15 his forces carried out a highly successful surprise landing at Inchon, the port of Seoul, far behind the North Korean lines, while at Pusan, the American and South Korean armies attacked in great force. Large segments of the North Korean army were thus trapped in a gigantic pincer, while the rest of the army was forced to retreat rapidly, suffering enormous losses. On September 28 Seoul was liberated, and the following day Syngman Rhee re-established his government there. Three days later, on October 1, MacArthur ordered his troops to move north of the thirty-eighth parallel, calling on the North Koreans "forthwith to lay down your arms and cease hostilities under such military supervision as I may direct."

On October 15, 1950, the President flew out to the American base at Wake Island in the Pacific to meet with MacArthur. There the confident General told the President that the war would be won and the conquest of all Korea completed by Thanksgiving. The Chinese Communists, he assured the President, despite some buildup of their troops in Manchuria and their protests over the crossing of the thirty-eighth parallel, would not intervene in the war. The next day, on October 16, unknown to the U.N. command at the time, the first military units of Chinese "volunteers" crossed into Korea. Meanwhile the U.N. forces pushed north. On October 26 the first U.N. troops, a contingent of Koreans, reached the Yalu River, the border between China and Korea. Through the darkness they peered across the river into Communist China. The main U.N. force was still some 20 to 30 miles south. Soon after their arrival at the Yalu, the advance group of Koreans was ambushed and driven back with heavy losses by Chinese soldiers—actually units of the Chinese army denominated volunteers to preserve the fiction that China was not officially entering the war. The following night several full divisions of Republic of Korea troops were attacked and forced back; when United States Eighth Army troops went to the aid of the R.O.K (Republic of Korea), they too were assaulted and forced south. When all U.N. troops had to be pulled back to a distance of some 50 miles from the Yalu, it became evident that the Chinese Communists had entered the war in force. In retrospect it is clear that the decision on the part of the United States and the U.N. to advance north of the thirty-eighth parallel was a mistake. Nothing, in the end, was gained by it and, in view of the Chinese warnings, it is highly probable that they would not have entered the war if the North had not been invaded.

THE KOREAN WAR,
JUNE 25—NOV. 24, 1950

→ U.N. offensive of Sept. 15–Nov. 24

Both as a military operation and as a symbol of united action against aggression, the war was completely changed by the Chinese intervention. The triumph of U.N. persistence, power, and audacious strategy at Inchon was suddenly followed by a series of costly and humiliating defeats as the U.N. forces were driven back down the peninsula and forced, once again, to evacuate Seoul. (Only gradually during 1951 were strengthened U.N. forces able to push north of the thirty-eighth parallel once more.) It was clear that unless the Chinese, who poured into Korea in tremendous numbers after early November 1950, could be halted, September's hope of completely clearing Korea of Communists would have to be abandoned.

Aware of this fact, MacArthur increasingly importuned Washington for permission to attack the Chinese across the Yalu, in what he referred to as their "sanctuary." But Truman and Acheson, acutely aware of the obligations of the U.S.S.R. to China under the mutual security pact of February 1950, and afraid of tying down American forces in a war on the land mass of China, with its enormous population and army, believed that any such action would expand the war into a global conflict. Though it went unnoticed at the time, it was true that neither the Chinese nor the Russians attacked the American sanctuary in Japan, though that country was a vital staging area for the successful prosecution of the war in Korea. The Russians refrained probably for the same reason that the Americans respected the Manchurian sanctuary: to keep the war from becoming a nuclear exchange between the great powers.

CHINA

River

Yalu

NORTH KOREA

Chongchon R.

SEA OF JAPAN

Pyongyang

Armistice line, July 1953

38° — 38°

CHINA

Seoul

Inchon

Han R. retreat

Line of U.N.
Jan. 24, 1951

YELLOW SEA

THE KOREAN WAR,
NOV. 25, 1950–JULY 27, 1953

Kum R.

SOUTH KOREA

Taegu

Communist offensive
of Nov. 29, 1950–Jan. 24, 1951

U.N. counteroffensive
of Jan. 25–Nov. 27, 1951

Pusan

But if the nation was spared a nuclear war, a limited war in a place far from American shores imposed frustrations and tensions upon a people accustomed to drive for victory and to demand the enemy's unconditional surrender. In December 1950 a draft board in Montana refused to call up another man until General MacArthur was authorized to use the atom bomb as he saw fit in China. Truman's popularity, as measured by public opinion polls, during his first five years in office went up and down over a wide range, but after January 1951 a majority of the people consistently opposed him. After the Chinese invasion, "Truman's War," as the conflict in Korea was dubbed, became increasingly unpopular. Not even during the War of 1812 had Americans been called upon to accept such indefinite and limited goals in their warmaking. Never before had the limits of American power been so frustratingly evident. They would be again, however, in Vietnam.

The Dismissal of MacArthur. One measure of the discontent stemming from the war was the furor stirred up by Truman's removal of General MacArthur from his command in Korea in April 1951. For several months the General had been privately and publicly proclaiming his irritation at having to refrain from striking at the Chinese at their staging areas in Manchuria. Although such statements by the United Nations commander evoked alarm among the other powers supporting the U.N. effort in Korea, Truman hesitated to take any strong action against the popular MacArthur other than warning him against such remarks in the future. But the President could no longer ignore MacArthur's insubordination when a letter from the General criticizing administration policy was read from the floor of the House of Representatives. MacArthur's removal from command by Truman was swift and public.

The domestic reaction was equally quick and revealing. Within 12 days after the announcement, over 27,000 letters and telegrams had been received at the White House, as compared with fewer than 2000 after the announcement of Roosevelt's court-packing plan in 1937. Congressmen received telegrams instructing them to "Impeach the little ward politician stupidity from Kansas City"; "Run the United Nations back to Switzerland"; "Impeach the imbecile." In San Gabriel, California, a crowd hanged the President in effigy; in Los Angeles the City Council adjourned "in sorrowful contemplation of the political assassination of General MacArthur." In Ohio and Massachusetts, flags were lowered to half-staff. Upon his return to the United States, the General received a stupendous welcome in New York and throughout the country; the two houses of Congress respectfully invited him to address them. The Armed Services and Foreign Relations Committees of the Senate scheduled elaborate hearings to inquire into his removal.

In the course of the hearings from May 3 to June 25, some two million words of testimony from the principal military and diplomatic figures in the country were entered in the record. The public press and air waves were filled with criticisms of limited war in Korea and with revelations of American strategic plans and capabilities. Yet when the record was complete, it was evident that MacArthur's recommendations amounted to carrying the war into China in order to oust the Communists from all of Korea. But as General Omar Bradley said, speaking for the Joint Chiefs of Staff, of which he was chairman, to have extended the fighting to the mainland of Asia would "involve us in the wrong war, at the wrong place, at the wrong time, and with the wrong enemy." Later Truman put it this way: "I knew that in our age, Europe, with its millions of skilled workmen, with its factories and transportation networks, is still the key to world peace." After all, the recovery of Europe under the Marshall Plan had only begun and the threat of Russia there had not yet completely receded. To become involved in a war with China might expose Europe to attack.

The Effect and Significance of the Korean War. Before the armistice was negotiated in mid-1953, American deaths, not to mention those of the other nations fighting in the rugged hills through the frigid winters of Korea, reached over 37,000; the wounded and missing reached levels several times that figure. To many Americans the war remained a bewildering and frustrating experience. It was sneeringly called "Truman's War," or "that police action," in derogation of the evasion that the President used to answer the charge that he had committed the country to war without Congressional authority. In fact Senator Robert A. Taft, the leading Republican in the Senate, publicly accused the President of usurping authority in sending troops to the Korean

War. The limited character of the war and the resulting frustration were also used by Communist hunters like Senator McCarthy to lend credence to their charges that the administration was not whole-heartedly fighting Communism at home or abroad.

Yet some real gains had been made. The war was, after all, the first war ever fought by an international organization dedicated to preserving peace with an international army. By the end of 1950, some 20 nations had sent units or assistance of some kind to Korea; by the time the fighting ended, 42 nations had offered assistance in the defense of South Korea. Moreover, the war demonstrated that collective security backed by American power would work, for the North Korean invasion was halted and turned back. The Chinese Communists, it is true, gained prestige in Asia by stopping the U.N.'s drive to the Yalu, but the price they paid was the inability to achieve their announced intention of reclaiming Formosa by invasion.

The war also stimulated American military preparedness after a period of Congressional economy that had reduced the military establishment to a dangerously low level. By June 1952 some 2.2 million men and women had been added to the armed forces of the United States. The Air Force, long languishing for lack of funds, expanded enormously. Moreover, NATO, slow to get started, suddenly leaped into a state of readiness after the Korean War began.

Domestically, the war forced the administration into economic controls once again, though not to the degree or extent familiar in World War II. Both income and excise taxes were raised in 1950, and in January 1951 the President signed into law a new excess profits tax. In early 1951 the government was compelled to restrict civilian use of steel, rubber, and aluminum to keep war production going. Wage increases were also discouraged in an effort to prevent price rises. But the rigid price controls and rationing procedures that had been used during the Second World War were not necessary in this much smaller struggle. Indeed, by the end of 1952, though the fighting continued in Korea, the military production buildup had reached its peak, and economic controls were gradually eliminated. In fact, many people in the United States, if they had no relatives in the armed forces in Korea, hardly knew there was a war at all—a fact that made the war even more frustrating and unpopular among those whose sons or husbands were fighting in Asia.

The End of the Korean Fighting. Once the intervention of the Chinese made evident that a conquest of the whole peninsula by the U.N. forces was out of the question, the administration tried its best to conclude the fighting as speedily as possible. The Communists, however, were not so eager; they were willing to talk about an armistice, but they were not willing to agree to it without argument and bargaining. As a result the war, now virtually a military stalemate on a line just north of Seoul, dragged on into the new administration of Dwight D. Eisenhower. In the middle of 1953, despite a last-minute maneuver by Syngman Rhee, who opposed some of the armistice terms, the fighting halted along a line that gave the South Koreans slightly more territory than they had possessed before the attack three years earlier. The extreme nationalists inside and outside the Republican party attacked the Eisenhower administration for agreeing to the armistice, just as they would have attacked Truman had he worked one out. But the new President was sufficiently popular personally and unassociated with the frustrating war in the first place to be able to win acceptance for something less than full victory. Truman probably could not have won popular support for such a conclusion to a war.

The armistice of July 1953 terminated the fighting, but it did not end the split in Korea; that, like the division of Germany, could not be healed until the deeper and more significant antagonism between Russian power and the United States was ended throughout the world.

The "New Look" in Foreign Policy

A Republican Version of Foreign Policy. Although in many respects the new Eisenhower administration continued the foreign policy goals established under Truman, it sought to introduce new means. As representatives of the party that had long criticized containment as too passive, Eisenhower and his Secretary of State John Foster Dulles wanted to try more active means to defeat the Russians. In theory the party was interested in doing more than simply countering Russian or Communist advances, but in practice it was not united on how a new approach to foreign policy should be carried out. As will be shown in the next chapter, the Republican party in 1953 and after was deeply split between the internationalists, represented by Eisenhower and Dulles, and the neo-isolationists, or continentalists, of whom Senator Taft (and later that year, Senator William R. Knowland of California) was the spokesman and Senator Joseph R. McCarthy of Wisconsin was a vociferous extremist. This latter group in the party — and sometimes it virtually dominated in foreign affairs — generally resisted foreign aid and doubted the value of NATO and other commitments in Europe. Hence it was usually unprepared to support more vigorous action in foreign affairs, despite its emotional hostility to the allegedly passive policy of containment. Furthermore, the Republican party as a whole was historically the party of business and conservatism, a fact that made it reluctant to spend larger sums of money or to break new paths.

Convinced that the Democrats under Truman had been too eager to spend money, the new administration wanted to balance the budget and to reduce expenditures in general, and in foreign affairs and defense in particular. Since the Defense Department was the most costly agency in the government, it received the first attention of the economizers, despite warnings that cuts in military expenditures might endanger national security. This urge to economy among Republicans of both wings of the party put a restraint upon the party's and the administration's ability to break out of the policy of containment.

The "new look" in foreign policy, as it came to be called by the press, was a deliberate attempt to reduce expenditures for defense at the same time that new approaches to foreign policy were introduced. Behind the new look lay the assumption that by a careful and deliberate use of the new technology of war—that is, rockets, nuclear weapons, jet aircraft, and carriers—security could be purchased at a lower financial cost than under the Democrats. An irreverent reporter summarized it as "a bigger bang for a buck." The administration, especially Secretary of the Treasury George Humphrey, was convinced that unless the international commitments of the United States were brought into line with its economic capabilities, the well-being of the nation would suffer. Eisenhower later wrote in his memoirs that maintaining economic strength, of which a balanced budget was an important element, was part of national defense. The United States, said Secretary Humphrey, had "no business getting into little wars. If a situation comes up where our interests justify intervention, let's intervene decisively with all we have got or stay out."

Early in 1953 the administration tried to break out of the containment policy of Truman by announcing that the Seventh Fleet, patrolling the waters of the Formosa straits, would no longer inhibit an attack by Chiang Kai-shek's troops upon the Communist Chinese mainland. Although this action, known as "unleashing" Chiang, had long been demanded by the extremists in the party, it did not galvanize the Nationalist government on Formosa; two years later the administration felt it necessary to put Chiang "back on the leash." In April 1953 Secretary of State Dulles told the world that the United States did not consider the "captive peoples" of eastern Europe "a permanent fact of history." The implication was that the United States would not accept forever a policy of merely containing Russian power; it looked to a time when that power would be rolled back.

Furthermore, although Eisenhower and Dulles represented the internationalist wing of the Republican party, they thought that the Democrats had been too eager to have the United States assume the heaviest burden of European defense. Actually, in the last years of the Truman administration, the Democrats, under the prodding of Secretary of State Dean Acheson, had also been moving to build up Europe's self-defense. Acheson, for example, had urged German participation in NATO in order to counter Russian superiority in ground forces. That course, however, had not been acceptable to the western European nations. Instead, the western European countries suggested a new European Defense Community in which the armies of all the participants, including Germany, would be pooled. In this way fears of a revived and independent German military power would be assuaged. In 1953 this European Defense Community was being debated by the nations of western Europe, though French fears of any form of German rearmament raised serious doubts that it would be accepted. Piqued by what he considered French irresponsibility in the face of a common menace, and mindful of the administration's desire to cut United States military expenses, Secretary of State Dulles in December 1953 publicly threatened an "agonizing reappraisal" of American policy toward Europe unless France accepted the European Defense Community. The French parliament, nevertheless, in August 1954 voted down EDC. The military cooperation of the nations of western Europe was salvaged only by a compromise plan offered by Anthony Eden, Prime Minister of Great Britain. Eden suggested a looser "Western European Union" and, in a notable departure from British tradition, committed four British divisions to permanent station on the Continent. German rearmament, also provided for in Eden's proposal, began at the end of 1954.

The Policy of Massive Retaliation. Perhaps the most notable expression of the new look in foreign-military policy was Secretary Dulles' threat of retaliation against the Soviet Union or Communist China directly, regardless of where an attack began. Secretary Dulles set forth his new position in a public address on January 12, 1954, before the Council on Foreign Relations. "The basic decision," he said, "was [sic] to depend primarily upon a great capacity to retaliate, instantly, by means and at places of our own choosing." With such a policy, he explained, the Department of Defense could shape military policy to fit American needs. "That permits a selection of military means instead of a multiplication of means. As a result, it is now possible to get, and share, more basic security at less cost."

The new policy had the whole-hearted concurrence of the civilian head of the Defense Department, Charles E. Wilson. One general has written that he heard Wilson say, "We can't afford to fight limited wars. We can only afford to fight a big war, and if there is one that is the kind it will be." The administration's new look placed heavy emphasis upon air power—a shift that was quickly reflected in the distribution of expenditures among the three services. Between 1953 and 1955 the size of the ground forces was cut one third and the Navy 13 per cent, while the Air Force was increased. The budget for 1955 showed a decrease of over $4 billion for the Army, a $1.5 billion cut for the Navy, but an increase of $1.2 billion for the Air Force.

The crisis in the Middle East, which will be discussed later in this chapter, required the Eisenhower administration to halt temporarily the reduction in the number of ground troops, but the policy of depending mainly upon the Air Force and nuclear retaliation prevailed throughout the second as well as the first Eisenhower administration. This narrowing of options available for the defense of the country and for the conduct of foreign policy was strenuously opposed by three of the chairmen of the Joint Chiefs of Staff. All of them —Generals Matthew Ridgeway, James Gavin, and Maxwell Taylor—wrote books criticizing this policy after their retirement from the service. Later, Maxwell Taylor became an adviser to President Kennedy when that President reversed the new look approach to defense. During 1957 Secretary Wilson announced two 100,000-men cuts in the armed services, and after the Middle East crisis of 1958, the Department of Defense informed the nation that the growing perfection of long-range missiles (intercontinental ballistic missiles) had allowed the Department to put into effect "a new concept" of United States global military strategy. This new plan placed greater emphasis upon the I.C.B.M. as compared with the intermediate-range vehicles. A week later the Secretary of Defense recommended reductions of 71,000 men for the coming year. In subsequent years Sherman Adams, Eisenhower's principal Presidential Assistant, pointed out that the President believed that nuclear weapons would be used in any large war of the future and that to keep a large standing army was wasteful. In Eisenhower's mind expenditures for such an army jeopardized the government economy that he wanted to characterize his administration.

The Middle East crisis, however, did compel the administration to recognize that "little," or limited, wars might require some adjustment in defense plans. As a result a new Strategic Army Corps was established in 1958, composed of 150,000 paratroopers and infantrymen who were maintained within the continental United States for instant air transportation to trouble spots anywhere in the world. But it was not until the Kennedy years and the Berlin crisis of 1961 that the new look, with its dependence upon air power and nuclear weapons, was definitely abandoned in favor of a broader range of military responses to threats to American interests.

A New Era in International Affairs

The Death of Stalin. On March 5, 1953 — the same year that the Eisenhower administration took office in Washington — Josef Stalin died. As many informed sources anticipated, several months of confusion ensued before it became clear who would be Stalin's successor. At first it seemed to be Georgi Malenkov, the new Premier and a slavish follower of Stalin. Also prominent from the first was Nikita Khrushchev, the short, stocky, uneducated son of an impoverished miner. Reacting strongly against the terroristic iron rule of Stalin, which had engulfed even the immediate subordinates of the old dictator, the new rulers played down any particular one of their group. Instead, they talked about "collective leadership." As was learned later, however, a struggle for dominance by one man was going on behind the scenes. Early in July 1957, it was announced that Malenkov, Molotov, and one other old supporter of Stalin, all of whom had been prominent in the new collective leadership, had been dismissed from their posts in the government and in the party. Malenkov, in a decided improvement over the usual Stalinist practices, was not killed but was appointed director of a remote hydroelectric station, while Molotov, reputed by Secretary Dulles to be one of the world's great diplomats, was sent as Soviet ambassador to Outer Mongolia. Now that his possible rivals for power had been removed, Khrushchev emerged in March 1958 as the successor to Stalin's one-man rule. He became Premier as well as First Secretary of the party.

In addition to sparing the lives of his rivals, Khrushchev showed in other ways that he was quite a different kind of leader from Stalin. Ebullient where Stalin was taciturn, outgoing and talkative where Stalin was suspicious and secretive, the new leader proved to be Communism's and Russia's most persistent and tireless world salesman. He traveled to as many non-Communist countries as would have him, including the United States, where, in 1959, he talked with everybody, parrying criticisms with humor or heavy sarcasm. Everywhere he predicted the triumph of Communism and praised his country's achievements. Stalin, on the other hand, except for a brief trip to Teheran in 1943, never left the Soviet Union after taking power in 1924. With the rise to power of Khrushchev, Soviet policy, if it did not change in fundamentals, altered greatly in style. It became flexible, energetic, quick to take advantage of changes in the world scene, cleverly attuned to propaganda advantages, and especially resourceful in appealing to the interests and fears of the emerging, anticolonial nations of Asia and Africa.

The advent of Khrushchev marked more than a change in personality; it also announced a new Soviet view of international relations. At the Twentieth Congress of the Communist party of the Soviet Union (1956) at which he denounced Stalin and his use of terror, Khrushchev also announced that the old Marxist-Leninist dictum that war between socialism and capitalism was inevitable no longer held. "At the present," he told the Congress, "the situation has changed radically," by which he meant the new power of the Soviet Union in the world. Capitalist states, he admitted, would still act in a belligerent manner. "But war is not a fatalistic inevitability." This shift in the old line was pregnant for the future, since it indicated for the first time that the Russian leaders recognized that no one could win a nuclear war. That change in Russian outlook was to be not only the basis for the ideological split between the Soviet Union and Communist China, which first became noticeable in 1959–1960, but also the foundation for a new relationship between the United States and the Soviet Union.

Thus in both Washington and Moscow, the year 1953 marked a dividing line between two eras. By then the world had moved from the atmosphere of the immediate postwar years, in which the issues left over from the war were paramount, into an era in which new forces were at work. Perhaps the most striking alteration was that Europe by now had definitely ceased to be under serious threat from the Soviet Union—and everyone knew it. The European Recovery Plan, NATO, and a new, expanding prosperity had done their work. At last, men of all classes were enjoying the fruits of the industrial might of Europe. Automobiles, refrigerators, washing machines, television sets, and a thousand and one products of a consumers' society were now coming into the homes of the European working class for the first time. With a booming economy and a prosperous people, western Europe had regained its confidence; the fear of a Russian thrust to the rim of the Atlantic had virtually disappeared. In fact, the nature of the Soviet and Communist threat was now quite altered. The danger of military aggression was being replaced by threats of internal subversion and exploitation of unrest in the new nations emerging in Asia and Africa.

Testing the New Look. As we have seen, dependence upon air and naval power and the massive destructive power of nuclear weapons constituted the heart of the Eisenhower-Dulles alternative to containment. That policy, in large part, was dictated by a concern for financial economy and a desire to use the new technology of war to maximum advantage. The flaw, however, in attempting to employ the threat of nuclear war in dealing with any act of aggression, regardless of its size or place, was that the American monopoly of nuclear and hydrogen weapons no longer existed. By 1953 the Soviet Union had exploded both fission (nuclear) and fusion (hydrogen) devices and was presumably in a position to inflict upon the United States as much damage—if not more, considering the concentration of the American population and industry—as American forces could upon Russia. The "balance of terror" which thus ensued undermined the ability of any policy of "massive retaliation" to meet local and limited acts of aggression, Russian inspired or not.

The hard truth of the dilemma, even without nuclear weapons being involved, was evident in March and April of 1954 in the crisis in French Indochina. The French forces there, having fought the Communist-led Vietminh ever since 1945, found themselves about to suffer a decisive defeat at Dienbienphu. In response to French appeals for air assistance from the United States, several military and civilian figures in the administration, including Vice-President Nixon, counselled support, though not with nuclear weapons. Public opinion, however, when informed of the matter, was violently opposed to American involvement. President Eisenhower took the same view, and no American air support was sent. Without American military assistance, the French forces capitulated. During the summer at a conference in Geneva, the French agreed to a cease-fire, which ended French power in Indochina.

Alarmed by the loss of French Indochina, Secretary Dulles sought to bolster resistance to Communist penetration in the rest of southeast Asia by a new multination defense treaty (Southeast Asia Treaty Organization), signed by Thailand, Australia, New Zealand, the Philippines, Pakistan, and the United States. Concluded in September 1954 and modeled after the NATO agreement, SEATO expanded American military commitments tremendously but did little to increase the available power for meeting those obligations. Conspicuous by their absence from the new organization were other important states of southeast Asia: Indonesia, India, Ceylon, and Burma, all of which preferred to stay out of such an agreement in the interest of retaining their neutralist foreign policies.

The Geneva Conference, 1955. One sign that a new stage had been reached in the Cold War was the interest among the Western nations in holding a meeting of the heads of government of the Big Four powers, especially the United States and the Soviet Union. A meeting at the summit, as Winston Churchill called it, might help bring some relaxation of tensions and some progress in the long, fruitless search for a disarmament formula. By the summer of 1955, the administration was prepared to consider a meeting at Geneva with the Russians, the French, and the British. Eisenhower by this time was hopeful that some step might be taken which would reduce the suspicion between the West and the East and put a halt to the arms race, especially in nuclear weapons. The meeting took place in July 1955 with Khrushchev and Nikolai Bulganin, at that time the Soviet Premier, representing the Soviet Union.

Although the public statements that issued from the conference were optimistic, and the pictures of the four heads of state always showed them smiling, it was evident by the third day that the differences between the West and East were not being appreciably reduced by the discussions. The Russians, though, were apparently impressed by the earnestness of Eisenhower and perhaps for the first time began to question their unceasing public assertions that the West wanted war.

On the fourth day Eisenhower made a dramatic effort to bring the conference off dead center. After reading some remarks about American disarmament policy, he laid down his papers, took off his glasses, and, looking directly at the Russian delegation, offered a new proposal for disarmament. Obviously deeply sincere and almost beseeching in his effort to reach the Russians, Eisenhower suggested that both nations "give to each other a complete blueprint of our military establishments from beginning to end, from one end of our countries to the other; lay out the establishments and provide blueprints to each other. Next, to provide within our countries facilities for aerial photography to the other country . . . where you can take all the pictures you choose and take them to your own country to study. . . ." The suggestion was intended to be only the beginning of a broader plan to relieve both sides of the oppressive fear of another and more devastating Pearl Harbor. Since both superpowers were developing missiles capable of delivering nuclear and hydrogen bombs within a matter of minutes, the fear was realistic. The proposal, however, despite Eisenhower's high hopes, aroused only suspicion in the Russians. Six years later Khrushchev told President Kennedy that he thought the plan was no more than a way to carry on espionage in the Soviet Union. The Americans were so fearful of another Pearl Harbor that within a year after the Russian rejection of the open skies idea, Eisenhower authorized secret reconnaissance flights across Soviet territory. In 1960 these flights would turn out to be more than simply a means of getting intelligence.

Although the open skies idea had practical difficulties and reflected Eisenhower's naïveté in international relations, it certainly demonstrated the willingness of the United States to think anew about disarmament, and it convinced millions of people of the President's genuine desire to dissipate the dark and sluggish cloud of war that hung over the world. The open skies proposal, like the conference itself, also offered evidence that the administration was adjusting its policy in the face of the new posture of Russians since 1953.

The Suez and Hungarian Crises. Two tests of American policy occurred, almost simultaneously, in November 1956. The most important occurred in Egypt. Ever since 1952 Egypt had been going through a revolution from above, led by young, nationalistic army officers. The revolutionary leaders wanted to rid their country of its historic dependence upon Great Britain and to efface the humiliating defeat at the hands of the Israelis in the Palestinian War of 1948. Politically, the revolution reached a climax with the deposing of the corrupt King Farouk in 1953 and the proclamation of a republic. The new republic, bent upon ridding Egypt of all vestiges of British power, pushed for the withdrawal of British troops from the Suez Canal, a goal that was reached in July 1954, when the British promised to bring home, within two years, all their troops in the canal region. That same year a young, ardently nationalist colonel, Gamal Abdel Nasser, became head of the revolution and the government. Ambitious and bold in behalf of his country's nationalist goals, Nasser appealed to both the Western powers and the Soviet Union for military and economic aid. At the same time that he was negotiating with the United States for financial assistance to construct a giant dam on the upper Nile at Aswan, his government recognized the Communist government of China. Irritated by this playing of both sides, Secretary Dulles cancelled the negotiations for American aid in the building of the Aswan dam. One week later, in July 1956, and two months after the departure of the British troops, Nasser moved to take over the Suez Canal. Contrary to its treaty obligations, Egypt nationalized the canal, which was owned largely by French and British stockholders. The European powers, heavily dependent upon the Middle Eastern oil that passed through the canal, protested vehemently. Then, on October 25, Israel, provoked by repeated minor acts of aggression by Egyptian forces on their common border and encouraged secretly by England and France, crossed the Egyptian frontier in force. Ten days later, as planned, British and French paratroopers dropped on Egyptian soil in an effort to recapture control of the canal and, hopefully, to oust Nasser.

At almost the same time that British and French troops were invading Egypt, Russian tanks were entering Budapest in Hungary to put down a revolt of the Hungarian people against the Communist regime there. Relentlessly and ruthlessly, the Russian army crushed the heroic Hungarian rebels, while Khrushchev threatened Britain and France with nuclear bombing by long-range missile if they did not withdraw their forces from Egypt.

Both the Suez and Hungarian incidents took the United States government by surprise. The French and British, unsure of the American attitude toward their intentions in the canal area, had failed to inform Washington of their plans. Angry that allies of the United States should ignore his views, and deeply concerned over the possible Russian response to the armed attack on Egypt, Eisenhower threw the influence of the United States government, at home and at the U.N., against the French and British. With both American and Russian as well as world opinion aroused against them, the British and French governments agreed to a cease-fire and the withdrawal of their troops. Israel also withdrew its troops in response to a resolution of the U.N. Assembly. A United Nations force was hastily created to patrol the border between Israel and Egypt—the first such force in history. Nasser's army, much less prepared than he had led the world and his own people to believe, was thereby saved from certain defeat.

Preoccupied with the Egyptian situation, the United States and the Western powers were unwilling to take any action about Hungary other than to publicize the plight of the Hungarian people in the United Nations. Actually, the circumstances and the location of Hungary in the center of Europe, far from any Allied territory, precluded any action short of direct war with the Soviet Union. Later Eisenhower wrote that he had feared that Russian insecurity about Poland and Hungary, both of which were resisting Communist rule, might be triggered into a world war if the United States made any threatening action. To assuage Russian apprehensions, the United States reaffirmed its earlier promise not to ally itself with either Hungary or Poland against the Soviet Union.

The Eisenhower Doctrine. The attack upon Egypt by Britain, France, and Israel threw Nasser and those countries which supported him, like Syria, into

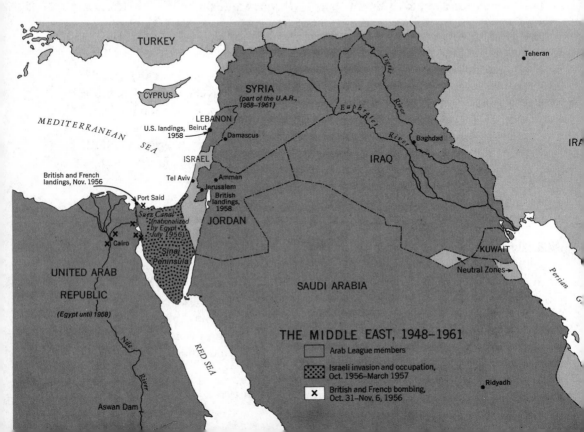

THE MIDDLE EAST, 1948–1961

▢ Arab League members

▨ Israeli invasion and occupation, Oct. 1956–March 1957

✕ British and French bombing, Oct. 31–Nov. 6, 1956

closer association with the Soviet Union, which was credited with stopping the invasion by its missile rattling. Rumors of Soviet infiltration of the Middle East through friendship with Nasser circulated in late 1956 and 1957. Washington became increasingly worried about the possibility of Russian influence becoming permanent and extensive in that unstable and turbulent region. As a result in March 1957, in response to an appeal from President Eisenhower, Congress passed a resolution affirming American intentions to aid any country in the Middle East that seemed to be threatened by Communist penetration.

The test of the "Eisenhower Doctrine," as it was soon called, came in the spring of 1958. During May, in the former French colony of Lebanon on the shores of the eastern Mediterranean, the pro-Western government came under increasing threats from its few local Communists and Arab nationalists and from the pro-Nasser government of neighboring Syria. Fearful that it could not survive, the Lebanese government appealed to the United Nations for support. Before any action was taken at the U.N., the pro-Western monarchy of Iraq was overthrown by a friend of Nasser's. To Eisenhower and his advisers, this latest eruption in the Middle East seemed to be a prelude to a Nasser-Russian attack on Lebanon. As a result, the United States on July 15, under the authority of the Congressional resolution of the preceding year, rushed 3500 troops to Lebanon. The same day the British flew 2000 men into Jordan to bolster its pro-Western regime against possible attack. No attacks occurred, and by August the crisis was over with the pro-Western governments in the two countries secure. American and British troops were entirely withdrawn in October.

By 1957, then, the administration had come full circle in its attitude toward Russian expansion. Once extremely dubious, if not contemptuous, of the validity of containment, it was now prepared to do its best to carry out that doctrine, since it had found the policy of massive retaliation too cumbersome a tool for dealing with the kind of local crises that seemed to characterize the Communist threat after the Korean War. One other lesson had been learned. After the Middle Eastern crises of 1956 and 1958, it was evident that Moscow was not the only source of instability in the world. Rising nationalism in western as well as eastern Asia, not to mention in Africa, was injecting a new and dangerous element into world politics.

The President as Missionary. One sign of the influence of the new nations was the strenuous efforts of the two superpowers to win their support. Khrushchev, for example, in the late 1950's, made several tours of Europe and Asia, especially to professedly neutral countries like India, to "sell" the Russian position on war and peace. Whether influenced by Khrushchev's example or by his own concern over the accelerating arms race, Eisenhower, despite two heart attacks and a serious abdominal operation in the preceding four years, undertook three extended foreign tours within six months.

These attempts to win the approval of world opinion for American policy were related to Dulles' resignation in April 1959 because of ill health. Dulles had always been the most adamant member of the administration in dealing with the world and the Russians. He had opposed, for example, the meeting of heads of government at Geneva in 1955. With Dulles gone, a more personal and relaxed approach to foreign policy came to the fore. Even before Eisenhower embarked upon his trips, and within three months of Dulles' resignation, Vice-President Nixon made a trip to Moscow, where he presented the American view of world affairs to the Russian people at the opening of the United States exposition at a trade fair.

The President was acutely conscious that his years in the White House were fast drawing to a close. Though he never reveled in the job, he saw it as an opportunity; personal visits might further his great ambition to secure a lasting peace. He told the American people just before he left on the first trip in December 1959, "During this mission of peace and goodwill, I hope to promote a better understanding of America and to learn more of our friends abroad."

The first trip, which was to India, the Middle East, and southern Europe, was the longest in time and distance: 19 days to stop in 11 countries on 3 continents, for a total of 22,000 miles. His welcome in India was perhaps the most overwhelming in a career studded with mass greetings; an estimated one million people turned out to hear and see him in New Delhi; crowds almost as large met him in Karachi, Pakistan, and in Teheran, Iran. In late February 1960 he embarked upon a two-week tour of Latin America, where he was well received, though only a year before Vice-President Nixon had been stoned and spat upon in Peru and Venezuela. The President's third visit—to Asia—in June 1960, however, was quite different from the previous two.

For some months anti-American sentiment in Japan had been growing among students and left-wing organizations. It came to a climax on June 11 when James Haggerty, the President's press secretary, arrived in Tokyo to make preparations for the President's arrival some days later. Haggerty's car was surrounded by a yelling, prancing, stone-throwing mob at the airport, necessitating the rescue of the American officials from their besieged automobile by a U.S. Marine helicopter. Later demonstrations against the United States reached such proportions that the Japanese government requested the President to cancel his scheduled visit to Japan. As a consequence the President visited only Taiwan, the Philippines, and Korea.

The U-2 Incident. The Japanese riots against the United States that summer were undoubtedly encouraged by a spectacular failure of American foreign policy earlier in the spring. On May 5, less than two weeks before the heads of the three Western powers were scheduled to meet with the Russians at another summit meeting in Paris, the Soviet government announced that its armed forces had shot down an American espionage plane deep within Soviet territory. The United States at first denied the allegation, saying that the unarmed plane—a U-2, a high-altitude reconnaissance plane—had been on nothing more than a routine weather mission along the borders of the Soviet

Union. This answer to the Soviet charge proved to be highly embarrassing to the United States. The next day, May 7, Premier Khrushchev triumphantly and indignantly informed the Soviet parliament that the pilot of the American plane was alive and in the hands of the Soviet authorities. Moreover, Khrushchev said, the pilot confessed that his mission had been to fly across the Soviet Union from Pakistan to Norway, photographing military installations. The plane had been brought down at Sverlovsk, 1200 miles inside the Soviet border.

Confronted with the evidence, the United States admitted the truth of the Soviet charges but defended them—in Eisenhower's phrase—as "a distasteful but vital necessity" to protect the world against another Pearl Harbor. The flights had actually been going on since 1956, but heretofore, apparently, no Soviet rocket had been able to reach the high-flying U-2. The administration's aberrant interpretation of international law evoked much opposition inside and outside the United States and was, in effect, abandoned when Eisenhower announced on the eve of the Paris summit meeting that the flights were being halted. (President Kennedy later refused to renew the flights on the ground that the risks involved were not worth the information gained.)

The whole U-2 affair dealt American prestige a heavy blow, since it caught American authorities in a deliberate, official falsehood. Moreover, considering the closeness in time of the flight to the convening of the Paris meeting, it seemed to suggest a recklessness in American activities that most people in the United States and in the West in general did not associate with the hitherto cautious Eisenhower administration. Some of the opprobrium piled upon the United States government both at home and abroad, however, dissipated on May 16, when Khrushchev broke up the conference before it began by demanding an apology from Eisenhower for the flights. Two days later, when it was apparent that the President was not going to apologize, Khrushchev held a two-and-a-half-hour press conference during which he furiously castigated the United States and the President for permitting the flights. Back in Moscow in June, Khrushchev insulted the President personally during a press conference and brought Soviet-American relations to a new impasse. A majority of the Senate Foreign Relations Committee, after holding hearings on the U-2 incident, concluded that the administration had mishandled the matter and that without the incident the Paris conference would probably have been held as scheduled. Eisenhower's cherished hope of a new relationship with the Soviet Union went aglimmering.

Troubles Nearer Home. Also during 1960 American relations with a new regime in Cuba deteriorated ominously. Ever since 1956 a young revolutionary, Fidel Castro, had been fighting a guerrilla war in the Sierra Maestra Mountains against the regime of General Fulgencio Batista, the dictator of Cuba. Castro's forces grew in strength as more and more people recognized the corruption and tyrannical character of Batista's regime. On January 1, 1959, the rebels moved out of the hills and mountains; Batista, seeing the handwriting on the wall, fled the country. The following day Castro's bearded revolutionaries entered Havana to proclaim a new order in Cuba. The United States, hopeful that Cuba was now on the way to a more honest and democratic government, recognized the new regime in a matter of days. Castro, a striking giant of a man with a full beard, made an unofficial good will tour of the United States during which he received an enthusiastic welcome, both publicly and privately, visiting even with Vice-President Nixon and other dignitaries of the government.

Events back in Cuba, however, aroused American misgivings about the new regime. Arbitrary military trials that ended in the execution of hundreds of so-called war criminals and widespread confiscations of property were especially disturbing. That summer the United States officially expressed its concern to Castro over the new agrarian reform law which, the United States asserted, was taking American property without adequate compensation.

The American protests did not stop the Cuban confiscations. Indeed, during 1959 and early 1960, the Cuban government assumed an increasingly anti-American attitude in both word and deed. Over a billion dollars worth of American business assets in Cuba were confiscated without compensation. That the Cuban government harbored Marxists and was very friendly toward the Soviet Union and Communist China did not diminish American anxieties. (Later, in his memoirs, Eisenhower said that he had refused to see Castro during his visit in 1959 because he believed the Cuban to be a Communist sympathizer.) A visit to Cuba by a high Soviet official in February 1960 resulted in the extension of $100 million in credits and an agreement by the Soviets to purchase five million tons of Cuban sugar over the next five years. Fearful that these and other trade arrangements with the Soviet bloc were precursors of Soviet economic and political domination, the United States took strong measures to express its disapproval. In late May the United States ended all economic aid to Cuba, and in July at the recommendation of Congress, the President cut the imports of Cuban sugar by 95 per cent. Sugar was not only Cuba's main export, but the United States was the island's biggest customer. The immediate Cuban reaction was more name calling and public displays of anti-Americanism in the plazas of Havana. By the close of 1960, Cuban-American relations were a source of widespread public and Congressional concern, irritation, and frustration.

Deeply disturbed by the increasingly anti-American and pro-Soviet character of the Castro regime, the administration quietly undertook countermeasures. In March 1960, two months before the public announcement of the cut in the sugar quota, it approved a plan for the secret military training of anti-Castro Cuban refugees for an invasion of the island. The training took place in remote sections of Guatemala, under the direction of the U.S. Central Intelligence Agency. The actual invasion was postponed because of the American presidential elections, but both the military leaders in the government and the CIA pressed the new President, John F. Kennedy, for an invasion early in 1961. The aim was to mount the invasion before the arrival in Cuba of new, Soviet-built jet airplanes, which would threaten the success of the invasion.

Kennedy found himself in a quandary about the invasion; he had not been privy to its organization, yet he was now expected to countenance it. New in the job, and desirous of not appearing weak in the face of military insistence upon going through with the plan, he agreed to it. His one requirement was that United States forces not be involved in the actual invasion, though he permitted them to assist in bringing the refugee-soldiers from Guatemala to the point of invasion. Actually, the invasion was badly planned and even more ineptly executed. For one thing, the newspapers in the United States learned of the secret training camps and so eliminated the element of surprise. For another, the size of the force was wholly inadequate, and American intelligence as to Castro's strength and popular support was wide of the mark. The 1500 Cubans who landed at the Bay of Pigs in April 1961 were easily crushed in a matter of hours by Castro's superior air and ground forces. The invaders neither got to the hills to carry on guerrilla warfare, nor did their attack trigger the popular uprising they had expected. Castro was simply stronger militarily and politically than the Cuban refugees and American intelligence had believed.

The Bay of Pigs was a fiasco from any point of view. As a power play, it was inexcusable, since no real power had been committed by the United States; thus the scheme was bound to fail. As a violation of international law and the inter-American agreements, it put the United States in the position of supporting the kind of subversive activity that it condemned when perpetrated by Communist states. Kennedy was shaken by his first venture into foreign policy. Manfully, he accepted full responsibility for the humiliating experience, but he recognized that he had accepted advice he should have questioned closely. Two days after the fiasco he asked Theodore Sorenson, his close assistant, "How could I have been so far off base? . . . All my life I've known better than to depend on the experts. How could I have been so stupid, to let them go ahead?" But because he had let them go ahead, he felt a deep responsibility for the invaders who languished in Castro's prisons, and he later managed to arrange for their return to the United States.

The Bay of Pigs incident had an enormous impact on Europe. American prestige, already shaken by the U-2 incident, plunged to a new low. As happened in the U-2 incident, the United States was again caught in an official lie, which called into question the government's future credibility. At the United Nations, Adlai Stevenson, the American representative, had categorically denied that his country was involved in the attack when the charge was made by the Cuban delegate. In Latin America the Cuban fiasco undercut the strenuous efforts of the United States to overcome Latin American hostility, which American intervention and Dollar Diplomacy had aroused in the early years of the century. Now, after 30 years of practising the Good Neighbor policy, the United States had given new ground for cries of "Yankee Imperialism," which went up from Mexico City to Buenos Aires.

The Bay of Pigs did more than lower American prestige in Europe and Latin America; it prepared the ground for a more dangerous confrontation in the Western Hemisphere with the Soviet Union itself.

SUGGESTED READING

The complexities and myriad details of the international politics of the 1950's are clearly discussed from somewhat different points of view in Jules Davids, *America and the World of Our Time* (revised ed., 1962) and John Spanier, *American Foreign Policy Since World War II** (2nd revised ed., 1965), the latter taking a "hard-nosed" *Realpolitik* approach. Less interpretative, but more complete is Wilfrid F. Knapp, *A History of War and Peace, 1939–1965* (1967), the work of an English scholar. Louis J. Halle, *The Cold War as History* (1967) surveys the postwar international situation with detachment and insight, arguing for an abandonment of the fears and anxieties that have caused the United States to overextend itself around the world. Evan Luard, ed., *The Cold War: A Reappraisal** (1964) is a collection of comments by English and other scholars. Hugh Seton-Watson, *Neither War Nor Peace** (1960) is a comprehensive and informed survey of the international situation during the 1950's. A. Doak Barnett, *Communist China and Asia: A Challenge to American Policy** (1960), Edwin O. Reischauer, *The United States and Japan* (3rd ed., 1965) and Cecil V. Crabb, Jr., *The Elephants and the Grass: A Study of Nonalignment** (1965) are good introductions to particular areas of American concern as the Cold War spread beyond Europe.

The literature on the Korean War is a fast growing one, and only a few items can be mentioned here. The best general account of the war is by a Briton David Rees, *Korea: The Limited War* (1964). T. R. Fehrenbach, *This Kind of War** (1963) is a detailed military history, drawing the moral that the United States must never let down its guard. Douglas MacArthur, *Reminiscences** (1964) and Matthew Ridgway, *The Korean War* (1967) are the recollections of the two U.S. commanders in Korea, who each saw the war in quite a different light. John W. Spanier, *The Truman-MacArthur Controversy and the Korean War** (1959) is the best study of perhaps the most critical episode in the history of civilian-military relationships in the United States. The best work on the Chinese intervention is Allen S. Whiting, *China Crosses the Yalu* (1960), which shows that the Chinese gave ample warning of their intention to counter the move north of the 38th parallel. Allen Guttmann, ed., *Korea and the Theory of Limited War** (1967) is a good introduction to the crucial place of that war in strategic military thought.

Eisenhower's foreign policy is rather hostilely analyzed in Norman A. Graebner, *The New Isolationism: A Study in Politics and Foreign Policy Since 1950* (1956). Paul Peeters, *Massive Retaliation: The Policy and its Critics* (1958) is a defense of the

*Available in a paperback edition.

administration's foreign policy under Dulles. Very critical of Dulles is Herman Finer, *Dulles Over Suez* (1964), which deals with the Middle East crisis of 1956. James M. Gavin, *War and Peace in the Space Age* (1958) and Maxwell D. Taylor, *Uncertain Trumpet* (1960) are books by high Army officers who objected to the Eisenhower administration's policy of "more bang for a buck." David Wise and Thomas B. Ross, *The U-2 Affair* (1962) is an exciting play-by-play journalistic account of that regrettable incident. Richard M. Nixon, *Six Crises* (1962) discusses in a sympathetic manner some foreign policy decisions within the administration. Dwight D. Eisenhower, *Waging Peace* (1965), which is the second volume of his memoirs, is indispensable for the administration's point of view on foreign policy. See also other studies of the Eisenhower administration discussed in the Suggested Reading for Chapter Three.

The Transformation of Japan / Pictorial Essay

At the end of World War II, 40 per cent of Japan's urban areas had been destroyed. Most of Japan's merchant marine, on which the nation's industrial production depended for raw materials, had been sunk. Industrial production had fallen to one seventh of the 1941 level. These were the conditions at the beginning of the American occupation of Japan. The main objective of the occupation was to establish the conditions for a democratic government. The most dramatic and lasting reforms were aimed at developing in the Japanese a sense of individuality and personal rights. If successful, such a program would, the occupation authorities argued, be the best defense against the revival of authoritarian government in Japan.

Women, who were given legal equality and the right to vote, were quick to take up their new rights. Today, more women than men vote in Japan, and many women have been elected to office. As educational opportunities were equalized, more women entered business and professional life. One consequence of these changes was a rapid alteration in traditional social customs. Women now generally walk abreast of their husbands, and the husbands are often seen carrying their share of babies and bundles.

Other social reforms affected young people. The oppressive powers of heads of families over adult family members were abolished. Educational re-

Hiroshima, 100 feet from ground zero. *Photo: Department of Defense*

Western clothing predominates in these two pictures, although two of the women are wearing traditional dress. Note the father tending the baby. One indication of the close relationship with the United States is the English traffic signs in the picture of the young couple. *Photos: Hiroshi Hamaya-Magnum; Below: Marc Riboud-Magnum*

forms encouraged intellectual independence in young people, who were also encouraged to develop as individuals with less deference to their elders. The younger generation was also quick to pick up Western attitudes and customs. As prearranged marriages declined, Western customs of dating became common. Western dress

Expressway in downtown Tokyo. *Photo: Wide World. Below:* Toshiba electronics plant outside of Tokyo. *Photo: Burt Glinn-Magnum. Opposite page:* Luxury hotel south of Tokyo. *Photo: Wide World*

was widely adopted, even to the "jeans" and "sneakers" of the girl on p. 75. American music and baseball (always popular in Japan) flourished. Japan has become a meeting ground of cultures, which has been confusing and upsetting for Japanese of all ages and classes.

Equally spectacular and a further measure of Western influence has been the dramatic growth of the Japanese economy. Japan has developed into the world's fourth largest industrial power. The land reforms of the occupation developed a middle class among the peasantry, thereby expanding markets and encouraging industrial growth. When the United States increased its purchases from Japan during the Korean War, the economy received further impetus to a sustained growth rate that, since the middle fifties, has not fallen below 10 per cent a year. This economic boom has turned Japan in the sixties into a modern nation. Yet even in the modern skyscrapers, the old influences can be seen in pagoda-like roofs, just as the temples, art, and literature of the past mingle with Western ideas and culture.

Japan's future, like its present, is filled with contrast and paradox. Since Japan is more technologically advanced, it logically should assume the leadership among the non-Communist Asian countries, but its past as an aggressor inhibits the Japanese from easily assuming this role.

CHAPTER THREE

A REPUBLICAN INTERLUDE

DEMOCRATS AND REPUBLICANS in 1948 had both urged upon General Eisenhower the acceptance of their respective party's nomination for the presidency, and he had respectfully and steadfastly refused both. At one point he painstakingly set forth cogent reasons why a military man like himself, who had spent his whole life outside of civilian pursuits, would not be the proper man for the office. Cogent as his arguments may have been, they could not erase from politicians' minds thoughts of Eisenhower's immense popularity and the respect in which he was held. For—as the journalist Marquis Childs has pointed out—the American adoration of Eisenhower in the postwar years was only comparable to the English idolization of the Duke of Wellington after his defeat of Napoleon. Nor was it forgotten that the Iron Duke became England's postwar prime minister.

The Election of 1952

After 1948 the Democrats were no longer interested in Eisenhower, for in public statements as president of Columbia University the General had made clear that his political views were Republican. He deprecated, for example, the Democrats' concern with social security and health insurance by saying that those who wanted security could find it in prison. Thus the Republicans had a clear field in trying to convince him that it was his duty to run for President in 1952. Even his appointment as Supreme Commander of the North Atlantic Treaty Organization forces in December 1950 did not seriously interfere with the mounting Republican effort to nominate him. Especially interested in his candidacy were leading members of the eastern, international wing of the party, which had supported Thomas Dewey in two previous campaigns. In fact, it was Dewey himself in 1950–1951 who did most to talk up Eisenhower's candidacy, despite the General's refusal to commit himself.

The Eisenhower Story. Born in 1890 in Denison, Texas, Dwight David Eisenhower was raised in Abilene, Kansas, one of five brothers in a family of decidedly modest income. It was the mother who held the family together and who left the enduring impression on the five sons. Never a studious boy, but much interested in sports and physical activity, Dwight went to work after high school. Then, at the age of 20, and largely by chance, he was successful in his try for an appointment to the United States Military Academy. At West Point he was hardly a model cadet; he broke rules, though never to the extent of being dismissed and was no more than a fair student. In sports Eisenhower excelled and, but for an injury, might well have become one of Army's star football players. After West Point his life followed the pattern of officers in the peacetime Army: frequent changes from one dull post to an even duller one, with promotions slow in coming and pay barely adequate. For a while in the thirties, he served in Paris and in Manila under General Douglas Mac-Arthur. After 20 years of active duty, Eisenhower had reached only the rank of major. Then came the Second World War, bringing new activities, rapid

Eisenhower with Chiang Kai-shek in Formosa. *Photo: Wide World* promotion, and a new sense of purpose. As a kind of protegé of General George C. Marshall, the chief of staff, Eisenhower now moved up quickly in rank; within two years he went from colonel to full general and to the command of the mightiest army ever assembled. With victory in Europe, his name became known to every American and most Europeans; his popularity may well have exceeded that of any public figure in the twentieth century. Eisenhower's radiant smile, warm manner, and genuine interest in and respect for people made him a natural political candidate. Moreover, his meteoric rise from truly humble origins fitted in well with the American tradition of presidential nominees.

The Republican Convention. During the spring of 1952, despite the General's refusal to say whether he was a candidate or not, those who wanted him continued to act as if he were. And, sure enough, just before the Republican nominating convention opened on July 11, Eisenhower resigned his military commands and announced his willingness to try for the nomination. His most formidable opponent was Senator Robert A. Taft, the acknowledged leader of the Middle Western isolationist wing of the party, which dominated the grass-roots organizations. But, as had been true for the preceding two conventions, the eastern, internationalist faction of the party controlled a majority of the delegates. In the very first days of the preliminary meetings, the Taft supporters were beaten on a procedural matter; it was thus made clear which way the balloting would go. Despite valiant efforts to prevent it, and amid many public, as well as private, expressions of bitterness by the Taft forces, Eisenhower was nominated on the first ballot. His partner in the race was Richard M. Nixon, senator from California, who as a congressman a few years before had made a name for himself as the member of the House Committee on Un-American Activities who had unmasked Alger Hiss.

The Democrats' Problem. The Republican Congress in 1947, remembering Franklin Roosevelt's four terms, succeeded in adding the Twenty-Second Amendment to the Constitution. Harry Truman, however, as the incumbent of the office, did not come under its limit of two terms for the presidency. Nevertheless, in March 1952 he announced to the country that he was not a candidate. Truman's first choice for his successor was his friend, Chief Justice Fred M. Vinson, but Vinson would not leave the Court. Early in 1952 Truman began to talk of the possible candidacy of the first-term governor of Illinois, Adlai Stevenson. The Governor was not widely known outside of his state and Washington D.C., where he had worked during the war. Moreover, he was genuinely interested in completing his record as governor. Repeatedly, Stevenson told the press and the politicians who were interested in his candidacy, that he was not available. But for lack of a more popular candidate and because Stevenson was an accomplished speaker, an exceptionally literate writer, and a good campaigner, the pressure upon him continued. Not quite prepared to remove himself irrevocably from the race, Stevenson found himself drafted for the nomination after a three-ballot fight with Estes Kefauver of Tennessee. Stevenson's draft was probably the first true draft since Garfield's in 1880. In an effort to heal the wounds of the 1948 campaign over civil rights, the convention named a moderate Southerner, Senator John J. Sparkman of Alabama, as Stevenson's vice-presidential candidate.

A Popular Campaign. During the conventions and campaign in 1952, more people than ever before watched at first hand the process of choosing a President. The extensive television coverage of the two conventions, which incidentally cost $11 million, enabled viewers to have better seats at the mammoth gatherings than most of the participants themselves. The most spectacular use of television during the campaign was Senator Nixon's defense of his probity. Early in the campaign, a newspaper revealed that a group of wealthy California businessmen had been contributing to a special fund for Nixon while he was a senator. Inasmuch as Eisenhower in his campaign was making much of the lax financial standards of the Truman administration, the revelation about Nixon could not be passed over. Eisenhower, obviously taken aback by the incident, waited several days before deciding whether Nixon had become a political liability. Meanwhile Nixon appeared on a nationwide telecast in which he missed no opportunity to present himself as a wronged person who had never accepted a dishonest dollar in his life. Nor did he overlook a chance to cast innuendoes at the Democrats, as when he referred to his wife's "respectable Republican cloth coat"—a sly reference to the mink coat scandals of the Truman administration. So overwhelmingly favorable was the response to Nixon's fight for his political life, that Eisenhower quickly decided he was a definite asset in the campaign.

The Republicans attacked the Democrats from a number of angles. Since this was still the era of the Great Fear, charges of corruption and Communist infiltration of government were heard widely. But unquestionably the most telling issue was the Korean War, which was unpopular. "We are suffering from a new kind of K.K.K.," said Stevenson's manager late in the campaign, "Korea, Communism, and corruption." Since the Republicans had not had a President since Hoover, the Democrats hammered home the poor record of the Republican party in the Great Depression. Recognizing the powerful appeal of this argument, Eisenhower acted to counter it. Again and again during the campaign, he promised to mobilize the resources of government to combat a depression if one should occur while he were President. His promise signaled his public acceptance of the New Deal revolution.

Almost from the outset Stevenson was running behind the General. Yet his serious attention to what he considered the issues of maintaining domestic prosperity and securing a permanent peace abroad, and his literate, often witty speeches captured the imagination of millions of people who had never heard of him before. Not since the days of Woodrow Wilson had the voters been treated to the urbanity and precision of language which characterized almost every one of Stevenson's carefully prepared and lucid speeches. A

Roper poll showed that in answer to the question of whether each of the candidates was a "man of really high intelligence," Stevenson's percentages of "yes" went from 38 in August to 48 in late October; Eisenhower's went from 52 to 53.

Recognizing that Korea was the key to the election, Eisenhower in late October announced that if elected he would immediately "forego the diversion of politics . . . to concentrate on the job of ending the Korean War. . . . That job," he pointed out, "requires a personal trip to Korea. I shall make that trip. . . . I shall go to Korea." Whether that dramatic promise or merely the widespread dissatisfaction with the Korean War was responsible for Eisenhower's victory is hard to say. But there seems little doubt that the continuance of the war was the heaviest burden which Stevenson and Sparkman had to carry as the heirs of the Truman foreign policy.

Pre-election polls and post-election analyses amply demonstrated that the war was actively disliked by most Americans, not so much because it was a war, but because it was being fought under circumstances Americans found hard to accept. In October 52 per cent of those polled voluntarily listed Korea as the main issue in the election. Moreover, as the MacArthur hearings had made clear, most Americans did not like the limited aims and therefore the self-imposed restrictions under which the administration chose to carry on the war. With no victory in the usual sense possible, the war had a hopeless air, which the Republicans did not hesitate to emphasize. As one Truman supporter told a reporter in 1952, "I'm against this idea that we can go on trading hills in Korea indefinitely." One southern Democrat put it more directly: "If the war is settled by November, I'll be for Stevenson. If not, it's Ike. If we can't get a truce I figure we'll need a military man around to clean things up." Even the prosperity, which ordinarily works to the advantage of the party in power, was turned against the Democrats that year. Many voters felt that the good times at home were being purchased at the cost of American blood in Korea. In short, the charges of corruption and Communist infiltration of government were only secondary. But in conjunction with the war, they added up to an unsuperable handicap for Stevenson, especially when placed beside the fame and prestige of Eisenhower.

The Measure of Eisenhower's Victory. The popular vote for Eisenhower was overwhelming: 33.9 million to Stevenson's 27.3 million; this disparity was even exceeded by that in the electoral college: 442 to 89. Eisenhower's vote-getting power was attested by his running 15 per cent ahead of his party's vote for Congress and by his decisively breaking into the solid South for the first time since 1928. Border states like Missouri, Kentucky, and Maryland, middle southern states like Tennessee and Virginia, and deep southern states like Texas and Florida all trooped into Eisenhower's column. Despite his internationalist position, he even captured the isolationist belt of the Middle West. Of the 57 counties in the nation which had consistently deserted the Republicans ever since 1928, Eisenhower gained back 31; he carried counties

THE ELECTION OF 1952

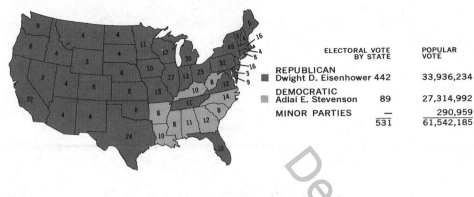

	ELECTORAL VOTE BY STATE	POPULAR VOTE
REPUBLICAN Dwight D. Eisenhower	442	33,936,234
DEMOCRATIC Adlai E. Stevenson	89	27,314,992
MINOR PARTIES	—	290,959
	531	61,542,185

in both the North and the South which had never voted for a Republican President. Eisenhower, was the first Republican since 1928 to attract substantial support from all classes as well as from all sections of the country.

In voting for a general, the country was giving voice to its weariness with partisan politics, for in America, unlike in continental Europe, Army officers have been almost ostentatiously detached from politics. Many U.S. Army officers, like General George Marshall and Eisenhower himself before 1948, refrain from voting in order to symbolize their lack of political partisanship.

Eisenhower's break into the South was still another measure of the increasing role of urban voters in elections. Studies have shown that 85 per cent of white-collar voters in southern cities voted for Eisenhower—an echo of early twentieth-century political history, when northern cities had been a stronghold of Republican voters. Moreover, in 1952 urban, middle-income voters in the South, long strongly Democratic, swung to Eisenhower. Furthermore, the lack of unions in the South meant that the urban working class there, traditionally conservative anyway, would not follow the pattern of northern urban workers, whose unions closely tied them to the Democratic party.

Across the nation Eisenhower sliced into the old Roosevelt-Truman coalition by capturing substantial Irish and German (both Catholic and Protestant) votes and making inroads in the traditional Democratic allegiance of Poles. Women of all classes and backgrounds seemed to favor Eisenhower as a more attractive personality than Stevenson, who was divorced. In November women voted heavily for Eisenhower, and their ballots made up a larger proportion of the electorate than men's.

Despite the magnitude of Eisenhower's victory, Stevenson still won more votes than any presidential candidate in history, except for Roosevelt in the landslide of 1936. Part of the explanation is that he benefited from the increase in population, but the more important explanation is that he held the great majority of those who formed the hard core of the Democratic coalition, which Franklin Roosevelt had first put together in the 1930's. The northern cities, organized labor, Negroes, Jews, and the rural South hardly broke ranks under the Eisenhower attack.

As befitted a victory of such proportions, Eisenhower entered the White House with Republican majorities in both houses, but because he was unable to carry Congressional candidates to victory with him in his personally successful invasion of Dixie, these majorities were rather slim. On the other hand, many of the Southerners, though Democrats in name, were more sympathetic to the Republican program than to some of the liberal aims of their own party. With these men Eisenhower could work.

Building a New Republican Party

The Republican Problem. Ever since the Depression and the advent of the Second World War, there have been two Republican parties rather than one. The division between them has been evident in both foreign and domestic policies. Although by the 1940's the majority of Americans accepted most of the New Deal measures as permanent features of American life, conservative Republicans continued to reject them. Nevertheless, as we have seen, by 1948 a significant segment of the party leadership, headed by Thomas Dewey of New York,, Earl Warren of California, and Harold Stassen of Minnesota, was quite prepared to accept the New Deal revolution as a fact of political and social life. Moreover, after 1941 this same wing of the party, best represented by Senator Arthur Vandenberg, espoused an internationalist position in foreign policy, supporting the United Nations, the Marshall Plan, and NATO. Yet this eastern, liberal, internationalist wing, though it managed to control the presidential conventions beginning in 1940, did not constitute a majority of Republicans. Indeed, the tendency of the typical Republican was to follow the lead of figures like Senator Robert A. Taft of Ohio, a moderate conservative in domestic politics (see above, pp. 18) and a continentalist, if not an isolationist, in foreign policy. At one time Taft denounced NATO as "so dangerous as to commit the United States to a cause beyond its capacity," while he denounced the U.N. as "an utter failure as a means of preventing aggression." His book, *A Foreign Policy for Americans,* published in 1951, set forth his deeply felt conviction that American commitments in Europe, if not to be abandoned completely, should at least be severely curtailed. After 1950 when Senator Vandenberg, the Republican architect of bipartisanship in foreign policy, withdrew from the Senate because of a fatal illness, Taft's views dominated Republican councils in Congress. After Taft's death in 1953, his views were perpetuated by William F. Knowland of California, whose literal-minded singleness of purpose equalled Taft's, but who fell far short of the Ohioan's sharpness of mind and intellectual discipline. Taft and Knowland also enjoyed the enthusiastic support of extreme anti-Communists and supernationalists from the Midwest like Senators Joseph McCarthy of Wisconsin, John Bricker of Ohio, and William Jenner of Indiana.

One of the potent arguments advanced to persuade Eisenhower to run in 1952 was that he alone would be able to tame the party's lingering isolationism and remake the Republicans into a party ready to meet contemporary issues with modern principles. Unless that could be done, advocates of his nomination pointed out, their party would never be anything more than a minority in the politics of the nation. The challenge appealed to Eisenhower, and for the first years of his administration he tried, with some success, to remake the Republican party. But in all his actions as President, the division within the party complicated his mission and limited his success.

Eisenhower the President. One of the persistent themes of the Democrats during the campaign had been that a military man like Eisenhower would be sure to assume a dangerously aggressive tone in dealing with Congress, the nation, and the world. Experience revealed, however, that nothing was less to be feared. From the beginning of his tenure until the end of his second term, Eisenhower in the White House was the opposite of the stereotype of a general. Indeed, he refused to lead Congress; it is difficult to talk about an Eisenhower program since most of the legislation of the Eisenhower years originated, not in the White House, but in Congress. Newspaper reporters, used to the vigorous leadership of Harry Truman and Franklin Roosevelt, were astonished when Eisenhower refused to comment upon pending legislation, on the ground that to do so would be to interfere with the legislative branch during its deliberations. The President consciously subordinated his own ego, usually giving credit for ideas and plans to the Cabinet or the administration rather than to himself. He not only seemed to think of himself as an equal member of a team, he even went so far as to remove himself from active involvement in the functions of government. His second-in-command, Sherman Adams, kept problems away from the President as much as possible, bringing only the truly unresolvable to the chief executive for decision. A hundred years after the demise of the Whig party, politically sophisticated observers were surprised to find a Whig in the White House again.

Actually, a large part of the explanation for Eisenhower's limited conception of his office stemmed from his military experience. People forgot that his military experience had never included the field command of men in battle, but rather the coordinating of huge, disparate armies and the reconciling of differences among allied nations joined in a common military enterprise. His great service as Supreme Commander of NATO forces, as during the war, had been his unsurpassed ability to reconcile diverse interests and secure cooperation between conflicting personalities. As a general he had acted as a mediator and a compromiser of differences, and under the circumstances probably nothing else would have worked. As President he operated in a similar fashion.

Leaders Under Eisenhower. At a press conference in January 1954, the President set forth in general terms, in the involved syntax for which he became famous, the philosophy of his administration. "When it comes down to dealing with the human in this country and his government, the people in this administration believe in being what I think we would normally call liberal, and when we deal with the economic affairs of this country, we believe in being conservative." In practice the administration showed itself to be more liberal than many Democrats had expected. But it was also true that Eisenhower was deeply concerned with avoiding the unbalanced budgets of Truman, for balancing the budget was what the General meant by being conservative in economic affairs. He would not, however, balance the budget by sacrificing military defense, though some of his Republican supporters seemed willing to do so. Early in his administration, the President complained about the short-sightedness of businessmen who insisted on tax cuts or other concessions in the face of military needs.

In keeping with his economic principles and the character of the Republican party, Eisenhower chose a preponderance of businessmen for his Cabinet officers. One of the quips of the day was that it was a Cabinet of eight millionaires and a plumber, the last being a reference to Martin Durkin, Secretary of Labor. Durkin, whose appointment was described by the forthright Taft as "incredible," was a union leader and a Democrat. Eisenhower appointed him as a gesture of national unity in case of labor strife. Durkin resigned after eight months because of differences over the Taft-Hartley Act; he was replaced by a businessman. Despite the influence of Taft in the party, in the Cabinet his only ally was Ezra Taft Benson of Utah, the Secretary of Agriculture. Benson was an ardent advocate of free enterprise in agriculture as in business, and during his tenure he undertook a campaign to have farm price supports steadily reduced in the interest of reducing the mounting farm surpluses. In this endeavor, however, he was opposed consistently, and usually successfully, by the farm interests in both parties in Congress.

The two most influential members of the administration were Secretary of State John Foster Dulles and George Humphrey, the Secretary of the Treasury. Dulles, who had long experience in diplomatic affairs under several administrations, virtually controlled American foreign policy during his years with Eisenhower. Again and again, Eisenhower told the press that Dulles, in his estimation, knew more about foreign policy than any man in the nation. Before 1941 Dulles had been an outspoken isolationist, but as Secretary of State he extended the military and moral commitments of the U.S. farther than any of his predecessors.

George Humphrey dominated domestic policies as Dulles did foreign. A self-made millionaire from Ohio, Humphrey, like the President himself, was raised in a small town, but in an upper-middle-class family. As a businessman Humphrey was firmly committed to the removal of government interference from business enterprise. A balanced federal budget was as much his goal as it was Senator Taft's. From the beginning Humphrey conceived of himself as the watchdog of the Treasury. At the time of his appointment, he is supposed to have made one request of the President. "I want you," he told

Eisenhower, "if anyone asks you about money, to tell them to go to see George."

Immediately below Humphrey in influence within the administration was Charles E. Wilson, the Secretary of Defense. As president of General Motors, Wilson had made a good record as an executive willing to work fairly and responsibly with labor unions. Brought to Washington because of his recognized capabilities in industrial procurement, he found it hard to adjust to political life in the capital. Blunt and undisciplined in speech, he committed several egregious errors in public relations that made him the butt of the nation's newspaper cartoonists and an embarrassment to the administration. Moreover, like Humphrey, he conceived of his job as the head of the national defense establishment as largely that of financial watchdog. Wilson was in complete agreement with the policy of depending upon a few advances in military technology, which would allow defense expenditures to be reduced. Many generals in the Pentagon thought him rigid in his conception of the proper defense for the nation. One embittered chief of staff later said of him, "He was the most uninformed man, and the most determined to remain so, that has ever been Secretary."

Removing Government from the Economy. The first Eisenhower administration intended to be a businessman's government in the best sense of that phrase. It was not intended that government should be subservient to business interests, as was often the case in the 1920's, but rather, that the interests of business would be consulted and the interference of government in business minimized. Thus as early as February 6, 1953, the administration abandoned all economic controls left over from the early days of the Korean War. The administration also curtailed or abandoned any government manufacturing enterprises which competed with private business, preferring, instead, to have government buy its supplies and services whenever possible from private enterprise. At one time the President even entertained a hope of selling the Tennessee Valley Authority. In March 1953, for example, he told the Cabinet, "By God, if ever we could do it, before we leave here, I'd like to see us *sell* the whole thing, but I suppose we can't go that far."

Paramount among the new administration's policies was the drive for a balanced budget. At the time, and later when he came to write his memoirs, Eisenhower saw a balanced budget as the principal achievement of his administration and the essential difference between the administrations of his Democratic predecessors and his own. To achieve a balanced budget, however, something more than minor economies were necessary if taxes were not to be raised. Almost as soon as he took office, Eisenhower cut back the amounts allocated in the Truman budget for foreign aid and military equipment—the amount provided for foreign aid alone was reduced by over a billion dollars. Despite his concern for economy, however, the new President would not cut spending sufficiently deeply to balance the budget immediately, because to do so would endanger national security. As will be seen a little later, this compromise quickly got him into trouble with his party, which wanted a balanced budget the very first year.

Other policies and acts of the administration strengthen this picture of a government trying to minimize governmental interference in and restrictions on business. In agriculture, for example, Congress was asked to enact flexible price supports so that the President would be empowered to lower farm prices as a means of reducing the surplus that had been piling up for years as a result of the price supports. Over the long run, the administration hoped to bring agricultural prices under the control of the market, something that had not been true since 1933. With the so-called Dixon-Yates contract, the administration also sought an alternative to the expansion of public power facilities. It refused to approve a new steam plant for the Tennessee Valley Authority in 1953 when it became evident that more power was needed in the Memphis area. Instead, the government made a contract with a private power syndicate (Dixon and Yates) to supply the electricity. In time the Democrats in Congress succeeded in invalidating the contract, which they viewed as an attack on public power in general and the TVA in particular. They had not forgotten that Eisenhower had once described the TVA as an example of "creeping socialism." In the field of nuclear energy, the administration also favored private over public enterprise. In 1956 the Atomic Energy Commission authorized the development of electric power from atomic energy by private industry. By the end of the year, 17 plants were planned or under construction by private firms.

Similarly, on the matter of offshore oil rights the administration supported the position of oil companies and businessmen in general. The Truman administration had convinced the United States Supreme Court that the oil-rich, submerged lands off the Gulf coast belonged to the federal government and not to the states. Conservationists and liberals in general believed that federal administration of this natural resource would be less liable to private pressure and abuse than control by the states. Hence they supported the Truman policy; the states, of course, and the oil companies opposed it. The Eisenhower administration, acting on the principle that the states should be given as much jurisdiction and authority as was consistent with the national interest, supported legislation that overturned the Supreme Court decision and awarded control over the disposition of offshore oil to the states, notably Texas and Louisiana.

In domestic policy Eisenhower, in short, was clearly a conservative. In some respects he was even more conservative than Senator Taft. For example, in 1960 the President admitted to his chief assistant, Sherman Adams, that he could not have gone along with Taft in such matters as federal aid to education and support of public housing, both of which Taft strongly supported. In Sherman Adams' words Eisenhower saw his administrations as "the first great break with the political philosophy of the decades beginning in 1933."

In at least two respects, however, Eisenhower and his supporters accepted New Deal-Fair Deal policies without question. One was the willingness to take governmental measures to avoid a depression. When in 1954 the economic indices showed a decline in the economy, Eisenhower urged his advisers and subordinates to prepare plans for the necessary antidepression measures. When in March the number of jobless reached 3.7 million, or 5.8 per cent of the labor force, the President in the privacy of the Cabinet meetings expressed grave concern, indicating that Republicans as well as Democrats by now agreed that halting a depression was a prime responsibility of government. The President and the Republican Congress also supported an expansion of the social security system in the very first year of the new administration.

The President and Congress. For most of his eight years in the White House, Eisenhower did not enjoy a Congress composed of a majority of his own party. Yet in some respects, his two years with a Republican Congress caused him more pain and difficulty than his six with a Democratic one. Certainly it is true that the Democrats, somewhat awed by his enormous popularity, and themselves generally dominated by moderates and conservatives, did not find working with Eisenhower difficult. This was not true of the conservative members of his own party who ran Congress in the years 1953–1954. Senator Taft, until he relinquished his Senate leadership in 1953 because of failing health, was the acknowledged head of the conservatives in the party and in the Senate. The President, determined to work closely with the party in an effort to heal its deep split, encouraged Taft to see him as often as he wished and without appointment. But the President's cultivation of Taft and his supporters could not eliminate all the conflicts between executive and legislature, or between the two wings of the party. Even more than the administration, for example, Taft wanted a balanced budget. That first year Eisenhower, despite many cuts in expenditures, could not achieve a balance between income and outgo. When informed of this at a meeting with the President, Taft exploded, banging the table and shouting, "Now you're taking us right down the same road Truman traveled. It's a repudiation of everything we promised in the campaign." Thunderstruck and inwardly incensed by the outburst, the President outwardly controlled himself. Patiently he tried to explain that any further cuts would endanger the national defense. Taft was not convinced, but he did not denounce the administration's policy in public.

The Republicans in Congress took much the same attitude as Taft. Although the President voluntarily cut more than a billion dollars from the mutual security budget inherited from the Truman administration, the Republicans in Congress were still not satisfied. Even after the President went before Congress to plead for his bill without any cuts, the fiscal conservatives joined with the extreme nationalists to slash still another billion from the foreign aid budget. The President's recommendation for a three-year extension of the reciprocal trade agreements was cut by the Republican Congress to one year. His request for new housing was also sharply cut by Congress. *The Congressional Quarterly Almanac* for 1953, taking note of how often the President was opposed by his own party in Congress, calculated that the Democrats saved the President's measures some 58 times in that single year. So uncooperative were the Republicans that in the middle of 1953 Eisenhower was talking privately about the desirability of forming a new party which would more accurately reflect his views.

The most striking and dangerous example of the conflict within the Republican party and between Congress and the President was the controversy over the Bricker amendment. In 1953 Republican Senator John Bricker of Ohio offered a constitutional amendment that would have seriously reduced the treaty-making power of the President. In the case of *Missouri* v. *Holland* (1920), the Supreme Court had held that through treaties the power of the federal government could be enlarged beyond the limits otherwise set by the Constitution. The Court based its judgment on the constitutional provision that treaties were "the supreme law of the land." In fact, however, treaties had never been used to enlarge federal powers in any important field. And there were few instances even in minor fields where federal power had been expanded through treaties. Nevertheless, Senator Bricker and his supporters feared that radical social and economic changes would be introduced through the "backdoor" of the treaty-making power. The Bricker amendment would have postponed the effective date of all treaties until Congress or the states passed supporting legislation that would be valid without a treaty.

President Eisenhower and Secretary of State Dulles strongly opposed the amendment on the ground that it would greatly hamper the conduct of foreign policy. But in the era of the Great Fear, a majority of congressmen agreed with Bricker. In 1953 the administration was able to force a postponement of a vote on the issue, but early in 1954 the proposal for an amendment came up again, this time with widespread support from members of Congress and from patriotic organizations throughout the country. Although a majority of senators voted for it, their numbers were insufficient to make up the necessary two thirds. A modified, but still objectionable form of the amendment was offered by a conservative southern Democrat a little later. It was defeated by only a single vote in the Senate: 31 to 60. Of the supporting votes, Republicans cast more than half.

The President and His Party. Conflicts between the President and his party in Congress, like that over the Bricker amendment, were actually skirmishes in the long war waged by the President to refashion the Republicans into an internationalist party. One way the President sought to influence the party was by campaigning for its candidates. In the Congressional elections of 1954, he took the unprecedented action of touring the country in vigorous support of Republican congressmen. Over and over again he called the voters' attention to the disadvantages, not to mention dangers, inherent in a government divided between two parties, and hence the desirability of his having a Republican Congress with which to work. (In point of fact, however, the Democratic congressmen often supported him more consistently on foreign policy than the Republicans.) The Congressional elections in 1954, despite Eisenhower's campaigning, ran true to form in that the opposition party made gains. But the Democratic majorities that were returned in both houses and the seven new Democratic governors boded ill for the success of the President's "modern Republicanism."

The Election of 1956. By 1955 the great majority of Republican leaders, regardless of their attitudes toward Eisenhower's political philosophy, knew that he was their greatest popular attraction since Warren G. Harding. Naturally, they assumed that he would run again in 1956. But that confident assumption collapsed on September 24, 1955, when the President suffered a sudden heart attack. While the world waited to learn whether he would live or die, the government ran along under the direction of the Cabinet, presided over by Vice-President Nixon. Within days it became known that the President would recover, but he was unable to attend a Cabinet meeting before November 22.

Once Eisenhower was back at work and making a strong recovery, the hopes of Republican leaders for his candidacy in 1956 revived. The President, however, was not sure he wanted to run again; he had long looked forward to retirement from a long and active public life and, in fact, had intended from the beginning of his presidency not to serve more than one term. Yet he could not forget that the great achievement he cherished for his administration still eluded him. He wanted to help bring real peace to the world. The 1955 Geneva Summit Conference had given him reason to believe that he had established a better relationship with the Russian leaders than any American leader since the Cold War began. Then too, another term might make permanent the changes he wanted in his party. At the end of February, he announced his candidacy. At the convention that summer he was immediately —almost gratefully—renominated, with Richard M. Nixon once again his running mate.

Meanwhile, the Democrats had already chosen their candidate, who was also the same as in 1952—Adlai E. Stevenson. Despite some opposition, Stevenson was chosen on the first ballot. Stevenson then deliberately tossed the choice of a vice-presidential candidate into the lap of the convention, which immediately went into a night and a day of furious and intense politicking and balloting. The final struggle was between Senators John F. Kennedy of Massachusetts and Estes Kefauver of Tennessee. Although deserted by the delegates from his native South, Kefauver, who had made two earlier unsuccessful bids for the presidential nomination, received the support of the convention. That Kennedy, a Roman Catholic, should have been strongly supported by the southern delegates suggested that the South's historic opposition to Al Smith in 1928 on religious grounds was now more history than political warning. The Democrats sought to avoid the rupture of 1948 over civil rights by remaining silent on the controversial question of the Supreme Court's decision on the desegregation of schools. The party was to suffer among southern Negro voters for its silence.

Stevenson, eager to run this time, carried on a whirlwind campaign which did not throw off as many intellectually exciting and witty speeches as his first contest. But he had been warned that wit in politics did not add up to victory. The Republicans depended upon having produced "Peace and Prosperity," as their slogan phrased it, but the real appeal was the President, as the great number of people, especially teen-agers, wearing "I Like Ike" buttons attested. Stevenson tried to counter the popular cult of Ike by seriously discussing the dangers of further testing of nuclear and thermonuclear bombs, but the administration officially and the Republicans unofficially squelched him by contending that a cessation of tests would endanger the national defense. The Hungarian and Suez crises, which broke into the headlines just before the voters went to the polls, did little to harm Eisenhower's high place in the public mind, despite the fact that both events constituted rather obvious failures in the conduct of American foreign policy. If the two crises had any effect, it was merely to reinforce the feeling of most Americans that at such times the General was more needed than ever.

The Strange Victory. As the public opinion polls had predicted, Eisenhower won easily; his percentage of the popular vote had been surpassed only by Roosevelt in 1936 and Harding in 1920. Stevenson's total vote of 26 million was slightly smaller than in 1952. The vote in the electoral college was 457 to 73. Once again Eisenhower broke into the now less than solid South, taking Virginia, Tennessee—though the latter was Kefauver's native state —Louisiana, Florida, and Texas, among the states of the old Confederacy. Somewhat of a surprise was the decided shift of Negroes in the South to Eisenhower, probably because of the Supreme Court decision on school segregation. The shift was especially evident in the cities, where Eisenhower's strength in the South was concentrated.

The real surprise was that, despite his tremendous personal victory, Eisenhower was unable to bring a Republican Congress back to Washington with him. Even his former Secretary of the Interior, Douglas McKay, running in Oregon for the Senate, was defeated. The Democrats retained their small, but sufficient, majorities in both houses. Not since 1848, more than a hundred years before, had a President failed to carry at least one house in his election; for a popular President like Eisenhower to fail to do so was unprecedented. The common explanation for the paradox was that the majority of voters were still wary of the Republican party, especially on domestic issues, but that they trusted Eisenhower. In the minds of many liberal Republicans, the Old Guard of the party, which had opposed welfare legislation under Roosevelt and Truman, still dominated Republican councils; such voters would not support the party, but they would vote for the President. In short, Eisenhower had still not altered the old image of the party in the minds of the independent

THE ELECTION OF 1956

	ELECTORAL VOTE BY STATE	POPULAR VOTE
REPUBLICAN Dwight D. Eisenhower	457	35,590,472
DEMOCRATIC Adlai E. Stevenson	73	26,022,752
☐ Walter B. Jones	1	—
MINOR PARTIES	—	194,166
	531	61,807,390

voter. It was also true that Eisenhower's real appeal had always lain in his apparent lack of partisanship; probably many voters who supported him did not take him seriously when he said he needed a Republican Congress. After all, hadn't he gotten along quite well with the Democratic Congress? (Actually, Eisenhower's strong partisanship has often been underestimated. In his memoirs, for example, he wrote that the defeat of Richard Nixon in 1960 was "my principal political disappointment. . . . I cannot ascribe any rational cause for the outcome," since in his opinion Nixon was clearly the better man. He also made a strenuous effort, he tells us, to prevent Douglas Dillon from serving in the Kennedy Cabinet, because Dillon was a Republican and a former member of Eisenhower's Cabinet.)

Eisenhower's Second Term

Divided Government. Throughout his whole second term, Eisenhower had to work with a House and Senate controlled by Democrats. (In the midterm elections of 1958, Democratic majorities in both houses reached proportions not seen since the middle 1930's. Leading Republican conservatives like Senators William Knowland and John Bricker lost their seats in 1958. That same year only two Republican newcomers managed to counter the nationwide Democratic tide: Nelson Rockefeller, running for governor of New York, and Barry Goldwater, contesting for a Senate seat in Arizona.) As a result the President conceived his job to be the protection of the taxpayer from the potentially, if not actually, wasteful Democratic Congress. When Congress passed salary increases for government employees in 1957, the bills were all successfully vetoed by the President. Early in 1958 when a recession that had begun the previous August began to evoke Congressional and public apprehension, labor and business groups alike demanded tax cuts as a means of pumping more purchasing power into the economy. The seriousness of the recession was attested by the report in April from the Federal Reserve Board that the index of industrial production had dropped 11.7 per cent since the previous August—the biggest decline since the Great Depression. Despite this fact, the President refused to endanger his first balanced budget by recommending tax cuts. Only with great reluctance did he sign a $3.375 billion federal highway bill which the Democratic Congress passed as an anti-recession measure.

When in August 1958 it became clear that the recession was over, the President returned quickly to his adamant stand against spending. Characteristically, he saw the issue of spending in moral, not modern economic terms. In January 1959, for example, he told legislative leaders that Democratic spending had to be held down. "We've got to convince Americans that thrift is not a bad word." In 1959 he vetoed a public works bill, which he stigmatized as a pork barrel; the House sustained his veto by a single vote. When he vetoed a second such bill, it was passed over his veto—the first overridden veto in his experience as President. That same year he killed two housing bills on the grounds that they were excessive and inflationary; a third one, which had been altered to meet some of his objections, he signed. At the close of the session, on September 19, he publicly criticized Congress for having been too "lavish" in its spending and chided it for failing to increase postal rates to end the deficit in the Post Office Department. Right down to the end of his tenure, he was resisting Congressional spending. In June 1960 he vetoed a 7.5 per cent pay increase for federal employees, but the veto was overridden, largely because it was an election year, by the Democratic Congress. As we have seen earlier, a similar concern for economy was evident in administration policy on military expenditures.

The Griffin-Landrum Act. One of the three principal pieces of legislation of Eisenhower's second administration was the Labor-Management Reporting and Disclosure Act. (The other two were the Civil Rights Act of 1957 and the National Defense Education Act of 1958. See pp. 96-97 and 104) Since February 1957 a Senate Committee on Improper Activities in the Labor or Management Fields, headed by John McClellan of Arkansas, had been listening to evidence of racketeering, corruption, and extortion by certain labor unions. By 1959 the public and Congress had heard enough; a bill designed to curb such activities was offered by the committee. In a sense the bill was a continuation of the philosophy of the Taft-Hartley Act, since the underlying assumption in both acts was that labor unions and especially their leaders needed to be federally controlled for the protection of union members and the public. Many labor unions whose records and practices the McClellan committee admitted were above reproach quickly conceded the need to clean up those unions which hired criminals and thugs to intimidate employers or rank and file members. At the same time these honest unions were wary of the committee's bill on the ground that it infringed upon legitimate rights of unions. Their wariness deepened when they recognized that many of the most ardent advocates of the bill were either conservative Democrats from nonindustrial southern states or Republicans who were known to be unfriendly to any labor unions, honest or corrupt.

The bill which emerged from the prolonged debates in both houses was supported by the administration. Liberal Democrats, like Senator John F. Kennedy, did their best to minimize the restrictions on labor in the bill, which became law on September 14, 1959. The act set up a bill of rights for union members to protect them against assessments and coercion by their leaders. It also required unions to make public, largely for the benefit of their members, all expenditures and all payments made to officers. Unions were also required to hold regular elections of officers. The law forbade union members to charge extraordinary fees to employers for performing ordinary work—a provision which grew out of extensive testimony in the McClellan committee hearings on "shakedowns" of employers by unions. The act was one of the achievements to which the Republicans pointed with pride in the campaign of 1960.

Democratic Independence. As the 1960 elections approached and the Democrats were under a growing necessity to make a record for themselves, they became increasingly critical of the President's leadership on domestic affairs, though they criticized him only obliquely, if at all, on foreign affairs. Sometimes their efforts to override his objections succeeded—as in the already mentioned pay increase for federal employees—but more often they did not. Thus the President was sustained in 1960 in his veto of a bill to aid areas of the country with substantial unemployment. Furthermore, an effort by the liberal, urban-based wing of the Democrats in Congress to pass a bill for medical aid to the aged through the social security system failed because of administration opposition. Similarly, a bill to increase the national minimum wage was beaten down in Congress.

Since many conservative Democrats joined with the President and the Republicans in defeating these welfare measures, it was evident, as the election of 1960 approached, that the Democrats, as well as the Republicans, suffered from division in their party's philosophy.

The New Movement for Negro Rights

The Supreme Court Decision of 1954. On May 17, 1954, in the hushed, ornate chamber of the Supreme Court of the United States, Chief Justice Earl Warren read a unanimous opinion. The case was *Brown, et al.* v. *Board of Education of Topeka, et al.*, in which Negro children contested statutes that required their segregation from white children in public schools. The heart of the question, the Chief Justice said, was, "Does segregation of children in public schools solely on the basis of race, even though the physical facilities and other 'tangible' factors may be equal, deprive the children of the minority group of equal educational opportunities?" The answer of the Court was, "We believe that it does." These historic words marked the climax of a half century of persistent effort by Negro rights organizations to reverse the Court's acceptance of racial segregation. Specifically rejecting the conclusion in the case of *Plessy* v. *Ferguson* of 1896, the Court now announced that "in the field of public education the doctrine of 'separate but equal' has no place. Separate educational facilities are inherently unequal" in 1954, whatever they may have been in an earlier period when the Fourteenth Amendment was adopted.

Although the Court's decision was momentous, the substance of the decision was not a complete surprise. Ever since the late 1930's, the Court, under the guidance of four different chief justices, had been striking down discriminatory laws and practices. In 1938, for example, the state of Missouri was told that an out-of-state law school for Negro Missourians did not meet the requirement of the Fourteenth Amendment for equal treatment of all citizens. Then in 1944 in *Smith* v. *Allwright*, the Court decided that Democratic primaries in the southern states, which were the real elections because the Republican party was virtually nonexistent there, could not exclude Negroes. Four years later, the Court specifically refused to uphold real estate agreements that discriminated against buyers on grounds of race. In 1950 Texas and Oklahoma were told that their separate law schools for Negroes were not equal to those open to white students and hence were unconstitutional. The culmination was the great decision of 1954 on public school segregation.

Though quite definite in its condemnation of segregation, the Court was still fully aware of the difficulties that would arise in carrying out the decision. As a result the Court postponed for a year its specific orders to the school districts for which the decision had been made. Meanwhile though, communities in West Virginia and Delaware, and the cities of Baltimore and Washington, none of which was directly involved in the case, voluntarily began to desegregate their schools in September 1954. In its second school segregation decision on May 31, 1955, the Court laid upon the local school boards the responsibility for drawing up plans for desegregation; the boards were also to bear the burden of proof for any delay in desegregating. The Court called upon the states, through their school boards, to end segregation within a "reasonable time," but it refused to set a deadline for the completion of the change. For all those who regretted this omission by the Court, there were many others who were thankful that the Court had given the South, where the changes would be most resisted, time in which to adjust to the alteration in well-established educational practices. One consequence, though, was that the delay permitted the formation of organizations and pressure groups determined to resist desegregation. During 1955 and 1956 white citizens' councils formed all over the South, dedicating themselves to obstructing desegregation through every legal means, and sometimes through illegal intimidation of officials and school boards as well.

Resistance to implementing the decision was strongest in the Deep South, where no effort was made to admit Negroes to previously all-white schools. Even in eastern Tennessee, not usually thought of as extreme on the race question, an angry mob at the little town of Clinton forced the halting in

September 1956 of the first attempts to desegregate the local high school. In February of the same year, a shouting, threatening crowd of students and townspeople forced the first Negro student at the University of Alabama to withdraw. By the middle of the year, some 350 school districts in nine states had desegregated, but none of these districts was in the Deep South; there the line was firmly held.

The Montgomery Boycott. At the very time that the Deep South was resisting the movement toward equalization of educational facilities, southern Negroes were displaying a new militancy which belied the argument of many southern whites that the Negro was content with the segregated status quo. On December 5, 1955, the 50,000 Negro residents of Montgomery, Alabama, began a boycott of the local busses in protest against segregation and discrimination by the bus company. The boycott, organized and led by southern Negroes, continued for months, with as many as 95 per cent of the Negro population of Montgomery participating, often at great personal sacrifice. Although 92 of the Negro leaders, of whom 25 were ministers, were arrested under an old law as a means of breaking the boycott, the Negro protest continued. The principal leader of the movement was the Reverend Martin Luther King, Jr., a young minister from Atlanta who had just come to Montgomery to accept his first church. A Doctor of Philosophy from Boston University, King won national recognition and eventually the Nobel Peace Prize for his advocacy of non-violence in the face of violence and riot. Militant in his determination to win equality for his race, he nonetheless counseled love instead of hatred for those who opposed him. Nevertheless, on April 4, 1968, King was himself the victim of a white assassin. The United States Supreme Court upheld a lower court on November 13, 1956, in striking down segregation on the busses of Montgomery.

Civil Rights Legislation, 1957 and 1960. Three years after the Brown decision, desegregation was still proceeding very slowly. Although a few school districts in western Texas, North Carolina, and Nashville, Tennessee, undertook the first steps in desegregating their schools in 1957, no moves in that direction had been made by any deep southern state. Nevertheless, the pressure for further breaks in the color line continued to mount. Now the drive was for protection for Negro voters in the South. After much extended debate and a delaying action by some southern congressmen, in August 1957 Congress passed the first Civil Rights Act since the days of Reconstruction. A large part of the credit for the passage of the act was due to the majority leader in the Senate, Lyndon B. Johnson, a Texan and a Democrat.

The act as passed, considerably amended from the administration's original and stronger version, limited itself almost completely to voting rights. Under the act judges were empowered to jail for contempt anyone — including state officials — who prevented a qualified person from voting. Persons charged with having illegally denied the vote to someone were entitled to a trial by jury. Such a trial was as strongly insisted upon by Southerners as it was opposed by liberal Northerners, who believed that southern juries would not convict a white man charged with keeping Negroes from the polls. The law also created the temporary Commission on Civil Rights which was to investigate violations of civil rights and to make recommendations for new legislation. In 1959 the commission issued its first report, in which it forthrightly criticized racial housing patterns across the nation. It especially noted that segregation of the races in housing was undesirable not only because it was discriminatory but also because the existing housing for Negroes and other nonwhites was simply inadequate for a decent life. (The question of housing, however, proved to be a sensitive one. When in 1966 the Johnson administration tried to enact an open housing law, it was first watered down in the House and then killed in the Senate.)

A second Civil Rights Act pertaining to voting was passed in May 1960, after a nine-day filibuster by southern senators. The act authorized the Justice Department to secure a court order to compel local officials to open voting records for inspection in order that discriminatory practices might be uncovered. If, upon the suggestion of the government, a court found a "pattern" of discrimination in voting, it could appoint a referee to register voters. The first suit under this new law, designed to overcome various evasive devices employed by southern election officials was filed in June 1960, against certain counties in Alabama.

Despite the new laws, voting by Negroes in the South remained far less, proportionately, than by whites. Part of this disparity, of course, resulted from the continued resistance, covert and overt, on the part of southern election officials, and from intimidation by local groups of whites. A large part, however, also stemmed from the Negroes' lack of interest and political experience. Hence Negro organizations and leaders organized campaigns to overcome the widespread political apathy and timidity among southern black people. Yet the resistance of southern whites to Negro voting was so obviously effective that within five years Congress and the national administration would feel it necessary to enact even stronger federal protections for Negro voters in the South.

The Little Rock Crisis. At a news conference on July 17, 1957, while Congress was debating a controversial provision of the Civil Rights bill, a reporter asked President Eisenhower whether he knew that under existing statutes he possessed the power to use federal troops to enforce the desegregation of the schools in the South. The President replied that he had been so informed, but then went on to say, "I can't imagine any set of circumstances that would ever induce me to send federal troops . . . into any area to enforce the orders of a federal court, because I believe that the common sense of America will never require it." Within two months the unimaginable occurred.

Arkansas is not a deep southern state, and it had already taken some steps toward desegregation. Indeed, in September 1957 five of the state's school districts, including one in the city of Little Rock, were scheduled to carry out plans for the grade by grade integration of the public schools. Five days before classes were scheduled to begin, on August 29, a state court forbade the Little Rock School Board to carry out its integration plan, on the ground that information from Governor Orville Faubus led the court to believe that violence would ensue if the plan were put into effect. A federal court countermanded the state court's injunction, but the night before the school was to open, the governor ordered contingents of the national guard to surround Central High School. When nine Negro students sought entrance, their way was barred by the troops. Because the federal court insisted that the school board's plan be put into effect, the situation at the high school was a direct clash between the authority of a federal court and that of the state. Men's minds leaped back across a century to Jackson and South Carolina's nullification.

President Eisenhower, who was vacationing at Newport, Rhode Island, was extremely reluctant to intervene in the explosive situation — he was a Whig, not a Jacksonian President. Moreover, he was not publicly committed on the issue of desegregation. Throughout his presidency he refused to express publicly a belief in the rightness of the Supreme Court decision of 1954, on the ground that to do so was improper for the President. In 1957 he rejected a private request from Martin Luther King that he go into the South to uphold the morality of desegregation as a means of countering the widespread white resistance. (Later, in his memoirs, the President said he had approved of the decision all along.)

Whatever his views on desegregation, however, Eisenhower never harbored any doubts about the supremacy of the federal government and about the necessity of upholding its courts. Now, for all his belief in limiting federal power, the President could not ignore Faubus' defiance of the federal court. After a request from the Governor for a conference, the President met him at Newport, where a temporary truce was arranged. Soon thereafter, the situation at the high school eased as the soldiers were replaced by policemen. On September 23 the Negro children were permitted to enter, but over a thousand protesters and rowdies surrounded the school, shouting and threatening. As a result the school authorities sent the Negro children home before the end of classes. The next day, when the crowd refused to disperse upon a presidential order, Eisenhower incorporated the Arkansas National Guard into the United States Army — thus putting them under his command instead of the governor's — and dispatched a thousand troops of the 101st Airborne Division to Little Rock. Grimly the paratroopers with fixed bayonets took up their position around the school, dispersed the mob, and for the next few weeks escorted the Negro students through the corridors of Central High to their classes.

The newspaper pictures of federal troops protecting nine young Negroes from an angry mob in the center of a large American city humiliated most

Americans and shocked the world. Little Rock became a worldwide symbol of the dangerous consequences of the unresolved conflict in the American mind between racism and equality. Not since the Civil War had public officials so openly defied the authority of the United States; not since the Civil War had the basic understanding which underlies all democratic government deteriorated to such an extent that only naked force could compel compliance with law. In order to reduce tensions in the community, the federal troops were withdrawn two months later and replaced by the federalized Arkansas troops, who remained on the school grounds for the remainder of the school year.

The immediate effect of the Little Rock crisis was a hardening of southern resistance to school desegregation. Arkansas and Virginia, for example, enacted "massive resistance" laws, which were intended to close the schools if integration seemed to be in the offing. As a result of such laws, Little Rock schools did not reopen all during the 1958–1959 session, and the schools in three Virginia cities closed down.

The prospect of the end of public education, and the unrest and unruliness aroused by the segregationists, produced a reaction against massive resistance. Conservative businessmen, ministers, mothers worried over the education of their children, and friends of law and order in general began to recognize the uselessness and the dangers of such resistance. Slowly, painfully, tentatively, the more moderate people in the South, of whom there were many, began to speak out and to organize. Massive resistance came to an abrupt end in Virginia in January 1959, when both the state and federal courts declared the "massive resistance" laws contrary to the state and federal constitutions. That fall several communities, including Norfolk, accepted Negroes in formerly white schools, though in Prince Edward County in the southern part of the state, the community closed all schools rather than integrate. At Little Rock in August 1959, all four public high schools opened, despite some sporadic dynamiting during the summer; six Negroes were in attendance, and there was no open opposition to them.

In 1960–1961 integration came to the Deep South for the first time. An attempt to begin integration at two primary schools in New Orleans in November 1960 resulted in the violent verbal abuse of a handful of Negro and white school children by a mob of white women. The vehemence of their protests insured a boycott of the schools by almost all the whites. Yet efforts by the governor and the legislature to prevent further steps toward integration in New Orleans proved ineffective; in the fall of 1961, two more schools opened with Negroes in attendance, and no white boycotts were attempted. After a riot against the admission of two Negro students at the University of Georgia in 1961, that state's resistance to the gradual integration plan for Atlanta collapsed. Georgia Institute of Technology admitted two Negro boys in September 1961 without a court order. Negro children entered the public schools of Georgia with white children for the first time on August 30, 1961, without incident. The three remaining states of the Deep South—Alabama, Mississippi, and South Carolina—did not permit any breaches of their pattern of segregation on any level of education until the advent of the Kennedy administration and further federal pressure. Outside of these three states, however, token integration at the college level had been proceeding in the South, virtually without incident, for several years. By 1960, of the 195 all-white institutions of higher education in 14 southern states, 124 were desegregated in practice or in principle.

The Sit-In Movement. Like the Montgomery bus boycott of 1955, the so-called sit-ins showed that the drive against segregation was something more than a protest by a few northern Negro organizations or a handful of southern liberals. Masses of Negroes in the South were joining the protest. No longer could it be argued that dissatisfaction with segregation was the result of northern agitators or was only the attitude of Negroes who had left the South. In February 1960 a completely unorganized group of Negro college students in Greensboro, N.C. instituted a new form of protest against segregation. They contested the exclusion of Negroes from lunch counters in the local Woolworth five-and-ten by simply sitting at the forbidden lunch counter and refusing to leave when denied service. The practice, which usually resulted in the immediate shutting down of the counter, was taken up by Negro students in other towns and cities. Sometimes they were joined by white students. The tactic quickly became a national form of protest. Violence rarely resulted because the sit-ins steadfastly refused to respond to taunts or provocations, even when white hoodlums physically attacked them or burned them with lighted cigarettes. Local authorities arrested as many as 1500 sit-in students for trespass all over the nation, but by the end of the year, several of the national chain stores had desegregated their lunch counters in 112 southern and border state cities.

Those stoical, well-disciplined sit-in students, quietly reading their books while making their protest, suggested a new self-control and high moral content in the Negro protest movement. Even some southern newspapers commented on the moral superiority of these Negro students over the rowdies and hoodlums who baited them. Very noticeable in this new means of protest was a religious undertone that echoed the important part that Negro ministers in the South were playing in most of the demonstrations and protest activities. A deep religious commitment had long been associated with southern Negroes; it was now being reshaped into a peaceful, but remarkably effective, weapon of social change.

The National Implications of the Negro Rights Movement. Ever since the First World War, the most common form of Negro protest against the segregation patterns and limited job opportunities in the South was migration to the North. By the end of the 1950's, Negro migration to the industrial cities of the North was creating problems there too. The Negro population of 14 of the largest metropolitan areas in the North grew almost 80 per cent between

1950 and 1960, while the total population of these areas increased only 19 per cent. Housing, schools, and recreational facilities open to Negroes streaming into Chicago, New York, Detroit, and other large northern centers did not expand proportionally. Increasingly, Negroes complained of being compelled to live in ghettos in the North and of being forced to attend inadequate, overcrowded schools. Moreover, many pointed out, the housing patterns in these northern cities, by separating the races, produced, in effect, separate and unequal schools, which sometimes were as inadequate as those established by law in the South. The large number of Negroes now concentrated in northern cities presented problems, not only because they were confined to black ghettos, but also because they were the poorest, least educated, and least skilled portion of the population. Organizations like the Negro-led Urban League pointed out that most Negroes were rural in background, and that in the 50 years since 1910 the Negro population of the United States had changed from being 70 per cent rural to being 70 per cent urban. That fact in itself was a demographic change productive of much social unrest. When Negroes came to the big cities, they were faced not only with the pressing disabilities of racial discrimination, but also with the challenges of a new urban environment. Clashes with the police and social maladjustments may not have been inevitable, but they were to be expected.

In short, as the South wrestled with its age-old problem of how to fit the black man into traditionally white America, northern cities were also finding out that legal segregation was not all that the Negro objected to or had a right to object to. Housing and job opportunities that were truly open to all would have to prevail if Negro discontent and protest were not to grow and fester in the North. A measure of the need as well as the lateness of the hour was the eruption of extensive violence in the Negro ghettos of northern cities in 1964 and after. (See p. 190)

Sputnikitis

One point frequently emphasized in the debate over segregation was that in a world in which the colored peoples of Asia and Africa were becoming increasingly important, the United States could no longer afford to discriminate politically, economically, and socially against Americans who happened not to be white. Nor did the propaganda of Communists and the press of Asia and Africa permit Americans to forget the contradiction between their social practices and the exalted words of the Declaration of Independence that asserted "all men are created equal." Abashed as many Americans might feel over the unsavory publicity which segregation and incidents like Little Rock brought them, they nevertheless felt they could justifiably be proud of the scientific, technological, and industrial advances which poured from the drawing boards and factories of their prosperous society. As the first people to achieve the marvels of splitting the atom and of fusing hydrogen, Americans believed themselves to be, in their scientific achievements as in their economic life, second to none. Then came October 4, 1957.

The Russian Sputnik. On that day the Soviet Union announced that Russian scientists and technologists had placed a man-made satellite in orbit around the earth. Sputnik I, the Russians called it. The American program for space exploration, as everyone knew, had not been expected to equal that feat for months. Even before the Americans could make an attempt to equal the Soviet achievement, Russian scientists on November 3 sent up Sputnik II, which was large enough to contain a live dog. In contrast, the first American effort, a Navy Vanguard rocket, exploded on the launching pad in early December. Not until January 31, 1958 were the anxious Americans at Cape Canaveral, Florida (now Cape Kennedy) able to launch the first Explorer satellite. Though it went higher than the two Sputniks, its weight was a mere 18 pounds as compared with 184 for the first Sputnik and 1160 for the second. Americans were dismayed by the demonstrated ability of the Soviet Union to surpass them technologically and shocked to reflect on what it meant militarily. Throughout the world Soviet scientists, long recognized among professionals as highly competent, received wide public acclaim. It would take time and much humility before the Americans would catch up with the Russians.

With the scientific and, to a lesser extent, the political prestige of both countries hinging upon successfully orbiting hardware, satellites were hurled into the skies in profusion during 1958. By 1961 the advent of the first Sputnik had evoked six separate series of American space efforts, each more ambitious than the preceding. In 1961 President Kennedy announced the beginning of the most spectacular—Project Apollo—designed to land a man on the moon by 1970. And, despite some cutbacks in funds during the 1960's, and the accidental deaths of three astronauts, the many American successes in orbiting men around the earth and photographing potential landing sites on the moon itself made it look as if 1970 might well see an American astronaut walking on the surface of the moon.

The Military Implications of Sputnik. The feverish activity in space was provoked by something more than a desire for international prestige, and scientific inquiry, though these motives were not absent. The heavy vehicles that the Russians shot into space in 1957–1958 indicated that they possessed a rocket of much greater power than anything available to the armed services of the United States. Thus, behind the space contest was a missile race. Before the first Sputnik was sent into orbit, President Eisenhower had depreciated a Russian announcement in August that the Soviet Army possessed a missile capable of attaining a speed in excess of 13,000 miles per hour and with a range of 5000 miles. Prior to the firing of Sputnik, the United States had twice failed to launch its Atlas intercontinental ballistic missile. And even when it was lifted off its pad, it traveled no more than 500 miles before plunging into the ocean in the south Atlantic missile range.

After Sputnik, public and Congressional pressure grew for an acceleration of the missile program. So strong was the national concern and dismay that the President felt the necessity on November 7, soon after the second Sputnik went up, to reassure the nation in a series of public addresses. He also named James R. Killian, president of the Massachusetts Institute of Technology, to be his special adviser on science and technology. On January 7, 1958, Eisenhower also asked Congress for $1.37 billion for expanding and accelerating the missile program. Congress almost immediately granted him all but $100,000 of his request. The budget of $73.9 billion which the President proposed for 1958–1959 was the largest peacetime budget in American history. As a result, the United States began to develop a new array of weapons.

The rocket arsenal of the United States, and presumably that of the Soviet Union, contained a spectrum of instruments, ranking from little bazookas, which enabled a single infantryman to stop a tank, through the short and medium range weapons like Nike and Thor which could be used against planes, troop formations, and ships, to the giant intercontinental ballistic missile (I.C.B.M.), which, as its name implied, could span oceans and devastate cities with its nuclear warhead. The most spectacular of all in the United States arsenal was the 1500-mile-range Polaris, which was capable of being fired from a submerged nuclear-powered submarine. Because the submarine would be constantly moving beneath the surface—it could remain submerged for months at a time—it would be an almost impossible target for an enemy to locate and destroy. The first of a series of such submarines, equipped with 16 nuclear-bomb-tipped Polaris missiles, went on regular patrol in the north Atlantic on November 15, 1960. Thus as a result of Sputnik, a missile race emerged between the two major world powers—a race which forecast a fantastic kind of push-button war in which only minutes might elapse between the declaration of war—if there was even that—and the slaughter of millions in a thermonuclear holocaust.

The Debate over Education. One further consequence of the Sputniks was a furious national debate on the character and goals of American education. Americans had always been deeply concerned with education, valuing it highly and relishing its successes in a new country composed of a great variety of nationalities and language stocks. Shocked by the recently demonstrated Russian superiority in technology and science, public figures and others proceeded to lay the blame for American inferiority in science and technology on the American educational system. Actually, criticisms of public education—the heart of the American system—had been widely heard some time before Sputnik. Books like Professor Arthur Bestor's *Educational Wastelands* (1953), Mortimer Smith's *The Diminished Mind: A Study of Planned Mediocrity in Our Public Schools* (1954), and Rudolph Flesch's *Why Johnny Can't Read* (1955), all attested to the growing feeling in the 1950's that American education was not demanding enough of the nation's children. Principally under attack was a misunderstood version of progressive education. In the 1920's and 1930's, some schools went to the extreme of making adjustment to life a central function of education and of offering courses appropriate to such an approach that were without meaningful content. As a result, all aspects of progressive education came under attack. Extreme and even unwarranted as many of the attacks on the schools undoubtedly were, it was nevertheless true that many schools were not requiring enough of their students intellectually. Thus the new educational critics like Bestor and Smith demanded more ''old-fashioned'' training: memorization, more intellectual discipline through the study of traditional subjects, and more emphasis in the curriculum on mathematics, languages, and sciences.

Thus when the Russian Sputniks began to orbit, the ground was well prepared for a thorough and often critical examination of American education. That same November in which the second Sputnik appeared in the sky, the United States government itself issued a 200-page study, *Education in the U.S.S.R.*, which quickly focused attention on the rigorous methods of Russian education. Noticeable in the report was the large amount of time spent in the study of sciences, languages, and mathematics by the children of the nation which had produced the first man-made satellites. Less than two months later, a report of the Rockefeller Brothers Fund, a highly respected research organization, recommended a complete examination of American education. The debate was on. So intense was the interest and the response that in April 1958 over half of the principals of the public schools of the nation told the Gallup poll that they were making changes in curricula and educational standards that year. Seventy-nine per cent of the principals thought that the high schools in America required too little of their students. Suddenly scientists became the darlings of press and public; as a result publicists vied with one another in trying to discover means by which young Americans could be encouraged to become scientists. Each year the newspapers reported with new pride the increasing percentage of graduating high-school students who elected to study science, mathematics, or foreign languages in college.

The administration and Congress responded to the national mood by enacting, on September 2, 1958, the National Defense Education Act, which suggested in its very title the new connection between national defense and the schools. The law authorized the spending of $887 million over a period of four years to encourage instruction and study in science, mathematics, and modern foreign languages. Included in that sum was $82.5 million in scholarships for graduate study in these fields and a $295-million loan fund for college students. It was the first major federal effort in support of higher education since the land-grant college act of 1862.

The shock of Sputnik not only awakened Americans to the desirability of study in science and languages, it also shook up the whole educational system, requiring trustees and teachers, professors and presidents, students as well as parents to think in fresh ways about the purpose and content of education. Above all, it placed a new accent upon high achievement and rigor in scholastic work. By the end of the Eisenhower administration, the debate was over; in the Kennedy and Johnson administrations the goal of a more demanding educational fare on all levels was accepted; the issue from then on would be how best to achieve that goal. As we shall see in the next chapter, the long-range effect of Sputnik was to propel the federal government as never before into the field of education.

The Election of 1960

The Campaign. Because of the Twenty-Second Amendment, 1960 was the first election year in which neither party was kept on tenterhooks waiting to find out whether the incumbent would run again. As a result even before the convention the Republicans had a good idea who their candidate was to be; Vice-President Nixon made no secret of his ambition to succeed Eisenhower. When toward the end of December 1959 Governor Nelson Rockefeller of New York, Nixon's only serious rival for the nomination, withdrew from the race, the field was clear for Nixon. His nomination was further clinched when Eisenhower let reporters know definitely during the spring that Nixon was his choice. As expected, at the Republican convention in Chicago in July, Nixon was nominated on the first ballot, with Henry Cabot Lodge, the United States ambassador to the United Nations, as his partner in the race.

The Democratic convention, which met earlier than the Republican that year, was much less decisive. Indeed, a number of hopeful candidates, especially Senators John F. Kennedy of Massachusetts and Hubert Humphrey of Minnesota, had been campaigning unofficially for almost a year before the convention and, in Kennedy's case, planning for it even longer. In the course of the six months before the convention met in Los Angeles, Kennedy succeeded in effectively eliminating Humphrey by winning the primaries in Wisconsin and West Virginia. Within certain segments of the party, there was still sentiment for Adlai Stevenson, who had captured the imagination and allegiance of many intellectuals and idealists, though Stevenson himself was once again troubled by self-doubt and indecision. The conservatives in the party, especially those in the South, gave their support to Senator Lyndon Johnson of Texas, the amazingly successful and shrewd majority leader of the Senate. But on the first ballot Kennedy's carefully organized campaign and months of hard talking paid off. He was nominated before the balloting was completed. In an astute move to unite the party and secure southern support in the election, Kennedy asked Johnson, who had won a third of the votes of the convention delegates, to run for Vice-President, which he agreed to do—much to the surprise of the public and the Kennedys.

The Democratic platform promised a continuation of the Fair and New Deals—the liberal program which had brought the party to power in so many previous elections. It called for a minimum wage of $1.25 and the "repeal of the anti-labor excesses which have been written into our labor laws" by the Republicans. If that was bait for the votes of organized labor, the farmers received the promise that inflexible price supports at 90 per cent of parity would be restored by the Democrats. A promise to revise the immigration laws in order to eliminate discrimination against eastern and southern Europeans was attractive to ethnic minorities who had long been a part of the Democratic coalition. Included also in the platform was a program of medical aid for the aged through the social security system. The platform strongly supported the Supreme Court decision against segregation in the schools and called for an end to segregation in all school districts by 1963. An additional appeal to Negroes was made in the praise of the sit-in demonstrations then occurring throughout the South.

The Republican platform was a defense of Eisenhower's administration, as it had to be under the circumstances. The emphasis was placed upon the peace and plenty which the country had enjoyed during the previous eight years. The Republicans also supported a high minimum wage without saying how high, and the ending of segregation without specifying a terminal date. The platform advocated the ending of all discrimination in jobs but was silent on the subject of the Fair Employment Practices Commission, which the Democrats had specifically endorsed. Both parties agreed that Communist China should not be admitted into the United Nations.

The campaign, despite extensive use of television and air travel by both candidates, proved to be unbelievably strenuous and physically demanding. Kennedy visited 44 states and Nixon all 50. An innovation of the campaign was a series of four television confrontations between the two young candidates (Kennedy was forty-three and Nixon forty-six). Although the debates, as they were called, hardly fitted the usual format of such encounters—there was no real attempt by either man to answer the arguments of the other—the public, which watched in tremendous numbers, obtained a close view of the candidates in action as well as a chance to evaluate the quality of the answers to newspaper correspondents' questions. The consensus was that Kennedy, who was not as well known nationally as the Vice-President, gained more from participation in the series. After the election Kennedy conceded to reporters that without the debates he did not think he could have won the election.

Kennedy's biggest handicap was his religion. In nominating him the Democrats decided that, despite their experience with Al Smith in 1928, a Roman Catholic could be elected President. Soon after the nomination of Kennedy, however, public and covert objections to having a Roman Catholic for President began to circulate. Unlike Smith, however, Kennedy from the outset admitted that his religion was a handicap and attempted to meet the opposition directly. Even in his primary fight in West Virginia, a state almost entirely old-line Protestant, Kennedy frankly raised the religious issue, saying plainly that religion, under the Constitution and in the American tradition,

THE ELECTION OF 1960

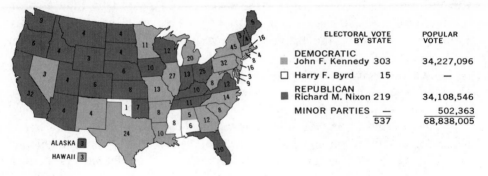

	ELECTORAL VOTE BY STATE	POPULAR VOTE
DEMOCRATIC		
John F. Kennedy	303	34,227,096
Harry F. Byrd	15	—
REPUBLICAN		
Richard M. Nixon	219	34,108,546
MINOR PARTIES	—	502,363
	537	68,838,005

ALASKA 3
HAWAII 3

should not be a factor in any election. Simultaneously, he made clear his own firm adherence to the traditional American conception of separation of church and state. His trouncing of his rival Hubert Humphrey in West Virginia on May 10 gave the Democrats and the country good reason to believe that religion might not be an issue in the coming campaign. Actually, as it turned out, that was not quite true. Always, though, Kennedy insisted upon meeting the objections to his religion from the high ground of principle. On September 12 at Houston, Texas, he addressed a group of Protestant ministers on the subject of his Catholicism, which had aroused much anxiety in the heavily Protestant South, just as Smith's candidacy had done 32 years earlier. "I believe," Kennedy told the assembled ministers, "in an America where separation of church and state is absolute . . . where no public official either requests or accepts instructions on public policy from . . . any . . . ecclesiastical source."

For the most part, the Republicans refused to use the issue of his religion against Kennedy. Nixon steadfastly adhered to his declaration made at the beginning of the campaign, that religion was not an issue.

A Close Election. On election day there was little confidence among pollsters or professional politicians as to the outcome. That night, as the polls closed across the nation, the early returns were equally indecisive. Not until early the next morning was the result definite, and even then the vote was so close that the final count was not clear for days. Kennedy's margin of victory turned out to be 113,057 out of some 69 million votes cast. It was the closest election in the popular vote since 1884; the electoral college vote was more decisive, however: 303 to 219. Although some Republicans held out for several days before conceding, Nixon himself, in what must have been, considering the closeness of the contest, a heart-breaking decision, conceded to Kennedy the day after the polling.

Analysis of the returns showed that Kennedy scored heavily in the industrial states that ran from Maine to Maryland, all of which contained a large Catholic population. Yet it is not certain that his religion won him many votes he would not have secured anyway. Surveys showed, for example, that his percentage of the vote in Catholic districts like Boston and elsewhere was not substantially higher than Truman's had been in 1948 (or than Johnson's would be in 1964). On the other hand, reliable surveys revealed that he lost as many as 4.5 million Protestant votes that were ordinarily Democratic. As political scientist V. O. Key put it, he won "in spite of his religion." Except for New Mexico, Nevada, and the new state of Hawaii, the only western states Kennedy carried were Michigan, Illinois, Minnesota, and Missouri. In general his strength was centered in the industrial cities — the heartland of the Democratic party — where Jewish and Negro voters, mainly urban-dwellers, strongly supported him. Indeed, the Negroes saved South Carolina for Kennedy, since Nixon came within 10,000 votes of capturing that once dependable stronghold of the Democratic party in the South. The usual Negro support of the Democratic party was increased greatly by an incident which occurred during the closing week of the campaign. When the Negro leader, Martin Luther King, Jr., was sentenced to four months in prison for a traffic violation in Georgia, Kennedy's brother Robert successfully intervened to secure his release. John Kennedy's courtesy call to Mrs. King was publicized to Negroes in two million pamphlets distributed at Negro churches throughout the country the Sunday before the election.

The slimness of Kennedy's victory was not reflected in the elections for Congress. The Democrats came in with huge majorities, counting 65 Democrats to 35 Republicans in the Senate and 262 to 174 in the House. But the avowedly reform-minded new President could not be sure that he would receive Congressional support for his program, since conservatives of both parties dominated the councils and the organization of both houses. Indeed, if anything, the election had returned more conservatives to Congress than in the previous session. This conservative domination would make the first two years of the new administration both a difficult period and one without much legislative achievement.

Yet it was clear from the election that the country was still — almost 30 years after the advent of the New Deal — strongly Democratic. It remained to be seen whether, without a vote-getter like Dwight Eisenhower, the Republicans could recapture the White House in the future, and, even if they did, whether they could ever hope for a Congress controlled by their party.

SUGGESTED READING

The Eisenhower years are still too close for a scholarly literature on its politics, but two journalistic accounts are important for understanding the political trends and issues of the early 1950's: Samuel Lubell, *The Revolt of the Moderates* (1956) and Louis Harris, *Is There a Republican Majority?* (1954). Both books are especially valuable on the election of 1952. The speeches of Adlai Stevenson, which did so much to win support for him among intellectuals, can be conveniently read in Adlai Stevenson, *Call to Greatness** (1962). Kenneth S. Davis, *A Prophet in his Own Country* (1957) is a favorable biography of Stevenson by a journalist; Herbert J. Muller, *Adlai Stevenson: A Study in Values* (1967) eulogizes the man and his ideals. There is no scholarly biography of Eisenhower as yet, but Marquis Childs, *Eisenhower: Captive Hero* (1958) is helpful, if highly critical. A sympathetic portrait of the leader of the conservative Republicans is by a newspaperman, William S. White, *The Taft Story* (1954).

The story of the Eisenhower administrations has to be pieced together from newspapers and contemporary periodical accounts, though some interim studies have appeared. Merlo J. Pusey, *Eisenhower the President* (1956) is favorable, while Dean Albertson, ed., *Eisenhower as President** (1963) is a collection of published articles, most of which are rather hard on the President and his administrations. Perhaps the best analytical study so far of the President is contained in a general work, Richard E. Neustadt, *Presidential Power: The Politics of Leadership** (1964), which also covers the Truman presidency. The book has value and interest also because of the influence it exerted upon John F. Kennedy. Much less useful, though it contains some valuable bits of information, is the racy, journalistic Jack Bell, *The Splendid Misery: The Story of the Presidency and Power Politics at Close Range* (1960). Richard H. Rovere, *The Eisenhower Years: Affairs of State* (1956) collects some penetrating columns by the *New Yorker* magazine's political reporter.

The most rewarding sources are the reminiscences of friends or members of the administration. Excellent is Robert J. Donovan, *Eisenhower: The Inside Story* (1956), which is drawn from Cabinet minutes and other confidential documents. Sherman Adams, *First Hand Report* (1961) is an account by the President's closest adviser in the White House; unfortunately, it is not very revealing or candid, tending to defend the President. Quite the opposite is Emmet John Hughes, *The Ordeal of Power* (1963), which is also written from inside the administration, but with a caustic pen and much disenchantment. Dwight D. Eisenhower, *The White House Years,* 2 vols. (1963, 1965) is the President's own memoirs; they are pedestrian and concede no failures, but cannot be overlooked.

The changing situation in education during Eisenhower's administration can be followed in Paul Woodring, *A Fourth of a Nation* (1957), James B. Conant, *The American High School Today** (1959), and Martin Mayer, *The Schools** (1961). Both Conant and Mayer were influential in bringing about reforms in school curricula. The controversy over public power is examined in a scholarly monograph, Aaron Wildavsky, *Dixon-Yates* (1962), in which the administration is absolved of any wrongdoing, but found culpable of serious ineptitude in handling the matter.

The early years and the mood of the Negro revolt can be glimpsed in Anthony Lewis, *Portrait of a Decade* (1964). It draws upon the columns of *The New York Times* to describe the upheaval in behalf of civil rights beginning in 1954. Louis E. Lomax, *The Negro Revolt** (1962) is a straightforward, sympathetic account by a

*Available in a paperback edition.

prominent Negro author. A more emotional and powerful statement of the Negro's grievances is contained in the collection of essays by the Negro novelist James Baldwin, *Nobody Knows My Name** (1961). The outstanding Negro leader of the decade has told his story of the Montgomery bus boycott of 1955 in Martin Luther King, Jr., *Stride Toward Freedon** (1958). Robert Coles, *Children of Crisis: A Study of Courage and Fear* (1967) is a psychologist's incisive study of the Negro children who undertook to desegregate schools in the South in the late 1950's and early 1960's.

Something of the conservative flavor of the Eisenhower years can be gleaned from two prominent books of the time. William F. Buckley, Jr., *Up from Liberalism* (1959) is a polemic by a young, truculent conservative, indicting the New Deal-Fair Deal liberals. The new conservative mood of the country is implicit in the scholarly study, Daniel Bell, *The End of Ideology** (1960).

The election of 1960 is covered in dramatic prose and astutely analyzed in Theodore H. White, *The Making of the President, 1960** (1961).

The first phase of the Negro revolution was directed against legal segregation, which by 1965 was substantially abolished by the civil rights acts. These laws made segregation illegal in schools and public facilities and abolished legal discrimination against Negroes at the polls and in jobs. While these laws were important gains, the situation of most Negroes was not immediately improved. In 1966 only 25.8 per cent of Negro pupils in the South attended school with white children; many adult Negroes still lacked the education and skills to get better jobs, even if employers ceased to discriminate against them. The main problem of most Negroes was their poverty, whether they lived on southern farms or in northern city ghettos.

Against the problems of poverty and the ghettos, the tactics of the first phase, sit-ins, demonstrations, and marches, were only of limited usefulness. More and more Negro leaders talked about the necessity of political action,

Negroes and whites joined the early sit-ins and marches, like the one below. *Photo: Matt Herron-Black Star. Above left:* Negroes line up to vote in Alabama. *Photo: UPI. Above right:* Demonstrators face fixed bayonets in Cambridge, Maryland. *Photo: Wide World. Opposite:* Fires smoulder in Washington, D.C., after the assassination of Dr. Martin Luther King, Jr. *Photo: Wide World*

Above left: A white woman pickets the consecration of a Negro bishop in New Orleans. *Photo: Wide World. Above right:* Whites protest an open-housing march in Chicago. *Photo: Wide World. Opposite:* Dr. Martin Luther King, Jr., testifies before a Senate subcommittee studying poverty and urban problems. *Photo: Wide World*

of "Black Power," as the only effective weapon to achieve real equality. At the same time the protests shifted from the South to the city ghettos in the North, where by the late 1960's an important proportion of Negroes lived.

Negro frustrations with the slow rate of progress toward full equality were evident in the riots that occurred in the nation's cities after 1963. As the Report of the President's Commission on Civil Disorders (1968) pointed out, most of the rioters in 1967 were young people, unemployed or employed in menial jobs, who were intensely proud of their race and who did not want to wait their entire lives for equality in an affluent society. Hostile toward white society and distrustful of the political system that ignored their situation, they let their frustrations explode against the symbols of white society in the ghettos, mainly small businesses and the police. Confrontations between young Negroes and armed police and national guardsmen, like the one pictured on p. 113, were frequent occurrences during the summers, reinforcing hostility between young Negroes and white authority.

As Negroes became more vehement in their demands for economic opportunity as well as legal equality, white resistance began to express itself and to organize in the North as it had in the South. The picture on p. 114, taken in New Orleans, captures the fierce racial hostility of some whites. The face of the man in the adjoining picture, taken during an open-housing march in Chicago, displays the same deep emotion, despite the assertion of such counterprotesters that their cause was not racial hostility but the freedom of the homeowner to sell to whomever he desires.

In this state of tension between the races, the 1968 assassination of Dr. Martin Luther King, Jr., in Memphis, Tennessee, set off a wave of riots throughout the country. King's assassination was ironic because he had continued to advocate nonviolence not only for moral reasons but also because he recognized, as did most Negro leaders, the futility of violence when the means of violence were overwhelmingly in the hands of the whites. Moreover, the effects of violence in the ghettos were felt almost entirely by the Negroes themselves, who made up the bulk of the killed, injured, and homeless. Yet it seemed that white society acted to remove the barriers to Negro equality and opportunity only when violence dramatically focused attention on the Negroes plea for recognition. The slowness of the whites' response and the Negroes' basic impotence as a minority enraged young Negroes and made them listen to the advocates of violence.

CHAPTER FOUR

INTO THE SIXTIES

DOMESTIC AND FOREIGN AFFAIRS UNDER KENNEDY AND JOHNSON

DURING HIS CAMPAIGN John F. Kennedy called for a new, youthful spirit in government and in the country at large; he never said it explicitly, but the fact was that Eisenhower was the oldest man ever to serve as President, and Kennedy would be the youngest ever elected. There was a decided emphasis on youth and vigor in the new President's short, pithy inaugural address: "Let the word go forth from this time and place, to friend and foe alike, that the torch has been passed to a new generation of Americans, born in this century, tempered by war, disciplined by a hard and bitter peace, proud of our ancient heritage. . . ."

A New Generation

Kennedy's emphasis upon youth was apparent in his selection of Cabinet officers. Although many of the new appointees were young, and far removed from the business background of the Eisenhower Cabinet, the new President was not doctrinaire on either ground. He selected as Secretary of Commerce Luther Hodges, who was a former business executive in his sixties—"the administration's only link with the nineteenth century," as Hodges phrased it. Kennedy broke boldly with precedent in the appointment of his brother Robert, even younger than himself, as Attorney General. Perhaps the most impressive Cabinet member was the Secretary of Defense, Robert McNamara, president of Ford Motor Company and a former professor. Kennedy and McNamara hit it off immediately, becoming good friends socially as well as mutually respected co-workers—a rare combination within the Kennedy administration. Also indicative of the new President's willingness to break with the usual practice was his appointment of Douglas Dillon as Secretary of the Treasury, even though Dillon was a Republican and a former member of Eisenhower's Cabinet. For Secretary of State, Kennedy passed over Adlai Stevenson to appoint Dean Rusk, a former State Department official and, at the time, head of the Rockefeller Foundation.

One of the striking facts about Kennedy's appointments on all levels was his dependence upon foundations and universities. Of the top 200 appointments, 18 per cent were drawn from educational institutions, as contrasted with 6 per cent in the previous administration. Newspaper columnists joked about the preponderance of Harvard men in the upper levels of the new administration, but there were also almost as many Rhodes scholars. Businessmen had made up 42 per cent of the top appointments under Eisenhower, but they constituted only 6 per cent under Kennedy.

An Uncommon Man. John F. Kennedy liked to think of himself as the representative of the generation born in the twentieth century, but in most ways he was far from typical of his contemporaries. Born in 1917 into a newly wealthy Irish Catholic family, he was educated at exclusive private schools and graduated from Harvard College just as Europe was descending into the night of World War II. His considerable talent as a writer and observer of

John F. Kennedy's inauguration. *Photo: Cornell Capa—Magnum*

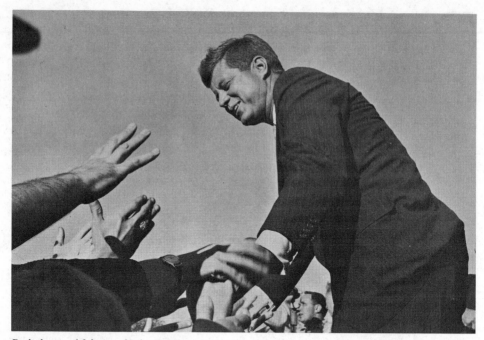

Both the youthfulness of John F. Kennedy and the magnetic attraction he had for people are caught in this picture of him taken during the 1960 campaign. *Photo: Cornell Capa—Magnum*

foreign events was displayed in 1939 by the publication of his senior thesis as the book *Why England Slept*, which was a study of the reasons for England's refusal to oppose the threat of Hitler during the 1930's. During the war he served as a lieutenant in command of a PT boat in the southwestern Pacific. When his boat was rammed and sunk by a Japanese destroyer, his devotion to his men and the hardships he incurred in order to get them back alive made him a minor hero. After the war his election to the House of Representatives from Massachusetts in 1946 brought him into national politics. In 1952 he was elected to the United States Senate after a hard and close fight against a favored Republican incumbent. Although the Senate suited his tastes better than the House, his ambition did not rest in the upper house. In 1956 he unsuccessfully competed for the Democratic vice-presidential nomination. After that defeat he began his campaign for the top place in 1960.

The ambition was one side of him. Another was his wit, which he turned against himself as well as against Republicans. "I understand that President McKinley and I are the only two Presidents of the United States to ever address such an occasion," he told the Republican-dominated National Association of Manufacturers in 1961. "I suppose that President McKinley and I are the only two that are regarded as fiscally sound enough to be qualified for admission to this organization on an occasion such as this." At another time, as he and his staff relaxed on the rear balcony of the White

House after making the harrowing decision to establish the Cuban quarantine, he lightened the gloom with the remark, "I hope you realize that there's not enough room for everybody in the White House bomb shelter."

There was also his pragmatism, his refusal to be tied down by theory or preconceived ideas, including those of his liberal supporters. In fact, he distrusted people who called themselves liberals, and when he himself was denominated a liberal, he quickly qualified the description to "practical liberal" or "pragmatic liberal." He never joined the liberal organization Americans for Democratic Action, for example, or even the American Veterans Committee, a liberal veterans group formed at the close of the Second World War. As a member of Congress, he had revealed a conservative streak when, for instance, he refused to vote for the repeal of the Taft-Hartley Act (though he had opposed it originally), and supported the Twenty-Second Amendment. (His much-commented-upon refusal to speak out against the actions of Senator McCarthy was dictated not by conservatism but by his concern for the opinion of his Irish Catholic constituents who idolized the Wisconsin senator.) Even before he became President, then, Kennedy evidenced the detachment that characterized his White House years. As one of his biographers, James M. Burns, has suggested, this detachment was a reflection of his divided origins. Although an Irish Catholic, born of conservative parents, he displayed the manners, the education, and the intellectual outlook of a member of the eastern establishment. One Massachusetts Democratic politician put it well: "Jack is the first of the Irish Brahmins."

As President, Kennedy obviously enjoyed his job; it never seemed too big for him, as it did in the beginning for Truman, or boring, as it appeared to be for Eisenhower. Kennedy thrived on the pressures of the presidency, gloried in its history, and welcomed its opportunities for leadership. In that way he was like F.D.R., though he lacked Roosevelt's nineteenth-century certitude. Realistic pessimism and ambiguity were never far removed from his thoughts or lips. Once after a successful press conference on television he told his assistant, "We couldn't survive without TV." His realism and intellectual honesty cringed at what public life sometimes demanded. After the Los Angeles convention, for example, he never used the phrase New Frontier again, either publicly or privately.

The Domestic Achievements of the Kennedy Years

Getting the Country Moving. During the campaign Kennedy had attacked the Eisenhower administration for failing to achieve a rate of economic growth commensurate with those attained by the industrial nations of Europe. As he pointed out, one of the social consequences of a relatively low rate of growth was high unemployment, which reached almost six million in the first months of the new administration. He proposed a number of measures to stimulate economic growth, but perhaps his most significant innovation was to call attention to the gap between the views of the new Keynesian economists on the proper and central role of government in the economy and the myths that businessmen and the public accepted as economic truths. Ever the pragmatist who scorned ideology because it interfered with understanding reality, Kennedy insisted upon educating the country in economics as no President before him had ever done. Like Theodore Roosevelt, he used "the bully pulpit" of the presidency to the fullest. His most notable effort in this connection was the commencement address he gave at Yale University in June 1962. His text was, "How can we look at things as they are, not through party labels or through position labels, but as they are—and figure out how we can maintain this economy so that it moves ahead?" His answer was: "What we need is not labels and clichés but more basic discussion of the sophisticated and technical issues involved in keeping a great economic machine moving ahead." The specific targets of his remarks were those members of Congress and the business community who thought balancing the budget was the most pressing fiscal task of government. To such people he pointed out that the national debt was actually a smaller proportion of the gross national product in 1962 than it had been in 1945, and consequently a much reduced burden. He also denied that business confidence in government was a necessary condition of prosperity, observing that the downturns of 1929, 1954, 1958, and 1960 came when Republicans, who were traditionally friendly to business, occupied the presidential office.

The steps Kennedy took early in his administration to stimulate the economy put these principles into action. In September 1961, for example, the minimum wage was increased to $1.15 an hour, with a further increase to $1.25 to go into effect two years later. The Housing Act of 1961 provided funds for urban renewal, low-income housing, and farm housing, thereby creating almost half a million jobs in the construction industry alone. In 1962 at his suggestion, Congress enacted the Manpower Retraining Act, which appropriated $435 million over the next three years, if the states would furnish a like amount, for the purpose of training the unemployed in new skills so that they could secure jobs. Finally, as an additional fillip to the economy, this same act authorized the President to spend up to $900 million in public works, which were to be located in those parts of the country where unemployment was especially high.

The principal measure for stimulating the economy that was enacted under Kennedy's administration and, indeed, the major domestic legislative achievement of his first two years in office was the Trade Expansion Act of 1962. Kennedy recognized that the success of the European Economic Community or Common Market, as it is usually called (made up of France, Italy, West Germany, and the Benelux countries), threatened to cut into American markets abroad. As a countermeasure, he proposed a drastic revision of the Reciprocal Trade Act, which expired that year. The Trade

GOVERNMENT SPENDING AND ECONOMIC GROWTH

Although the federal debt has continued to grow since World War II, the economy has grown much faster. The national debt is now only a fraction of the total amount of goods and services produced each year. On the other hand, as state and local governments have assumed larger roles in the economy (see graph on p. 13) their debts have risen much more rapidly than the federal debt. The largest percentage increase in governmental spending has been in the "other" category (including in 1966 the enlarged portion). This reflects the increasing expenditures of state and local governments, who pay for all or part of these services. *Sources:* Bureau of the Census. Treasury Department. Government spending includes all levels of government.

GOVERNMENT INDEBTEDNESS

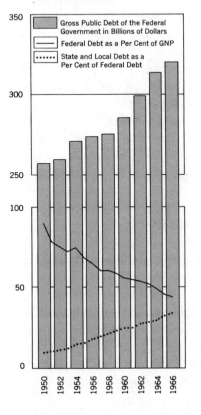

GOVERNMENT SPENDING
In Billions of Dollars

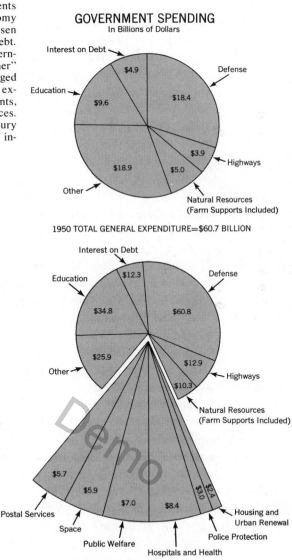

1950 TOTAL GENERAL EXPENDITURE=$60.7 BILLION

1966 TOTAL GENERAL EXPENDITURE=$189.4 BILLION

Expansion Act marked an even greater departure from protectionism than had the Reciprocal Trade Act of 1934. It gave the President new powers to cut tariff rates, although Congress had always heretofore guarded its prerogative in this area. It also provided for federal aid to those business firms and workers adversely affected by the resulting competition from abroad. Kennedy envisioned the act as a means of stimulating American economic growth by opening markets abroad. By permitting the importation of certain foreign goods, particularly from the Common Market, the administration hoped to secure in return wider and important markets for American goods, while increasing, through foreign competition, the efficiency of industry in the United States.

Kennedy's chief advice for stimulating the economy—a by-product of his acceptance of the new, Keynesian economics—was the reduction of personal and corporation income taxes. He recognized that, despite an unbalanced budget, a cut in taxes would leave more money in the hands of consumers, the spending of which would act as a massive stimulant to growth. And with growth, total government revenues, despite the cut in tax rates, would actually increase. The President advocated a tax cut in the summer of 1962 and repeated the proposal three times in 1963, but conservative legislators, led by Democratic Senator Harry F. Byrd of Virginia, would not vote a tax cut while federal expenditures were larger than revenues. Only under the Johnson administration was the cut enacted, and it then produced the precise effect Kennedy had predicted. Not only did federal revenues rise, but by 1967 the country was enjoying the longest boom in its history, and the annual rate of economic growth was up to a spectacular 5.6 per cent.

A Short Honeymoon with Business. Ever since the 1930's, the business community had been wary of, when not actively hostile toward, Democratic administrations. Unlike Eisenhower, Kennedy was no advocate of businessmen in government, but he did hope he could avoid the hostility that businessmen had felt toward Truman and Roosevelt. His hopes, however, were dashed in the spring of 1962 when business hostility reached a new high as a result of the President's handling of a dispute over wages between the steel industry and the steelworkers' union.

During March and early April, the administration had worked closely with management and labor in the steel industry to avoid a strike and an inflationary wage increase that everyone recognized would set back the slowly growing economy. Responding to government pressure, the steelworkers union agreed to sign a new contract with the companies without receiving the usual wage increases for the first year; the tacit understanding was that the steel manufacturers, therefore, would not raise their prices. Ten days after the strike had been averted, the president of United States Steel announced that his company was raising its prices. Kennedy and his advisers were incensed, convinced that they had been betrayed. At a press conference the next day he lashed out: "Some time ago I asked each American to consider what he would do for his country and I asked the steel companies. In the last twenty-four hours we had their answer."

Characteristically, the President did not confine his anger to words. Suddenly the antitrust division of the Justice Department began to investigate signs of monopoly in the steel industry; the Defense Department announced it would be awarding new contracts only to those steel companies that did not raise prices. The presidential indignation and the resultant threats had their desired effect, for other steel companies failed to follow the lead of United States Steel, which soon rescinded its increase. The business community, however, was up in arms over the incident.

Thus, like his Democratic predecessors, Truman and Roosevelt, Kennedy found himself at odds with business. And a sharp and deep drop in the stock market the following month did nothing to enhance his standing in business circles.

Kennedy and Negro Rights. In 1966 a public opinion poll revealed that John F. Kennedy was remembered by Negroes as having done more for the black man in America than even Lyndon Johnson, under whose administration more civil rights legislation has been enacted than during any administration in the previous 90 years. Yet there was justice in putting John F. Kennedy in first place. He was the first President in the twentieth century to make the cause of Negro equality his own and the nation's.

Kennedy's involvement in the Negro revolution came late, as it did for most white Americans in the twentieth century. It became noticeable during his campaign in 1960 when he made his famous gesture of concern for Martin Luther King. That act was followed up when he reached the White House by his appointment of a number of Negroes to important jobs in government. Moreover, as occasions arose in the course of the civil rights struggle in the South, the President supported his brother Robert's keen interest as Attorney General in the rights of Negroes. One instance of such support occurred in the spring of 1961 when Negroes and whites protesting segregation in interstate travel (Freedom Riders) in Alabama were attacked by mobs. The President saw to it that soon thereafter the Interstate Commerce Commission ordered the immediate desegregation of all waiting rooms in bus, plane, and railroad terminals.

The federal government's protection of Negro equality was not as easily extended to Mississippi. In the early fall of 1962, Kennedy was compelled to intervene with military force in that state just as Eisenhower had been compelled to do at Little Rock, Arkansas, five years before. When the state and the University of Mississippi refused to honor a federal court order to admit James Meredith as the first Negro student to Ole Miss, the President dispatched 300 U.S. marshals to protect his rights. The marshals were met by a barrage of rocks, bottles, and bullets from a howling mob of students and townspeople; the riot, in which two persons were killed and scores injured, lasted 15 hours before 5000 United States troops brought order to the university town of Oxford. Meredith was admitted when order had been restored and graduated in 1963. His enrollment was the first break in the heretofore solid resistance to desegregation in Mississippi; it was followed by the admission of Negroes to all levels of education in the state.

In May 1963 when police in Birmingham, Alabama, brutally used dogs, clubs, and fire hoses to break up Negro demonstrations, the resulting violence caused the President to send federal troops into that city to restore order. That and other acts of intimidation against Negroes moved him in June to advocate, in a nationwide address, additional federal legislation to carry forward the Negro revolution. His appeal was frankly ethical. Carefully he pointed out that equal rights for Negroes "is not a sectional issue," nor "a partisan issue. . . . We are confronted primarily with a moral issue. It is as old as the Scriptures and is as clear as the American Constitution." His address was given added, if unnecessary, point that same night by the ambush killing of Medgar Evers, the Negro leader of civil rights workers in Mississippi. On June 19 Kennedy sent his civil rights bill to Congress. He did not live to see it enacted, but it became law under the Johnson administration after a three-month filibuster in the Senate.

The Civil Rights Act of 1964 was the most ambitious and comprehensive ever placed upon the statute books in the United States. It prohibited racial discrimination in public places, like hotels, theaters, and restaurants; in employment; and in labor unions. Moreover, it provided for the withholding of federal funds from any agency of the state governments in which racial discrimination was practiced. This provision alone carried great persuasive power since hospitals, schools, and a number of welfare programs in the South, as elsewhere, were recipients of federal funds. The Attorney General was also authorized to institute suits in behalf of individuals who had been discriminated against, yet might be too poor to go to court to enforce their rights. Finally, the act prohibited discrimination in the application of voter-registration requirements and established the presumption that any person with a sixth-grade education was literate. In that way literacy requirements, which were often used as a device for disfranchising Negroes in the South, were nullified. The most obvious and immediate effect of the act was the opening of many public accommodations previously closed to Negroes. In at least some sections of the Deep South, Negroes went to the polls in large numbers for the first time in the twentieth century. For example, in 1964 in Tuskegee, Alabama, a black-belt community, Negroes succeeded in electing two members of their race to the city council.

The act was in fact the most sweeping affirmation of the American belief in equality ever enacted. It not only prohibited racial discrimination, but it outlawed discrimination in employment for reasons of sex, nationality, and religion as well. As never before, the federal government committed itself to equality for America's two most visible minorities: Negroes and women.

The Blighting of the Promise. Toward the close of 1962, the President and his administration were looking forward to the second half of his term. The broad program of economic reform announced in 1961 had not gone very well, for, despite the large Democratic majorities in both houses, many points of the program had run up against considerable resistance in Congress. Twice, in those first two years, Congress had rejected programs for medical care for the aged—despite two major public addresses in favor of them by the President. Similarly, Kennedy's plea for federal aid to education had also fallen on deaf ears in Congress. Moreover, the President's recommendation for a Department of Urban Affairs, which recognized the need for help to the cities, had also failed to pass. A similar fate overtook his further request for half a billion dollars in federal grants to those cities working out long-range plans for mass public transportation. Even in foreign affairs, where his record of achievement was brighter, Kennedy stumbled over Congressional resistance, particularly in the House, where conservative southern Democrats joined with Republicans in 1962 to cut the President's foreign aid program. Until the end of 1962, the only major achievement of the administration had been the Trade Expansion Act. Then, in November the administration received strong support from the country. Instead of losing 30 to 40 seats as was normal in an off-year Congressional election, the Democrats lost only a handful in the House and held their large majority in the Senate. For that reason, and because of the large amount of important legislation that was working its way through the Congressional mill, 1963 was full of promise. The tax bill, the aid-to-education bill, and the civil rights bill aroused expectations of a commendable achievement for the first Kennedy administration.

That promise, however, was killed by an assassin's bullet. On November 22, 1963, John F. Kennedy was shot to death in broad daylight while riding in an open car through the streets of Dallas. The motive for the shooting will never be known, since his alleged assassin, while in the hands of the police, was himself shot to death by a local resident said to be incensed by the President's murder.

The assassin's bullet killed more than the promise of the Kennedy administration; it murdered a man who had won the respect and deep affection of large numbers of his countrymen and people throughout the world. His death stunned the nation with its suddenness and irrationality. There had been so much, and now there was nothing. "Like a great green cedar," one eulogist said, "he came crashing down, still in full vigor and strength."

Johnson Takes Over

The New President. Neither in name nor in native state was the new President bringing anything novel to the office. But, as events would show, he differed greatly from the earlier Johnson and the earlier Texan in the White

House. Sworn into office just before flying back to Washington from Dallas, Lyndon Baines Johnson plunged immediately into the job of mastering an office he had long hoped for, but which had eluded him in 1960. The contrast could not have been greater between the young, eastern-born and urban-bred Kennedy, who had inherited his wealth, and Lyndon Johnson. Born on a farm in semiarid southwestern Texas in 1908, Johnson grew up in straitened circumstances, working his way through school and college by a variety of jobs, including teaching. As many of his speeches were later to attest, the wastefulness and emptiness of the Great Depression never faded from his memory; at the signing of almost every welfare measure, he alluded to his experiences as a child and young man in the depressed ranchlands of Texas and across the country during the 1920's and 1930's. His rearing in the agricultural South remained in evidence in his drawling speech and rural metaphors. His sentimental and effusive rhetoric, reminiscent of his father's Populism, contrasted sharply with the low-keyed, taut manner of Kennedy. A large man, possessed of enormous energy and will, Lyndon Johnson's ceaseless activity as President easily belied the fact that he had almost died of a heart attack in 1955.

Johnson began his public career as an officer of the National Youth Administration and came to Congress for the first time in 1937, where he was a loyal supporter of the New Deal and a fervent admirer of Franklin Roosevelt. Running for election to the United States Senate in 1948, he won his nomination to the Democratic ticket by fewer than 100 votes. Yet within four years he was Democratic floor leader of the Senate. There he displayed an ability to dominate that individualistic body unequaled since the days of Senator Nelson Aldrich at the beginning of the century. As his central role in the enactment of the Civil Rights Act of 1957 demonstrated, Lyndon Johnson, during the Eisenhower administration, was the effective legislative leader of the government. Later events would show that this was only the beginning of the momentous impact that this first southern-born President since Woodrow Wilson would have on the advancement of the Negro to equality.

A Firm Assumption of Power. As President, Johnson proved to be different from Kennedy in more than background and style; he was also able to move legislation through Congress at remarkable speed. The first 100 days of the new administration witnessed the passage of several important bills that previously had been stalled in legislative committees for months. Within those first 100 days, the reduction in personal and corporate income taxes that Kennedy had been advocating for over a year was enacted (February 1964). In the same period the foreign aid bill and the Higher Education Facilities Act (December 1963) were enacted, and the civil rights bill approved by the House. During the remainder of his first year in the White House, Johnson went on to make a record of legislative achievements that astonished a country accustomed to seeing a liberal President hamstrung by a conservative and tight-fisted Congress. At Johnson's request Congress raised the salaries of government employees again, passed a new low rent housing act, and enacted a new National Defense Education Act. Most significant of all was the passage through the Senate, after a three-month filibuster, of the Civil Rights Act of 1964, which has already been discussed.

Johnson also proved himself to be a remarkable persuader not only of legislators, with whom he had long worked, but of labor and management as well. When a railroad strike to prevent the removal of 40,000 surplus firemen from diesel engines threatened once again, Johnson personally worked behind the scenes to bring a settlement, which he triumphantly announced on April 22, 1964. Unlike the experience in 1963, Congress was not compelled to act to prevent a nationwide railroad strike. The Johnson settlement gave good promise, moreover, of at last bringing the wearisome five-year-long dispute to a close.

The War on Poverty. Like all Presidents who have succeeded to the office, Johnson promised to carry on the policies and principles of his predecessor. (He also retained virtually all of the Kennedy Cabinet members through his first year in office.) But almost from the outset of his administration, Johnson made it clear that he intended to put his own brand on the liberal Kennedy program. In his first State of the Union message in January 1964, Johnson called for a war against poverty as the keystone to the arch of the policies of his administration. Out of that proposal came the passage of the Economic Opportunity Act, which received his signature in August 1964.

The act was a recognition that most of the poverty in the nation was the result of lack of education, not of lack of jobs or opportunity for work. The act appropriated almost a billion dollars for various agencies and projects that would help young people continue their education or receive job training that would enable them to undertake jobs that required new skills. Under the act a Job Corps was created for training sixteen- to twenty-one-year-old unemployed youths. The act also set up VISTA (Volunteers in Service to America) to mobilize the skills and energies of young Americans in behalf of their poor and disadvantaged countrymen, much as the Peace Corps was intended to assist in the economic development of foreign countries. Funds were also made available under the act to those cities and communities that were working out educational and training programs to help the poor rise out of their cycle of poverty and despair.

Since there had been a Fair Deal and a New Frontier, it followed that there must be a name for the Johnson program. For a while the President seemed able to do no better than "the better deal," a term which he and his staff used several times in the early spring of 1964. But in a speech at the University of Michigan in May, he hit upon the title he would stick by. The Great Society, he said at Ann Arbor, was "a place where leisure is a welcome chance to build and reflect, not a feared cause of boredom and restlessness. It is a place where the city of man serves not only the needs of the body and the demands of commerce, but the desire for beauty and the hunger of community. . . . It is a place where men are more concerned with the quality of their goals than the quantity of their goods."

Not everything that the President sought in that first year was vouchsafed him. His efforts to fulfill Kennedy's commitment to medical care for the aged and to an increase in social security benefits did not pass Congress. Nor was he successful in pushing through an otherwise remarkably compliant Congress his bill to relieve poverty and arrest economic decay in Appalachia. But within a single year in office Lyndon Johnson had established himself as a strong and effective President in his own right.

The Landslide

The Rise of Barry Goldwater. While the President was working to build a record on which to base his campaign for a full term in the White House, the Republicans were preparing for their own campaign by subjecting his Great Society to severe criticism. As we have seen in Chapter Three, for over 20 years the party had been split between a conservative or Taft wing and a more liberal wing, which since 1940 had provided all of the party's presidential candidates. From time to time during those two decades, the bitterness of the conservatives over their exclusion from the presidential nomination had burst out, but without any effect.

In 1964 the time of the conservatives had come, and Senator Barry Goldwater of Arizona was their man. Barry M. Goldwater was a genial, earnest, gregarious, millionaire department store owner. As early as 1960, he was frankly calling himself a conservative in a society where it had long appeared that liberalism was the only acceptable label for a national candidate. Waggish opponents of the Senator suggested that his brand of conservatism was really nineteenth-century liberalism, centering as it did upon principles of laissez faire and states' rights. But in the prosperous atmosphere of the 1960's and in the frustrating age of the perpetual Cold War, Goldwater's references to the verities of the agrarian republic and his highly nationalistic approach to foreign policy evoked a warm response from many Americans. Incomes may have been up, but so were taxes; billions of American dollars had been lent and given to nations around the globe, yet wars still raged, while others threatened. The racial issue provoked violence, and the overcrowded cities, with their rocketing crime rates and spreading slums, threatened the safety and peace of mind of many who wanted to enjoy untroubled their new prosperity. For these Americans it was comforting to hear Senator Goldwater preach patience to the restless black ghettos, promise a reduced and balanced federal budget, and advocate a tough, military stand against Communist Russia and China.

The eastern wing of the Republican party, however, did not recognize the attraction Goldwater's conservatism obviously held for millions of frustrated and bewildered Americans. Nor did they understand that for many Republican politicians the conservative program was a welcome change after a quarter century of accepting the liberal reforms of the Democrats, with only the lame qualification that Republicans could carry them out more effectively. Such, in truth, had been the message of Thomas E. Dewey in 1948, Dwight Eisenhower in 1952 and 1956, and Richard M. Nixon in 1960. Why not, as the Goldwater supporters contended, present the electorate in 1964 with "a choice not an echo"? Provide a candidate who repudiated the principles common to the reforming Democrats from the New Deal to the Great Society, and the American voters' conservative instincts would produce a conservative Republican victory.

Precisely that conclusion was reached by the Republican convention in San Francisco in the summer of 1964. The convention nominated Goldwater on the first ballot and then proceeded to nominate for second place William Miller of New York, who balanced the ticket geographically, but hardly ideologically. Miller, despite his eastern origins, was of the same conservative persuasion as Goldwater, though lacking the genial humor and open manner of the Arizonan.

The platform the party adopted in San Francisco reflected the conservative domination of the convention; it called for an end to deficit spending, further tax reduction, enforcement of the Civil Rights Act of 1964, and a stronger foreign policy based on "a dynamic strategy aimed at victory," which was a reference to the increasingly frustrating war in Vietnam.

No Democratic Fight. The Democratic party's convention had no trouble in selecting its candidate: Lyndon B. Johnson was obviously the champion of the party. But the choice of his running mate created some suspense, if only because the President refused to divulge his preference until the last minute. His choice of Hubert Humphrey, senator from Minnesota, surprised many because of Humphrey's long association with the decidedly liberal wing of the party. The selection of Humphrey, which the convention accepted by acclamation, was interpreted as an earnest by Johnson that those groups, like organized labor, which had feared his conservatism in 1960, need have no comparable anxiety in 1964. The platform not only promised to carry out the principles laid down by Kennedy and Johnson, but also came out for full support of civil rights for Negroes, aid to education, medical insurance for the aged, full employment—and, of all things, a balanced budget! Unlike the Republicans, the Democrats went out of their way to specifically condemn extremism on the right and on the left—meaning the supernationalistic John Birch Society and the Ku Klux Klan (which seemed likely to support Goldwater), as well as the Communist party. The contest between the parties, in short, would not be confused by the customary balancing of philosophies in nominees or platforms.

The Campaign and the Election. Despite the clear ideological differences between the parties, there was no high-level discussion of the issues in the campaign, only platitudes and attacks. Moreover, Goldwater proved to be a

THE ELECTION OF 1964

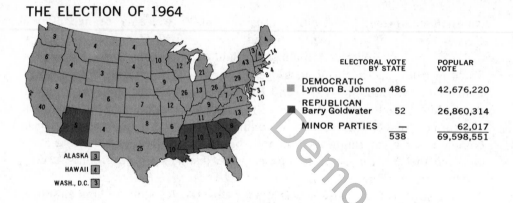

	ELECTORAL VOTE BY STATE	POPULAR VOTE
DEMOCRATIC Lyndon B. Johnson	486	42,676,220
REPUBLICAN Barry Goldwater	52	26,860,314
MINOR PARTIES	—	62,017
	538	69,598,551

ALASKA 3
HAWAII 4
WASH., D.C. 3

rather ineffective campaigner; his forte was clearly not the great mass rally and the frequent speechmaking that modern campaigning demands. Recognizing that some of the impromptu, ill-considered denunciations of New Deal legislation that he had made in the past were now hurting his strength, he tried to qualify his remarks and to assure the country that he was not going to sell TVA to private enterprise or to abolish the social security system after all. Johnson was more relaxed and bouyant if only because he was favored in the polls from the beginning. Nevertheless his penchant for folksy phrases and rural figures of speech dismayed many of his more sophisticated, urban supporters, who found his drawl, his lumbering generalizations, and his sentimentality undignified and even embarrassing. He was most effective, however, in charging that Goldwater was too impulsive and belligerent to be trusted with the foreign policy of the nation. Johnson's characterization of the Republican candidate received widespread credence because of Goldwater's refusal to vote for the test ban treaty in 1963, and his well-known advocacy of bombing raids on North Vietnam. The anxiety about the war in Vietnam, and the widespread fears that Goldwater would expand the war, that he would "shoot from the hip," as the popular phrase went, undoubtedly turned many voters, including Republicans, against him.

In fact, subsequent analyses of the elections revealed that Goldwater lost millions of Republican votes. Usually safe Republican states like Maine, Vermont, Nebraska, and Kansas went overwhelmingly for Johnson. To put the matter positively, Johnson's victory was the greatest in the twentieth century; he received 61 per cent of the vote, or more than F.D.R. in 1936 or Warren Harding in 1920. He carried the District of Columbia and 44 states; while 4 of the 6 states Goldwater did capture were located in the Deep South. Johnson's victory was equally impressive in Congress: 295 seats in the House as compared with 140 for the Republicans; the Senate was also lopsidedly Democratic: 68 to 32.

That the main Republican strength had been in the South showed how completely the traditional political alignments had been reversed. The Deep

South, smarting under the Democratic endorsement of Negro equality, turned in desperation to the once-despised Republican party, which, under Goldwater, ignored the Negro when it did not oppose him. Goldwater's emphasis upon states' rights also spoke to Dixie. So intense was southern interest in the election that the South was the only region of the country in which the turnout of voters was greater than in 1960. The decline in the vote throughout the nation resulted from the absenteeism of many Republicans who were unwilling to vote for either Goldwater or a Democrat. If Johnson's position on civil rights lost him votes in the South, it brought him the overwhelming support of Negroes in both North and South. (Goldwater had deliberately exposed himself to the opposition of Negroes by voting against the Civil Rights Act of 1964.) In no section of the country was Negro support of Johnson less than 95 per cent; in some cities of the North, the proportion reached 99 per cent.

Undoubtedly many Negroes voted for Johnson not just because of civil rights, but also because they were poor. For, especially in the big cities, the low-income groups, a mainstay of the Democrats ever since the New Deal, continued to vote overwhelmingly for the party of Franklin Roosevelt: the proportions hovered around 90 per cent. Old people in retirement areas like St. Petersburg, Florida, who had voted Republican for 20 years, deserted the party because Goldwater was believed to be a threat to the social security system. Even many of the well-to-do suburbs deserted their Republican allegiance when confronted with a conservative candidate who seemed to rely heavily upon military solutions to problems of foreign policy. Moreover, since Goldwater's commitment to laissez faire caused him to repudiate farm supports and governmental controls over agriculture, many farmers also abandoned the party on election day. In 23 states, later studies showed, the rural vote in each state went more heavily for Johnson than the state as a whole. The candidate who promised continued price supports, more rural electrification, and more soil conservation payments won the farmer.

Despite the Republicans' disaster in 1964, they made resounding gains two years later. They increased their seats in Congress by 47 and won 8 new governorships. Noteworthy, however, was the fact that almost all of the Republican winners had either opposed Goldwater's nomination in 1964 or simply ignored in 1966 the conservative ideology represented by the former Arizona senator. The results of the 1966 elections showed once again how costly the Goldwater candidacy had been in 1964.

On the Road to the Great Society

The Mandate. Johnson's overwhelming victory at the polls, together with his swollen majorities in both houses of Congress, gave him new authority to build the Great Society, the program which he set forth in his State of the Union message in January 1965. Bills which Congress had turned down in the preceding year now passed quickly and with ease. In March, for example, the

President signed the Appalachian Regional Development Act, which authorized $1.1 billion for the improvement of the thousand-mile-long mountainous region that runs through 11 states and in which poverty and poor education are endemic. Johnson's war on poverty was further advanced by the Public Works and Economic Development Act of August 1965. That law authorized the spending of $3.3 billion over a period of five years for the economic development of depressed cities and regions.

Two measures introduced originally by Kennedy were enacted into law soon after the new Congress convened. Twice during the Kennedy years the opposition of many Republicans and of the powerful American Medical Association had prevented the passage of bills to provide medical care for persons over sixty-five through the social security system. The new Congress, heavy with liberal Democrats and urged on by the President, pushed through a Medicare insurance law, which the President happily signed on July 30, 1965. The act provided that basic hospitalization costs, including nursing home care for all persons over sixty-five, would be paid for out of social security taxes. A supplementary plan, which cost the participant only $36 a year, was also set up to help meet additional medical expenses of persons over sixty-five. The President, ever conscious of the historical roots of momentous events, arranged to sign the bill in the presence of the aging former President Harry S. Truman, who in 1945 had first recommended a government health insurance program.

The second piece of Kennedy legislation that Johnson secured from the new Congress was the renovation of the immigration law. Kennedy and the Democratic platform of 1960 had both promised an end to the national origins system of quotas for immigration, but nothing had come of the proposal. The national origins quota system, which first became United States policy in 1924, not only limited the numbers that could enter this country, but also favored certain nationalities over others. For many years the policy had been opposed on the ground that it discriminated against Asians and southern and eastern Europeans, but the prospect of eliminating the discriminatory policy seemed remote. Truman, for example, had recommended such a change, only to have the McCarran Immigration Act, which reaffirmed the national origins principle, passed over his veto in 1952. Nor had President Kennedy's urging in the same direction been any more effective.

The Immigration and Nationality Act of 1965 provided for the gradual elimination of the quotas based upon national origins, to be completed by June 30, 1968. The total number of immigrants permitted was set at 170,000, with each country outside the Western Hemisphere having a maximum quota of 20,000. Priority of admission was to be given to relatives of citizens, persons with skills, and refugees. In short, the principle of limited immigration, which first went into effect in 1921, was continued. But the practice of basing quotas upon preferences for certain nationalities, which had been in effect since 1929, was now abandoned in favor of a system of priorities based on the dual

THE INCIDENCE OF POVERTY, 1966

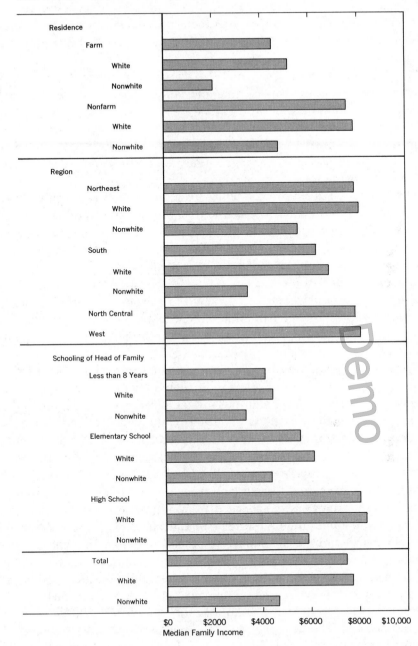

Median Family Income

Median family income means that half of the families received less than that amount while the other half received more. Poverty can be defined generally as a family income of less than $4000. It is evident that the South is still the poorest region, that rural dwellers are still poorer than urban dwellers, and that Negroes, no matter where they live, are at the bottom of the economic ladder. Education, however, is a prime source of economic improvement, a fact that helps to explain the strong interest in education by all levels of government. *Source:* Bureau of the Census, *Income in 1966 of Families and Persons in the United States.*

considerations of national economic need and of simple humanity. A significant change from the old law, also, and presumably a concession to proponents of the national origins idea, was the establishment for the first time of a quota of 120,000 for immigration from the countries of the western hemisphere.

The Education President. In 1964 Johnson predicted that the 88th Congress would be known as "the education Congress" because of the important legislation enacted in that field in 1963 and 1964. It seemed much more likely, however, that it would be Johnson himself who would go down in history as the principal advocate of federal aid to education. For, as one of his aides said, "Johnson has a passion for education of the same order of intensity as Kennedy's passion for stopping atomic testing."

In 1964 the old question of whether the federal government should aid the schools or leave the matter to the traditional local authorities ceased to be a live issue. That year a Congressional study revealed that the federal government was already spending $2.2 billion a year on education. Congress recognized the new role of the federal government when it passed the Higher Education Facilities Act in December 1963. The act, which originated under Kennedy, marked a new step in federal aid to education. It provided not only grants and loans for the construction of college and university buildings, but, for the first time, put the federal government into the business of helping to develop graduate centers.

As the need for educational facilities mounted in response to the rapidly increasing population and the new prosperity of Americans, the overburdened states and localities turned increasingly to the federal government for aid. The National Defense Education Act of 1964 marked another shift in emphasis that demonstrated anew the expanding federal interest in education. The original NDEA legislation, passed in 1958, had been sparked by the Russian Sputnik, and it appropriately provided loans and grants for the study of mathematics, science, and foreign languages in order to keep up with Russian advances in technology and science. By 1964, however, justifications for aid to education no longer required foreign threats. The NDEA of 1964 provided funds and scholarships in the humanities, too. The Elementary and Secondary Education Act of 1965 authorized the spending of more than a billion dollars over the next three years for grants to the states to raise educational levels in the low-income school districts. The act was a landmark in educational history because it provided aid, for the first time, to children in private, church-supported schools as well as to those in public schools. Because of the need for improved education in a technically advanced economy, the traditional objections to federal aid to church-supported schools, on the ground that it would violate the constitutional separation of church and state, were abandoned. The shift was not unrelated to the fact that in 1960 Americans had also shed for the first time their historic prejudice against electing a Catholic to the presidency. Appropriately and fortunately, however, a Protestant President advocated the inclusion of all children enrolled in recognized schools in the first federal program for education below the college level.

President Johnson's oft-stated conviction that every young American should have open to him as much education as he could absorb was partly realized in the Higher Education Act of 1965. To the already familiar provisions of loans to students, the new act added federal scholarships of up to $1000 a year for students otherwise unable to attend college. It was a kind of revival on a permanent basis of the program of the National Youth Administration, with which the President had first entered government service in the 1930's. Actually, it also continued the long trend toward popularization of higher education begun in the 1920's and further encouraged by the Veterans Readjustment Act of 1944 ("G.I. Bill"), which gave financial aid to returning veterans who wished to enter colleges and universities after the war.

A New Departure in Public Housing. In September 1966 the President realized his long-cherished wish to use federal funds to help pay for the housing of the poor. In 1965 he had urged Congress to pass a bill authorizing the federal government to supplement the rent payments of the poor living in privately owned housing. Only after a long and acrimonious fight was the law enacted, and not until 1966 were adequate funds forthcoming to implement the idea. At the signing of the $22 million appropriation bill, Johnson called the program "the single most important breakthrough in the history of public housing. . . . It is a clear-cut but compassionate solution to a pressing national problem." In effect, the act permitted the federal government to help pay the rent of those poor who lived outside public housing, and who otherwise might not be reached through the usual channels of the poverty program or the public housing laws. In the President's mind it was a part of his larger program to end poverty altogether.

A Southern President Champions the Negro. As congressman and even as senator, Johnson had supported the customary segregation practices of the South. But in the late 1950's he began to speak out against the mores of his region, his crucial support of the Civil Rights Act of 1957 being a notable example of this change in attitude. As President his record on Negro rights surpassed that of any President since Lincoln; his public avowal of Negro equality more than matched that of John F. Kennedy. Undoubtedly Johnson's strongest and most eloquent statement in behalf of Negro equality was his address at Howard University in June 1964. The goal of complete equality that he set forth in that speech has not yet been achieved anywhere or at any time. Freedom from slavery is not enough, he pointed out. "You do not wipe away the scars of centuries by saying: Now, you are free to go where you want, do as you desire, and choose the leaders you please. You do not take a man, who, for years has been hobbled by chains, liberate him, bring him to the starting line of the race, saying 'you are free to compete with all the others,' and still justly believe you have been completely fair. Thus it is not enough to open the gates of opportunity. All our citizens must have the ability to walk through those gates. This is the next and more profound stage of the battle for civil rights."

Johnson's actions in behalf of Negro equality matched his words. As we have seen, he pushed Kennedy's civil rights bill through a reluctant Senate in 1964. In his appointment of Robert Weaver to the Cabinet and Thurgood Marshall to the Supreme Court, Johnson brought Negroes into higher levels of the federal government than had any previous President. His principal effort to realize his commitment to Negro equality was devoted to protecting the franchise for southern Negroes. The Civil Rights Acts of 1957 and 1960 had not been effective enough in reducing the barriers to Negro voting which southern whites had erected, especially in the Deep South.

The Voting Rights Act of 1965. Southern Negro leaders believed that if Negroes could be protected in their right to vote, they would then be able to obtain justice from white sheriffs, justices of the peace, legislators and governors, who would then be dependent, in part at least, on Negro votes. As it was, intimidation, local tradition, and the Negro's ignorance of his rights conspired to keep the number of Negro voters far below the proportion that Negroes constituted in many southern states and counties. The voting act, as finally passed in the summer of 1965, provided for federal officials to register Negro voters in any county in which the Justice Department found that the number of Negroes voting in the presidential election of 1964 was less than 50 per cent of those old enough to vote. In this way the often deliberate delays in registration by local officials could be circumvented. Four days after the President signed the bill, federal examiners began to register Negroes in selected counties in Alabama, Mississippi, and Louisiana.

The Long Road Ahead. The enactment of the Voting Rights Act, however, did not immediately end the practical disfranchisement of Negroes in the South any more than the passage of the Civil Rights Act the year before had ended racial discrimination. Despite the increased registration of Negroes in 1966, strong segregationists won the governorship in Alabama and in Georgia, though at the same time a Republican moderate on the race question was elected governor in Arkansas, as a result of Negro support. Indeed, all over the country in the middle 1960's it appeared that as the nation created ever more powerful machinery for achieving the long-neglected goal of equality, both Negro impatience and white resistance mounted. As some gains were made by Negroes in their pursuit of full equality, they pushed ever more insistently for even greater and quicker improvement in their legal and social position. To whites, however, the very achievement of some gains suggested that the tempo of change ought to slow down, not increase. As ancient social patterns in both North and South were increasingly challenged and upset, whites became more apprehensive and often resorted to violence. White violence against Negro demonstrators in Alabama in the spring of 1965 caused President Johnson, like his two predecessors, to send federal troops into his native South to extend the protection that Alabama's segregationist governor would not provide.

Nor was the violence confined to the South. In 1964 riots broke out in Harlem, Rochester, Los Angeles, Brooklyn, Jersey City, Philadelphia, and other large northern cities, during which the black ghettos went on rampages, attacking the police, setting fires, and looting stores and homes. In 1964 many white liberals feared that the Negro demonstrations and riots in the cities of the North would produce a "white backlash" that would help Goldwater in his campaign for the presidency.

The backlash did not appear in 1964, but it showed evidence of coming into action in 1966. The first signs appeared during the summer as Congress was debating a new civil rights bill to prohibit discrimination in housing. White mobs jostled, hooted at, and stoned Negro demonstrators who sought to influence real estate agents in Chicago to give up their policy of refusing to rent or sell houses to Negroes in white districts. Martin Luther King, who led one of the demonstrations, later said that the hatred and violence he encountered on his march through parts of Chicago exceeded anything he had experienced in the Deep South. There were signs in other cities, too, that as the movement for Negro equality sought to break down the barriers in housing, which prevailed in most of the northern white urban and suburban districts, white resistance would become more, rather than less, violent. Significantly, a civil rights bill requiring open housing failed to pass the Senate in 1966 largely because of the white backlash. It was the first failure to pass a civil rights bill since the Negro revolution had begun a decade before. Also, the substantial Republican gains in the 1966 election in the House of Representatives and in the securing of several governorships gave evidence of white resistance to additional legislation in behalf of Negro rights. Furthermore, the resurgence of Republican strength in Congress strongly suggested that the administration's hope for a new civil rights bill on housing would not be realized in the new Congress. (The Democrats retained control of both houses in the election, but now conservative southern Democrats and Republicans were sufficiently numerous together to be in a position to defeat civil rights legislation as well as other measures of the administration.)

The history and prospect of violence in both North and South made clear that progress in civil rights, as in all great social changes, was uneven. Yet, if one compares the situation in 1966 with that in 1945, the shift in attitudes and practices regarding the black man on the part of people and government in white America was far from negligible. In that interim the whole legal basis of segregation was not only dismantled, but the very idea of segregation came under attack in the press and in practice. Soon after the passage of the Civil Rights Act of 1964, for example, hotels, motels, and restaurants in Jackson, Mississippi, were opened to Negroes for the first time in the twentieth century. Many northern employers who wanted to hire Negroes in 1965 complained of a lack of qualified applicants; the desirability or expediency of hiring them was no longer questioned. By 1965 desegregation of schools and universities had finally begun in every southern state. More Negroes were also voting in the South than ever before. As recently as 1960 only 5 per cent of Negroes voted in Mississippi; in 1965 the figure was up to 14 per cent. Throughout the South in 1965, Negro registration was 46.5 per cent of the eligible voters, as compared with 25.4 per cent in 1956. One result of the increased Negro registration was the election in 1966 of a Negro as sheriff of Macon County, Alabama, for the first time since Reconstruction.

Dramatic as the progress undoubtedly was, it was also clear that the Negro revolution was still far short of the goals that many Negro leaders and President Johnson had now set. For by 1967 the goals of the 1950's had been left behind. At one time the aim had been simply to remove from the Negro the disabilities of segregation in law and practice, but as that goal was on the way to achievement, it became apparent that the problems of the Negro were much deeper and would require more profound remedies. His poverty, for example, though often the consequence of a century of segregation, would not be removed simply by eliminating segregation. In fact, the most needed gains in behalf of Negro equality were still to be made; they lay in areas other than legal rights. The struggle for Negro equality and the war against poverty were really two sides of the same problem. Since most Negroes were poor, and their poverty was one of their principal disabilities, equality would become a reality in America only when the war against poverty was won. The ending of poverty, however, would be a considerably more difficult job than removing the legal basis of discrimination; it would, in fact, be the toughest test that the Great Society would have to meet. And it would point up the fact that all problems, like all solutions, are dynamic rather than static; before a problem can be "solved," it has already become a different one, and even in the process of dealing with it, new problems are encountered.

From New Deal to Great Society. Lyndon Johnson began his political career under the New Deal of Franklin Roosevelt. It was fitting, therefore, that his Great Society program should complete the revolution begun by his party's leader some 30 years before. Johnson's programs for federal aid to education, urban improvement, the war on poverty, and Negro rights certainly went far beyond anything contemplated by even the most advanced New Dealer, let alone Franklin Roosevelt. Yet they could be seen as implicit in the New Deal, especially in its novel use of federal power and revenues. What made the difference between the two was the prosperity of the 1960's. The New Deal's unavoidable preoccupation with depression was now gone. Moreover, with the economy booming, programs which were beyond the wildest dreams of New Dealers became not only possible, but imperative. Even the Negro revolution can be viewed as a product of affluence. Prosperity fired Negro aspirations and expectations, provided funds for Negro organizations and agitation, and impelled the federal government to take up its long-deferred commitment to equality.

In early 1968, as Lyndon Johnson neared the end of his first full term in office, it became evident that his Great Society program was not receiving from Congress or the country the support that it required if it were to be written into law. After the Democratic losses in the elections of 1966 and 1967, Johnson's ability to push legislation through Congress noticeably waned. In 1967 the House of Representatives, for example, now dominated by conservatives in both parties refused to grant the President's request for a tax increase to curb inflation, though Johnson gave the measure top priority. Only a few of the President's antipoverty measures got through Congress in 1966 and 1967 and then belatedly and after cuts in appropriations. Johnson's loss of popular support was also mirrored in the public opinion polls. By December 1967 less than 50 per cent of Americans judged him successful in his handling of the office, though his proportion of the vote in 1964 had been over 60 per cent.

The reasons for his decline in popularity were several. Part of his difficulty stemmed from his being blamed for the unresolved problems besetting the cities of the nation and for the violence accompanying the Negro revolution. (Both of these issues are discussed further in Chapter Five.) He also suffered from the growing disenchantment throughout the country with the frustrating and seemingly endless war in Vietnam. By the close of 1967, over 15,000 Americans had been killed there, and the financial cost of the war was reaching $20 billion or more a year. Such costs, which promised to mount rather than decrease as time went on, made it extremely difficult for the harassed President to capture attention and support for his domestic program.

An End and a Beginning: Foreign Policy Under Kennedy and Johnson

When John F. Kennedy entered office in January 1961, he found the Soviet Union at the height of its power and self-confidence. Its annual rate of industrial growth exceeded by a good measure that of the United States, its only rival in economic strength. It possessed not only the hydrogen bomb but the missile capability to deliver that devastating power anywhere in the northern hemisphere. Moreover, some of the new, underdeveloped countries, particularly those impinging on American interests, like North Vietnam and Castro's Cuba, were already enlisted in the Soviet camp. That January, Premier Nikita Khrushchev told his people that "there is no longer any force in the world capable of barring the road to socialism." Boldly he proclaimed Soviet support of "wars of national liberation" wherever they might break out among the underdeveloped nations of the globe.

Because of facts like these, Kennedy, during the campaign, had charged the Eisenhower administration with losing the initiative in foreign affairs.

Kennedy's own years in the executive mansion would be devoted to meeting the challenge of that Soviet power. Indeed, Kennedy made his most noteworthy contributions in the field of foreign policy. Foreign policy had always engaged his interest more deeply than domestic affairs. "The big difference" between foreign and domestic matters, he once said, "is between a bill being defeated and the country being wiped out." Secretary of State Dean Rusk later remarked that when he first met the President-elect to discuss foreign affairs, he was surprised "by the extent to which [Kennedy] wanted to look at everything from the beginning, from the ground up . . . the origins." Even more than Franklin Roosevelt, John F. Kennedy was to act as his own Secretary of State.

Kennedy recognized that the key to world peace was the relationship between the United States and the Soviet Union. From the beginning of his administration he sought to melt the hard freeze into which those relations had been locked by the U-2 incident. While writing his inaugural address he accepted the suggestion of using the word "adversary" in place of "enemy" in referring to the Russians. For the rest of his life, he employed the milder form. The essence of his approach toward the Russians was evident in other ways during that first year. In his speeches and actions, he rejected the clichés of an ideological war against Communism while firmly defending the vital interests of the United States. "Let us never negotiate out of fear," he said in his inaugural address, "but let us never fear to negotiate."

After the fiasco of the Bay of Pigs in April, Kennedy felt it was essential that he meet with Khrushchev, if only so that the two leaders might take each other's measure. It was at their meeting in Vienna in June that the untried President first learned of the Russian leader's determination to expel the Western Allies from their position in divided Berlin. Kennedy was so struck by the seemingly uncompromisable impasse between the two sides that upon his return he expressed his somber reaction in his report to the American people. "We have wholly different views of right and wrong, of what is an internal affair and what is aggression, and above all, we have wholly different concepts of where the world is and where it is going. . . . The question is whether these two systems can ever hope to live in peace, without permitting any loss of security or denial of freedom to our friends. However difficult it may seem to answer this question in the affirmative as we approach so many tests, I think we owe it to all mankind to make every possible effort." Within a matter of weeks one test would be made at Berlin.

Meanwhile two other tests had been inconclusive. As we have seen already in Chapter Two, the attempt to overthrow Castro in Cuba only brought the United States into disrepute. At about the time the Bay of Pigs crisis broke, Kennedy was confronted with Communist expansion in Laos, a new country created out of the former French colony of Indochina. The Laotian situation is properly a part of the later discussion of southeast Asia, but it is mentioned here because it was the first test of the administration in countering Communist expansion. By the end of the first spring, Kennedy could count half a success to his credit in Laos, where a compromise was worked out, and a complete failure in Cuba. The real test came in Berlin.

A World at Stake on the Autobahn. Germany was the source and the center of the Cold War. A divided Germany and a divided Berlin, by providing innumerable opportunities for confrontations between the two superpowers, offered the tinder for a global conflagration. In the summer of 1961, it looked as if the final confrontation might be at hand. Khrushchev announced that before the end of the year he would sign a treaty with his satellite regime of East Germany, which would close off all Allied ground and air access to Berlin. When Kennedy had heard of the Russian's intention at Vienna, he had told the Soviet premier that the United States could not abandon its rights, though it would not object to a treaty between East Germany and the U.S.S.R. that did not impair Allied movement in and out of Berlin. Khrushchev, however, was not entirely free to ignore the situation in East Germany, where the Communist government was extremely unpopular. Ever since the end of the war, Germans in the Russian zone had been fleeing to the West, mainly through Berlin, where flight was easiest. By 1961 perhaps as much as a quarter of the total population of East Germany had drained away, usually those persons most valuable to the economy: the young and the skilled. In May 1961 alone, 30,000 refugees flocked into West Berlin. At stake was the economic viability, as well as the prestige, of the East German regime.

Kennedy, however, would not abandon the rights which the Allies had won by conquest and agreement in 1945 and which had been further sanctioned by 15 years of practice. He viewed the Russian intention to sign the treaty with East Germany as more a test of his will than a vital interest of the Russians. Moreover, after his bungle at the Bay of Pigs, he apparently felt it imperative that he meet such a challenge with firmness. The difficulty was how to demonstrate his will without seeming to endanger the Russian position in Berlin, for to do so might well precipitate a war. The first part of his problem he met by asking for and receiving from Congress the power to call up 250,000 reservists in the event the Russians should attempt to drive the Western Allies from Berlin. The second part he attempted to meet by publicly acknowledging the Russians' interest in central Europe and vowing that he did not intend to threaten that interest. But clearly the American position was incompatible with the announced Russian intention of signing the treaty with East Germany.

The break in the impasse came on August 13, when the Communists solved their problem of the fleeing Germans by suddenly erecting a concrete-block wall all along the line between East and West Berlin. Although the Western powers, including the United States, were taken completely by surprise, no preventive action could have been taken or was even contemplated. Inhumane and divisive as the ugly wall undoubtedly was, the East Germans and the Russians were within their rights to erect it. The flood of refugees shrank to a trickle and then virtually stopped as the East Germans strengthened and extended the wall and staffed it with sharpshooters. Not sure that the wall was the end rather than the beginning of the Russian action, Kennedy, five days later, sent 1500 additional troops down the Autobahn from West Germany to the Berlin garrison. They would test Russian intentions and be a sign to the apprehensive West Berliners of continuing American support. The convoy was not stopped.

After some inconclusive discussion about Berlin between American and Russian diplomats in the early fall, on October 17 Khrushchev suddenly announced that there was no longer any need to insist on signing a treaty with East Germany. The threat of war was over. Yet at one dramatic moment in Berlin that summer, Russian and American tanks faced each other in hostility for the first time in the Cold War—indeed, for the first time in history. It was not to be the last. But, as Kennedy said later, the gradual easing of tensions and the ultimate avoidance of war in Berlin showed the value of endless "jaw, jaw."

Applying the Lessons of Berlin. During the election campaign Kennedy had made much of the "missile gap" that was supposed to exist between American and Soviet military capabilities. In February when Secretary of Defense Robert McNamara had a chance to examine the facts, he admitted that there was indeed a missile gap, but that it was in favor of the United States. More disturbing to McNamara and the administration, however, was his further discovery that, despite the belated efforts of the Eisenhower administration to move away from reliance upon massive retaliation, the military establishment of the United States was ill prepared to fight any war except one involving nuclear weapons. As McNamara wrote in his report to the President, massive retaliation with nuclear weapons was "a strategy believed by few of our friends and by none of our enemies. . . ." The dangers inherent in the new look approach to defense were later forcefully brought home to Kennedy in his talks with Khrushchev in Vienna in June 1961 and during the Berlin crisis. Suddenly the President recognized that in depending upon the nuclear deterrent alone, the United States, in confronting the Russians on the Autobahn or any other equally insignificant place, had a choice only between "holocaust or humiliation." A radical expansion of conventional forces would provide additional time in which to deal with a crisis and to decide if a particular issue was worth carrying to the point of nuclear war. The fuse of war, as one adviser put it, could not be removed, but it could be made longer. In May 1961 in a special State of the Union message, Kennedy asked for a massive increase in defense expenditures, all of which was to be used for nonnuclear armaments.

The Kennedy-McNamara strategy of defense made nuclear retaliation a very remote resort; conventional warfare was always preferable to reliance on the ultimate weapon. Kennedy also urged the development of counter-insurgency forces—which later came to be called the Green Berets. He recognized that future confrontations with Communist power might well involve guerrilla warfare as well as more conventional encounters. He himself read the works of Mao Tse-tung and of the Castroite Che Guevara on guerrilla warfare and recommended that the generals and officers in the Army do likewise.

During the three-year span of the Kennedy administration, defense spending rose $17 billion above that of the Eisenhower years, constituting one of the largest and swiftest buildups of military power in history. Under the dynamic and imaginative leadership of Secretary of Defense McNamara, military power and the needs of diplomacy were coordinated as never before. With a wide range of military responses now available, diplomacy achieved the flexibility required by a great power in the nuclear age.

Cuba Revisited. After the Bay of Pigs, Castro's hostility toward the United States understandably increased. In December 1961, for example, he announced that he was "a Marxist-Leninist and will be to the day I die." In January 1962 Cuba extended its trade pact with the Soviet Union and built up an army of a quarter of a million men. Fearful of subversion by Cuban agents throughout Latin America, the Organization of American States that same month expelled Cuba from membership. During the late spring and summer, rumors were rife in the United States that the Russians were setting up missiles in Cuba. Publicly the United States government discounted the stories, while extremely highflying U-2 reconnaissance planes periodically

This is one of the earliest air reconnaisance shots of Russian missiles being secretly emplaced in Cuba during the fall of 1962. This picture and others like it began the missile crisis. *Photo: Department of Defense.*

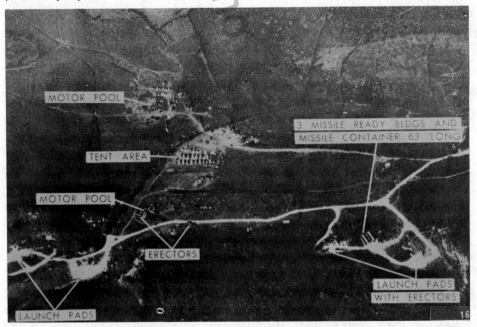

swept over the island checking for signs of missile sites. During September and early October, only surface-to-air missile sites were discovered, which, because of their short range, were not considered threatening. On Tuesday, October 16, however, the President was shown pictures of medium-range missile sites in the process of construction in Cuba. Such missiles had a range of 1100 miles or sufficient to reach a large part of the southeastern United States. He ordered the U-2 flights stepped up to several a day and initiated secret conferences among his closest advisers. Before the week was out, sites for intermediate-range missiles were also revealed by the U-2 photography. Such missiles, which had a range of over 2000 miles, could devastate most of the cities in the southern and northeastern United States.

To Kennedy the missiles constituted a dangerous shift in the balance of power in the Cold War. He rejected out of hand the idea that nothing should be done, refusing to equate the Russian missiles in Cuba with American missiles in Turkey. Actually, the presence of missiles in Cuba constituted no greater military threat to the United States than the intercontinental missiles based in the Soviet Union, which were capable of reaching any city in the United States. Once again, as in Berlin the previous year, Kennedy envisioned the threat as psychological, as a testing of his will to take firm action when challenged by an unnecessarily provocative shift in the balance of forces in the world. It was this view of the situation, rather than the supposed military threat, that convinced Prime Minister Macmillan of Great Britain to support Kennedy's action in the crisis. Kennedy was certain that if he did not act, the Russian pressure on the United States would increase, and the credibility of America as a great power with protective responsibilities for weaker countries would be shattered.

The discovery of the missile sites was not made public for over a week, while the President and some 15 close advisers met almost constantly to canvass the responses that were open to the United States. Quick action was necessary, for more missiles were on the high seas, and the sites would become operational within a matter of days. Once that occurred, the Russian move would be difficult to counter or reverse. A suggestion for bombing the sites was ruled out as too provocative and likely to alienate Latin Americans; an invasion of Cuba was considered too massive a response and unworthy of a great power in dealing with a small nation. Gradually the preponderance of opinion came to favor a blockade, or rather, as it was called, a naval quarantine of Cuba, which would stop the Russian ships before they could deliver the missiles. Kennedy, recognizing that this was once again a direct confrontation between the two greatest nuclear powers, wanted the most flexible arrangement possible, one that would provide the maximum opportunity for the Russians to back down without humiliation. Always in the minds of the American leaders as they discussed the various responses was the likelihood that the Russians would create a diversion in Berlin—or even more alarming—that the Cuban missiles were themselves only a diversion to mask a new attack on Berlin. No precipitate action must be taken that would provoke war unnecessarily or, alternatively, leave the United States unprepared to meet challenges elsewhere. By quarantining only offensive weapons—permitting even strategic materials like oil and petroleum products through the naval lines—the United States made evident its central concern with the immediate threat. No side issues must be permitted to cloud the naked risk and fundamental interest at stake. By setting up a naval quarantine many miles away from Cuban shores, the possibility of accidents or causes for war were kept to a minimum, for even if the Russian ships did not stop, the United States Navy ships were under orders to do no more than immobilize them by a shot to the rudder, thereby avoiding unnecessary loss of Russian lives or ships.

His decisions made, the President spoke soberly to the nation on television in the early evening of October 22, revealing the existence of the Russian missiles and announcing the imposition of the quarantine. He demanded that the Russians remove all offensive weapons from Cuba. One measure of the gravity of the situation was that the Organization of American States, now purged of Cuba, unanimously supported the American intervention, an almost unheard of degree of agreement where United States intervention in the Western Hemisphere was concerned.

The ensuing week was tense as the Russian freighters, with their missiles aboard, continued to steam toward Cuba, though under constant surveillance by United States Navy planes. When, after three days of watchful waiting, the ships stopped and then turned back in mid-Atlantic, the really tough question came to the fore: would the Russians remove the missiles already there and destroy the sites, as the President demanded? Would they abandon their first ally in the Western Hemisphere? Personal letters from Khrushchev and Kennedy flew back and forth, the continuation of a private, and until then secret, correspondence that Khrushchev had initiated a year earlier during the Berlin crisis. The rapport that had been built up between the leaders now paid off, for on Sunday, October 29, the Russians agreed to withdraw the missiles in return for a United States promise not to invade Cuba. The President also insisted that some Russian medium-range bombers, which the United States considered offensive weapons, also be removed from Cuba. On November 20, Khrushchev agreed to that ultimatum, too.

Even at the time, the missile crisis was recognized, as Prime Minister Macmillan said in the House of Commons, as "one of the great turning points of history." Twice the United States had been tested, once in Europe and once in its own backyard, and in both cases the President had acted coolly, cautiously, and with regard for the sensibilities of his opponent, though also with underlying firmness. As Kennedy would say a year later, "nuclear powers must avoid those confrontations which bring an adversary to a choice of either a humiliating retreat or a nuclear war." Recognizing the need for instant communication in the missile age, the Soviet Union and the United States worked out arrangements for the running of what came to be called the "hot line," that is, a direct, private teletype circuit from the White House through Scandinavia to the Kremlin, so that in any future confrontation there could be immediate communication to avoid any misunderstanding of intentions on either side. The line was first used in a crisis with notable success during the opening hours of the Israeli-Arab war in June 1967. Both superpowers made it clear to one another that they were not engaging in the fighting.

Detente. Once the basic agreement with the Soviet Union had been made, the Caribbean quickly cooled off. By the end of the year, the naval quarantine was lifted because the missiles and bombers were gone, and most of the Russian technicians had left. One sign of the return to a less superheated atmosphere was Castro's release, at the end of the year, of a thousand Cuban prisoners who had been captured during the Bay of Pigs invasion. For their release to the United States, Castro demanded and received some $50 million worth of medicines and drugs.

After Cuba, Kennedy was confident that the Russians understood that American power did not threaten genuine Soviet interests, and that the United States would not wilt before Russian challenges. As a consequence he worked for further relaxation of tensions. Perhaps his clearest statement of his hope for accommodation was his speech at The American University in June 1963. Pointing out that the Russians had the same fears of us as we had of them, he urged Americans to "deal with the world as it is, and not as it might have been had the history of the last eighteen years been different. . . . We must conduct our affairs in such a way that it becomes in the Communists' interest to agree on a genuine peace . . . to . . . let each nation choose its own future, so long as that choice does not interfere with the choices of others. . . . For, in the final analysis our most basic common link is the fact that we all inhabit this planet. We all breathe the same air. We all cherish our children's future. And we are all mortal. . . . The United States, as the world knows, will never start a war."

Although the speech was overshadowed in the United States by the civil rights address given by Kennedy the next night, in Europe, and especially in the Soviet Union, it was hailed as a significant break from the frozen rhetoric of the Cold War. Khrushchev told Averell Harriman that it was the "best speech by any President since Roosevelt." The Russian newspapers published the speech in full, and thereafter all Western broadcasts to the Soviet Union, even those in Russian, ceased to be jammed.

Clearing the Air. Kennedy's American University speech was delivered in the context of a concrete effort to moderate the Cold War. Ever since 1956, when Adlai Stevenson made the suggestion during his campaign of that year, there had been sporadic talk of halting nuclear testing by the U.S.S.R. and the United States. Such testing released large amounts of radioactive materials into the atmosphere, which were not only dangerous to the health of those nearby, but spread around the globe, to affect people far beyond the borders of the nuclear powers themselves. Two fears held up American acceptance of a ban on testing. One was that the Russians would continue to test secretly, and thereby forge ahead of the United States in the nuclear arms race. The other was that any cessation of tests, even if adequately monitored, was bad because it deprived the United States of the opportunity to acquire the knowledge necessary for improving its weapons systems. The first objection was taken care of by modern equipment enabling the United States to detect nuclear tests anywhere in the world, except, perhaps, those conducted underground. Therefore, if the Russians should cheat, the U.S. would know about it and could resume testing itself. The second point, that continued testing was necessary to improve weapons systems, was answered by the fact that the gains likely to be made by further testing were inconsequential compared with the dangers from continued contamination of the atmosphere. The Russians' primary objection was that their security would be breached by the inspection necessary for monitoring the ban, an argument that stalled the discussions between the United States and the Soviet Union for several months. The President's address at The American University in June broke the log jam. In July after talks in Moscow, the two nuclear powers signed a treaty agreeing not to test nuclear devices in the air, under the water, in outer space, or in any place that would permit radioactive debris to fall beyond the tester's borders. (Underground tests were still legal.)

Despite some preliminary opposition in the United States, the treaty was accepted overwhelmingly by the Senate in September 1963. In short order it was also signed by 99 other nations, with only France and Communist China, among the major nations, failing to agree to it. Their refusal was presumably dictated by a wish to develop their own nuclear devices; and in the next three years both Communist China and France exploded nuclear devices in the atmosphere.

Behind the drive for a test ban treaty, there had been a larger objective in Kennedy's mind: it was the limitation of the threat of nuclear war by keeping the number of nuclear powers as few as possible. In May 1963 Kennedy told one of his advisers, "If we don't get an agreement this year . . . I would think the genie is out of the bottle and we will not ever get him back in again. . . . Personally I am haunted by the feeling that by 1970, unless we are successful there may be ten nuclear powers instead of four. . . . I regard that as the greatest possible danger and hazard." The Johnson administration took up the cause of a nonproliferation treaty with the Russians in 1965. By the end of 1967, there was reason to believe that the U.S.S.R. and the United States were moving toward agreement on preventing the increase in the number of nuclear powers, though no agreements had yet been signed. In December 1966 the two countries did agree, however, to exclude all military activities from outer space.

Looking Beyond the Soviet Union

The Peace Corps. During his campaign Kennedy had promised that he would seek ways of tapping young Americans' idealism and sense of service to the world. In March 1961 he acted on his promise by issuing an executive order setting up the Peace Corps. The corps would consist mainly of American youths who would work on various projects for social and economic improvement in the underdeveloped countries of the world. It was clearly understood that there would be no paternalism in the operation; the Americans would live as the native population did; they would be paid very little by American standards; and what they were paid would be held for them in the United States. In September Congress approved the corps in a permanent form, appropriating $30 million for the first year. At the conclusion of that year, virtually all domestic critics and the foreign countries to which the Americans had gone to work adjudged the scheme a success, both in promoting friendlier feelings toward the United States and in making solid contributions to the improvement of the economies of the host countries.

The Alliance for Progress. America's troubles with Castro's Cuba redoubled Kennedy's resolution to grapple with the economic and political problems of Latin America. After all, the threat of Castro was not his military power, which was negligible when compared with that of the United States, but his example as head of a revolutionary state in a region in which widespread poverty, illiteracy, and great extremes of income provided fertile soil for subversion and revolution. Moreover, it was well known that Castro supported Communist subversion wherever he could, if only to end his diplomatic isolation in the hemisphere. On March 13, 1961, in addressing a group of Latin American diplomats, Kennedy suggested a plan "to satisfy the basic needs of the American peoples for homes, work and land, health and schools" through massive economic assistance from the United States. The plan, which soon received the title Alliance for Progress, was intended to be a partnership between the United States and the several Latin American countries, in which the latter would undertake to help themselves through necessary tax and land reforms while receiving economic aid and advice from the United States. The idea struck fire among the Latin American countries and was officially supported by the Organization of American States at Punta del Este in Uruguay in August 1961. In the course of the following year, the United States provided almost a billion dollars to get the program started.

The Alliance got off to an enthusiastic beginning, but progress was slow. By 1963 some American businessmen were complaining that hostility to foreign investors was still strong in certain Latin American countries, and that in the first nine months of 1962 net American investments there had dropped by $37 million, though one of the central purposes of the Alliance was to attract foreign capital. In 1965 President Johnson recognized that the original span of ten years proposed for the achievement of self-sustained growth through peaceful economic and social reform would be too short. He suggested that the timetable would have to be extended to 20 years. Five years after the Punta del Este conference the annual growth in gross national product of the region was still only 1.4 per cent, or half the rate of population growth. It was true that Cuba was still the only Communist state in Latin America, but few other major achievements of the Alliance could be counted five years after it began. Latin America remained a poverty-stricken region, beset by inflation, rapid population growth, and a low rate of economic advancement. But simply because the problems were so massive, improvement would take a long time, even with help from the United States.

A Johnson Doctrine. Not all threats to, or denials of, democracy in Latin America originated on the left. One of the worst threats from the right was the regime of Rafael Trujillo in the Dominican Republic in the Caribbean. For 30 years Trujillo ruled his island country with an iron hand, extracting from his impoverished people millions of dollars for his own use, while putting up a façade of modernization by building luxury hotels and public monuments to impress pleasure-minded tourists and unthinking citizens. Despite the elaborate precautions taken to protect the hated dictator, in the fall of 1961 Trujillo was assassinated.

The removal of Trujillo, however, did not bring political stability or freedom to the Dominican Republic. Uprisings and military coups overthrew seven governments in four years. In April 1965 a military-civilian revolt attempted to restore to power a liberal nationalist, Juan Bosch, whom conservatives and the Army had forcibly removed 19 months before. Fearful that the ensuing warfare between the rebels and the conservative-military regime would result in a Communist take-over supported by neighboring Cuba, President Johnson on April 28 sent 2000 United States Marines to the capital. Ostensibly sent there to protect American lives and property, the troops, as the President later admitted, were actually intended to forestall a Communist coup. The President's action was attacked vehemently in the United States and throughout Latin America as a violation of past promises against unilateral intervention in the affairs of the American states. To many observers the danger of a Communist take-over seemed remote and unsubstantiated by the evidence given by the State Department. Nevertheless, by early May there were 14,000 troops in Santo Domingo, the capital, with the number eventually reaching 30,000. At the United States' urging an Organization of American States peace-keeping force was created to join the United States forces in restoring order to the island nation. U.S. troops were not withdrawn until the middle of the summer as preparations were finally getting under way for free elections, and the last ones did not leave until the summer of 1966.

In Latin America and throughout the world, the Santo Domingo affair served to counter much of the good will that the Alliance for Progress had generated in the previous four years. The occupation of the Dominican

Republic was the first military intervention by the United States in Latin America since the enunciation of the Good Neighbor policy by Franklin Roosevelt over 30 years before. Johnson's action, which he defended in two television addresses to the country, obviously stemmed from his fear of another Cuba. The presence of an established Communist state in the Western Hemisphere had long been a basis for Republican criticism of the Kennedy and Johnson administrations; Johnson did not want to give his critics another stick with which to beat him. Where Communism was not involved, the President could reveal his sympathy with Latin American independence, as in his agreement in 1965 to negotiate a new treaty with Panama to recognize that country's sovereignty over the Canal Zone. It was also argued that American intervention in the Dominican Republic had not prevented the Dominican people from finally expressing their political preferences, as they did in the elections held in early 1966.

But more important than the example of Cuba in accounting for Johnson's precipitate intervention in the Dominican Republic was the fact that the United States was already engaged in a costly and expanding war in Vietnam. The President simply felt he could not afford to allow a triumph for Communism in the Caribbean, however remote that possibility might be. The war in southeast Asia was unquestionably the most significant development in foreign affairs and the greatest threat to world peace since the Cuban missile crisis of 1962.

The Mounting Commitment in Southeast Asia

Laos. When John F. Kennedy conferred with President Eisenhower, preparatory to assuming the presidency, the General admitted that he was leaving behind an important piece of unfinished business: the Communist threat to take over Laos. Eisenhower said that the allies of the United States seemed unconcerned about the little southeast Asian country, but he himself was determined to prevent a Communist victory there, even if it meant going to war without any allies. This conviction was held by Kennedy as well. In a televised press conference on Laos, the new President told the nation that though the United States would not be drawn into the civil war in Laos he knew "that every American will want his country to honor its obligations." The problem was that a weak, unstable regime, which was favorable to the West, was under attack from the pro-Communist Pathet Lao, an insurgent group supplied by Communist North Vietnam, and the Soviet Union, and supported politically by Communist China. Kennedy ordered military aid to be sent to the beleaguered government, thereby forestalling a take-over by the Pathet Lao while negotiations with the Russians and Chinese Communists were going on in Geneva. Out of these negotiations emerged an agreement in July 1962 to form a coalition government in Laos and to stop the civil war. Although the agreement did not end the war in Laos, it prevented the Communists from taking over the country.

The Growth of a Commitment. Laos was only a side show to the main event in southeast Asia. It was Vietnam that came to dominate American foreign policy. No more than a small noise in the wings under Eisenhower, the war in Vietnam came into the spotlight under Kennedy. With Lyndon Johnson, it filled the stage of foreign policy, directing the action and rewriting the script. Its cost of $15 to 20 billion a year threatened to draw funds from domestic programs, and its prosecution alienated Asian and European allies and friends. Even the British, who had publicly supported the war, raised objections to the expansion and intensification of the American effort. France openly denounced the American involvement as a threat to peace. An important Asian country like Japan found it difficult, because of popular opposition at home, to give more than minimal, formal support to the American cause. Thailand, the Philippines, South Korea, and Australia, it is true, were staunch supporters of American policy in Vietnam, but they were neither powerful nor internationally influential. Increasingly, in 1965 and 1966 Americans asked themselves how they had become involved in this second frustrating war in Asia that seemed without end.

The American involvement in Vietnam grew out of the Asian revolution and the Cold War; what one began, the other reinforced and complicated. As we have seen already in Chapter Two, a part of the Asian revolution involved the overthrow of French colonial rule in Indochina. The leader of the insurgents, Ho Chi Minh, and many of his followers, it is true, were Communists, but even after 20 years, it remains clear that the Vietminh was a genuine nationalist movement, a part of that broad movement of revolt against Europe that swept first Asia and then Africa.

But the rebellion of the Vietminh was not only nationalist in character. Many of its leaders were Communists, and after 1949 they were able to make contact with Communist power outside Vietnam. When mainland China was taken over by the Communists, they provided to the Vietminh not only moral and political support, but arms and secure places for training and regrouping troops as well. The French soon found that their difficulties in suppressing the Vietminh were greatly increased. Thus, the war in French Indochina became a part of the Cold War. This became evident in 1950, when the Communist North Koreans and then the Chinese Communists invaded South Korea. It was in connection with the threat from Chinese Communism in Korea that the first American military advisers were sent to Indochina in 1950 to aid the French in the event that the Chinese should seek to help the Vietminh. As the war in Indochina continued, the United States gradually increased its help to the French, on the ground that the Indochinese revolt was a part of the larger effort to expand Communist power in Asia, of which the Korean War was the spearhead. By the middle of 1952, the United States was paying for one fifth of the French war effort in Indochina; in 1954 the proportion was four fifths. President Eisenhower was so convinced of the need to resist the Vietminh, whom he considered more Communist than nationalist, that he was prepared to commit American troops to Indochina in support of the French if the French would grant unconditional independence to the Vietnamese once the war against the Communists was won. The French, however, were not yet ready to admit that colonialism was at an end.

When, at the Geneva Conference in 1954, the French abandoned the war, the United States refused to sign the agreement, apparently on the ground that it relinquished people to Communism, which many Vietnamese had made clear they rejected. The Geneva accord basically provided that Vietnam would be divided temporarily at the 17th parallel, with the Vietminh troops withdrawing to the north, and the French and their Vietnamese allies and several hundred thousand anti-Communist North Vietnamese collecting south of the line. Elections to determine the form of government and to unify the two parts of the country were scheduled to take place two years later. Actually, the elections were never held because the anti-Communist nationalists of the South, led by President Ngo Dinh Diem, refused to hold them, apparently for fear that the Communist Ho Chi Minh would win. For several years after 1955, when he organized the Republic of Vietnam, Diem carried on a strenuous and essentially successful campaign to organize and build up South Vietnam, suppressing dissident religious sects, bandits, and other groups who refused to acknowledge the central government at Saigon. Among the dissident groups he had to contend with were supporters of the Communist regime of the North, which was now allied with China and the U.S.S.R. Since Diem enjoyed the support of the Americans, his refusal to hold elections in 1956 gave him security against a change in regime. He used that security to strengthen his own power. Although a valiant nationalist, who had created a state in the South where the French had left chaos, he was also an autocrat who gave more and more power to his own family and ruled increasingly without reference to the wishes of his people or advisers. Those who disagreed with him he dismissed as agents of the Communists. Diem's personal government became so oppressive that in 1959 and 1960 rebellions in the countryside and in Saigon itself seriously challenged his authority.

Then, in December 1960 the North Vietnamese radio, broadcasting from Hanoi, announced the formation of the National Liberation Front "somewhere" in the South to overthrow the Diem regime. As its title suggested, the front was a coalition of anti-Diem groups, including the Communists. The heretofore sporadic opposition to Diem now became a highly skilled and effective guerrilla war that promised to topple the increasingly unpopular Diem government. Although the exact relationship between the National Liberation Front in the South and the Communist government in Hanoi was not clear, there is evidence that some of the support, and perhaps some of the direction came from the North. But prior to 1963, the great majority of those fighting under the banner of the NLF, or the Vietcong, as the Diem government called the rebels, was recruited in the South, and the great preponderance of its arms was American equipment captured from the South Vietnamese army.

The Vietcong won recruits by a combination of persuasion—promising land and other reforms—and terror—killing hundreds of officials and teachers and other representatives of the Saigon government in an effort to destroy its authority in the countryside. Unfortunately, the Diem government had dragged its feet in carrying out promised land and other reforms, so that it could count on small loyalty from the peasants.

By the time that Kennedy came into office it was evident that the Diem forces were losing ground, despite the growing number of American military advisers and economic and military aid of about $300 million a year. Kennedy accepted the vague commitment to support the independence of the South that he had inherited from Eisenhower. He drew the line, however, at committing United States troops to the area, despite a recommendation to that effect from his military advisers in 1961. Instead, he held troops in readiness for possible involvement, while tripling the number of American advisers there, and increasing military and economic aid. He also sent Vice-President Johnson to Saigon in 1961 to survey the situation and to bolster the sagging morale of the South Vietnamese. Other missions by high administration officials followed in the next two years, usually concluding with unduly optimistic reports on the progress of the war. But the military situation continued to slide downhill, even as American aid increased. From 2000 at the end of 1961, the number of American military personnel in Vietnam rose to 15,500 in 1963, with a commensurate increase in American casualties. Kennedy was not prepared to have Americans fight the war, but neither was he willing to abandon the South to the guerrillas.

In September 1963 the various oppressive acts committed by the Diem government caused the United States to dissociate itself from the internal policies of the Saigon government. Less than two months later Diem and some of his close supporters were murdered in a military coup; the military junta which took his place pledged itself to carry on the war, though with more regard for popular opinion. Military rule, however, proved even less stable than one-man dictatorship; several coups punctuated 1964 and early 1965, while the war against the Vietcong faltered. Meanwhile, the United States continued to be drawn ever more into the struggle. Twice, in early August 1964, American destroyers in the Gulf of Tonkin, off North Vietnam, were attacked by small North Vietnamese torpedo boats. The attacks brought not only an immediate naval response on the spot, but air bombardments of North Vietnamese shore installations as well. President Johnson asked Congress for a resolution supporting his authority to "take all necessary measures" to repel any new attacks and to resist further aggression. Congress responded immediately and overwhelmingly by passing the resolution.

As success in the war continued to elude the administration, American popular dissatisfaction grew. Some public figures advised a more vigorous effort to inhibit the support from the North, including bombing of military targets in that "sanctuary." Others, including prominent Democratic and

MONGOLIA

U.S.S.R.

Peking

Yellow

River

CHINA
*(Communist government
established, 1949)*

Shanghai

NORTH
KOREA
1948
Pyongyang

Seoul
SOUTH
KOREA
1948

JAPAN

Tokyo

BONIN IS.

INDIA
1947

Okinawa

BURMA
1948

Dienbienphu
Haiphong
Gulf of
Tonkin

Taipei
TAIWAN

Canton

Hong Kong
(Br.)

*(Nationalist Chinese government
established, 1949)*

LAOS
1954
Hanoi
NORTH
VIETNAM
1954

Hainan

Rangoon

Irrawaddy R.

THAILAND

Mekong R.

Bangkok

CAMBODIA
1954
Pnom
Penh

SOUTH
VIETNAM
1954

Saigon

PACIFIC OCEAN

MARIANAS

Manila

PHILIPPINES
1946

Guam

SOUTH CHINA SEA

CAROLINE IS.

Malaya
1957
Kuala Lumpur

Singapore
1959

Sumatra

MALAYSIA
1963

North Borneo

Sarawak

Borneo

Celebes

INDIAN

Djakarta
Java

INDONESIA
1949

New Guinea

TERR. OF
NEW GUIN
(Aus

PAPUA
(Austral.)

OCEAN

Darwin

THE FAR EAST, 1949–1966

☐ Countries allied with the U.S.

■ Communist countries

▲ Major U.S. air bases

Dates show when countries became independent.

AUSTRALIA

Republican senators, took precisely the opposite position, contending that the United States was hopelessly over committed to a war that could not be won without a massive invasion of the Asian mainland. Such an invasion might well result in a war with Communist China or perhaps even with the Soviet Union, both of which supported the Vietcong and North Vietnam. As we have seen, during the campaign of 1964 Johnson emphasized his restraint in Vietnam and held up to scorn the allegedly trigger-happy statements of Goldwater, who wanted to increase the military pressure on the North by bombing its military installations in order to cause it to withdraw its support from the National Liberation Front.

No Sanctuary. In February 1965 the war took on a new and ominous shape. For the first time President Johnson ordered American air forces in South Vietnam to bomb and strafe military sites and supply depots in North Vietnam. (It was the very policy that he had derided when Goldwater advocated it in 1964.) At the same time he announced that American military personnel in the South would be steadily increased. Apparently he had decided that without a commitment of greater American power the war could not be ended, for pleas for negotiation with Hanoi to call off its support of the South received no positive response. In April the President combined the stick of increased military power with the carrot of economic aid. At a major address at Johns Hopkins University, he asked for an end to the war on the basis of self-determination by the South and a massive investment of a billion dollars by the United States in the development of the rich Mekong Valley, which runs the length of the peninsula of southeast Asia. Significantly, and in emulation of George Marshall's famous Harvard address of 1947, he included North Vietnam in his promise of aid. All through 1965 and 1966, the United States and other governments pressed the Hanoi government to agree to negotiations, but without success. Because the administration viewed the war in the South as primarily a result of the aggressions of the North (which was at best a half-truth), it refused to deal directly with the National Liberation Front. But in view of the continued successes of the Vietcong in the South, there was really no reason why the North or the NLF should seek negotiation since that could only mean a loss of what otherwise seemed about to be won by war.

When the bombing of the North failed to bring the rebels and aggressors to the conference table, the administration turned to direct military involvement on the ground. On June 5, 1965, the State Department admitted for the first time that the rising number of United States ground troops in Vietnam were engaging in military action against the enemy. That summer the number of troops sent to Vietnam increased spectacularly, and draft calls mounted rapidly.

By year's end the United States was clearly enmeshed in a war that rivaled Korea in numbers and which promised to be considerably more difficult to conclude. Unlike the war in Korea, the struggle in Vietnam was without any clear lines of battle. Moreover, the Vietcong were dedicated and resourceful fighters, accomplished at striking and running. They deftly evaded the superior equipment of the Americans, and hit back hard when the Americans were unprotected by their planes or helicopters. For certain kinds of military equipment, the jungles and rice paddies were almost impenetrable; yet they provided excellent opportunities for Vietcong ambushes of Americans.

But as American equipment and men poured into Vietnam the tide began to turn in 1966; it became clear that the Vietcong could not win so long as the Americans stayed, though it was not equally clear that the American effort could end the war without still further measures. At a conference with the head of the South Vietnamese military junta, held at Honolulu in early February 1966, President Johnson personally committed the United States to victory for the South, with the understanding that political and economic reforms would be instituted to win the allegiance of the people. In pursuit of that goal, the Americans pushed the Saigon government to reëstablish a constitutional government, based upon popular elections. In the course of 1966 and 1967, a new constitution, modeled after that of the United States, was written, elections held, and a new civilian government installed. (The new president and vice-president, however, were generals, for the army remained the strongest force in the divided country.) Meanwhile the war continued inconclusively, though American deaths reached over 15,000 in late 1967 and the bombing of the North was stepped up to include as targets military installations in the major cities. Despite the increased punishment, the North Vietnamese refused to withdraw from the war as the United States demanded.

The Vietnam war presented a challenge more difficult to meet than any previous effort to contain the spread of Communist power. Although the Korean War had been fought in Asia, too, it had been a conventional war, in which American technical superiority could be employed to great advantage. In that war, moreover, the United States enjoyed the moral advantage of the backing of the United Nations and the knowledge that it was resisting a clear-cut case of aggression. In Vietnam, on the other hand, the struggle had begun as a civil war with only minimal support from outside, and it flowed directly out of the Vietnamese anticolonial struggle against the French. Ho Chi Minh was the best known nationalist leader in both sections of Vietnam, a fact that had the disadvantage of tying the United States' efforts there to the old French colonial war. Finally the absence of direct Russian involvement in the fighting precluded the kind of appeal to big power responsibility that Kennedy had used so effectively at Berlin in 1961 and in the Cuban missile crisis a year later.

The Broader Picture

If one reviews the international scene over the 20 years since the Second World War, the persistence of familiar problems is discouraging. The source of the Cold War—the division of Germany—remains. Berlin, now divided by the wall, is still a hundred miles inside East Germany, providing fertile ground for war-provoking incidents and big power confrontations. In Asia the United States is engaged once again in a costly war against a Communist enemy. The toehold of Communism in the New World in Cuba also remains. Indeed, the basic American strategy of containment that had been enunciated in Europe in 1947 is still the basis of American action in Vietnam and in Asia as a whole. The question that is now being decided in Vietnam is whether a policy that was crowned with success in Europe will work as well in the different social and military circumstances of Asia.

A New Age of Nationalism. Yet the persistence of the old factors pales into insignificance when measured against the great changes that have taken place in these two decades. Most of the changes can be regarded as manifestations of a new age of nationalism, of which the most obvious examples were the host of newly independent states in Africa and Asia. But a new sense of national identification was also evident among the older countries. Even the great alliance of NATO, which the nations of western Europe and the United States had constructed in the early years of the Cold War, was being disrupted by nationalism. The France of Charles de Gaulle, for example, in 1966 forced the removal of all NATO troops from its national territory. France could afford to express its nationalism in this fashion because the threat of Soviet Russia to western Europe had declined markedly by the 1960's. One reason that this danger had diminished was that nationalism was also rising within the Communist camp, fragmenting its hitherto monolithic weight in international affairs. In eastern Europe, Poland, Hungary, and Romania were definitely, if cautiously, exploring different roads to Communism and questioning Moscow's assumption of uncritical loyalty from all Communist countries. The most spectacular example of a nationalistic break in the Communist monolith was the split between Communist China and the Soviet Union. Their alliance in 1950 had seemed to presage unprecedented power for the Communist side in the world struggle, but by 1965 divergences of national interest between the two largest countries in the world had begun to assert themselves. Historically, there has always been friction between China and Russia along their 2000-mile common frontier. But to that there was now added a competition for the leadership of the Communist world. As a result nowhere in the world could it any longer be assumed that Communist ideology overrode national interest.

In substance the rise of the new nationalism has meant the decline of ideology on both sides in the Cold War. The decline has not been smooth or even steady, for the United States intervention in the Dominican Republic in 1965 can only be viewed as a reversion to an ideological approach to foreign policy. Certainly the encounters in Berlin and Cuba under Kennedy and Khrushchev were more frightening than any under Truman and Stalin in the early years of the Cold War. Yet at Kennedy's death it was evident to all the world that Russian-American relations were better than at any time since the days of the common effort against Hitler. Kennedy himself gave concrete evidence of his desire for a continuing rapprochement by sanctioning the sale of wheat to Russia in October 1963. Cultural and scientific exchanges, increased travel by private citizens in both countries, and the lifting by the Russians of the most extreme forms of censorship on news from the United States were all additional straws in the winds of change. That the new accommodation was more than simply a personal one between Kennedy and Khrushchev was shown by the continuance of the reduction in tension under Johnson and new Russian leaders after October 1964 when Khrushchev was unceremoniously removed from office, though, significantly, he was neither disgraced nor imprisoned.

Unquestionably, the explanations for the reduction of tensions between Russia and the West are manifold, but two developments are undoubtedly important. One is Russia's mounting ideological and nationalist conflict with its erstwhile ally and neighbor, China. The other is the realistic recognition by Khrushchev and his successors that a nuclear war would destroy the whole civilized world; and that therefore war between the major powers was no longer a realistic way to resolve conflicting national interests. The new Russian attitude was demonstrated in September 1965, when the Soviet Union volunteered to mediate a border war between India and Pakistan, against the wishes of Communist China. For the first time since the Communist Revolution in 1917, the Soviet Union undertook to offer disinterested mediation in a dispute between two states, one of which was supported by a Communist ally. With that gesture—the mediation took place at the end of the year—the Soviet Union entered the community of great powers, assuming responsibility for the maintenance of world peace.

But the detente with the Soviet Union in Europe was only part of the story. The threat of aggression in Europe, which had generated the Cold War initially, may have come to an end, but in western and eastern Asia the threat was still real. The aftermath of the short, but decisive Israeli-Arab war of June 1967 made it evident that the United States and the Soviet Union were serious rivals in the explosive Middle East. The Russians at the United Nations and in the forums of the world made it clear that they supported Egypt and the other Arab states in their insistence that Israel be branded as the aggressor in that war. Generally, though cautiously, the United States supported the Israeli demand for Arab recognition of its existence as a state and for a peace treaty between the belligerents in the recent war to formalize that recognition. In Vietnam the United States was only beginning its containment of Communist power. In 1966 President Johnson admitted that the United States was not an Asian power, but he emphasized that it was a Pacific power, as much interested in the future of Asia as it was in the future of Europe. In neither place, he asserted, would the United States permit the expansion of Communist power by force at the expense of other nations. For behind the war in Vietnam loomed the power of Communist China, on record as an implacable foe of the United States and as a self-proclaimed supporter of "wars of national liberation" wherever they might break forth.

The spread of the Cold War to Asia, and the threat of a third World War arising out of Vietnam were only the beginning of men's anxieties 20 years after the defeat of Hitler and Japan. Nuclear arms continued to be added to existing stockpiles, which were already large enough to destroy all life on earth many times over. But beyond these tangible sources of conflict lay an even greater source of international disorder and peril.

People and Food. The root of the danger lies in the enormous increase in world population. As man has learned to master his physical environment, control disease, and expand his food supply, his species has increased almost geometrically. In 1650 the estimated population of the world was 545 million; 150 years later it was not yet a billion, but in the next century it jumped to 1.6 billion, and by 1965 there were 3.3 billion people living on the earth, with 7000 being added each hour. At the present rate of population growth, there will be more than 7 billion people by the opening of the new century. The principal reason for the upsurge since the early nineteenth century is the advances in medical science, which lowered the death rate, once the principal check on the birth rate. Today no humane society can deny to people anywhere the advances of medicine and science, but the world is not prepared to feed the great explosion in numbers of people that these advances promise over the next decades.

How to feed the great masses of people being born around the world is the great social conundrum of the twentieth century. The pessimistic prediction of the late eighteenth-century English economist Thomas Malthus that population would outrun the food supply has not proved correct for the industrialized nations of the world. But in the new nations, still without the tools and techniques of modern agriculture, the increase in population presses hard upon the food supply, resulting in insufficient diet, mass starvation, or both. In eastern Asia, for example, the average annual increase in population between 1948 and 1951 was 1.3 per cent, while the increase in the food supply was less than one tenth of 1 per cent. Some areas of the world, such as North America and Europe, to be sure, managed to keep their rate of food production equal to or even greater than their rate of population growth. But the surpluses of these fortunate regions were not readily available to the less fortunate, which were usually too poor to pay for the food they needed but could not raise themselves. Throughout the 1950's and 1960's, the United States sold and gave away large quantities of food to hungry nations throughout the world, but even its overflowing granaries were being depleted. In 1966 the Secretary of Agriculture announced that, for the first time since the 1930's, a wheat surplus no longer existed in the United States. He authorized an increase of one third in acreage for food production for the coming year. Despite the acknowledged high productive capacity of American farms, at the

FOOD vs. POPULATION

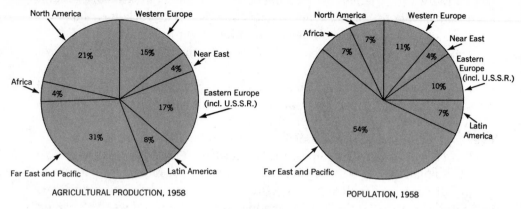

AGRICULTURAL PRODUCTION, 1958

POPULATION, 1958

With only 28 per cent of the world's population, the industrially advanced regions, North America and both Eastern and Western Europe, enjoy a surplus in food production, with 53 per cent of the total. However, the underdeveloped regions lack an adequate food supply. The Far East and Pacific, for example, with 54 per cent of the population, produce only 31 per cent of the food supply. *Source:* Food and Agriculture Organization of the United Nations.

present rate of population growth there will not be sufficient food in the world ten years from now to feed all the people on the globe.

Some countries of Asia, worried about the potentially disastrous effects of uncontrolled population growth could have upon their hopes for economic advancement, have begun programs for family limitation. India, Japan, and Communist China were all attempting to popularize contraceptive techniques; Japan, in its concern over the problem, went to the extreme of legalizing abortions. The Japanese effort did result in a lower birth rate, but few other countries seemed able to match that achievement, partly because cultural habits encouraged large families and partly because illiteracy and poverty prevented the dissemination of the information necessary for practicing contraception.

The United States was not unmindful of the threat to peace, order, and a decent life that the population explosion posed. In 1964 for the first time, government agencies began to provide advice on population control to those countries that requested it. Yet as recently as 1959 President Eisenhower had said he could not "imagine anything that is not a proper governmental activity" more than birth control. He announced that the United States would do nothing to foster such practices among foreign nations. (He has since changed his mind, as the threat of uncontrolled population growth has risen.)

In a notable address at Montreal in the spring of 1966, Secretary of Defense Robert McNamara spelled out how population growth, poverty, and the future security of the United States were intimately related. Security for the United States, he said, was ultimately not to be found through multiplication of weapons and military hardware. True security would come when the developing nations of the world achieved a decent standard of living and no longer provided occasions and causes for war. Surveying the history of the nations of the world since 1958, he noted that the poorer a nation was, the more likely it was to have experienced war or revolution in the previous eight years. Poverty and political instability were highly correlated. Yet, because of population growth, the poverty of the nations with the lowest per capita incomes was actually worsening in relation to the wealth of the industrial nations. By 1970, he emphasized, over half of the population of the world will live in the independent nations located in the southern half of the planet, where the poverty of the world is also concentrated. By 1975 the number of children alone in the Southern Hemisphere will equal the total population of the more advanced Northern Hemisphere. These children will grow up in abysmal poverty, with the attendant frustrations and tensions providing ready sources of violence and extremism. By the end of the century, at their present low rate of economic growth, the 80 poorest nations will reach a per capita income of $170 a year as compared with the projected per capita income for the United States of $4500. Communists may well exploit this poverty and resulting discontent for their own ends, he went on, but "it would be a gross oversimplification to regard Communism as the central factor in every conflict throughout the underdeveloped world." In fact, of the 149 serious internal revolutions in the preceding eight years, Communists were involved in only 38 per cent. The great unfinished business of the world, with a major responsibility resting upon the United States because of its wealth and military power, is achieving an enduring peace. But that goal, for which the United States has struggled ever since 1945, was inextricably bound up with the expectations of those millions of newly independent peoples who wanted a decent life for themselves and their children, and who knew that it was now in the power of man to eradicate poverty and disease from his world. The advancement of the underdeveloped nations must go on at the same time that the more active threats to peace, as in Korea or Vietnam, were countered and turned back. Potential aggressors would have to be taught that a united world would resist their efforts to bring about political or social change by coercion. "Can we achieve these goals with the Soviet Union and with Communist China?" McNamara asked toward the close of his address. "The answer . . . lies in the answer to an even more fundamental question. Who is man? Is he a rational animal? If he is, then the goals can ultimately be achieved. If he is not, then there is little point in making the effort. All the evidence of history suggests that man is indeed a rational animal—but with a near infinite capacity for folly. He draws blueprints for utopia. But never quite gets it built. In the end, he plugs away obstinately with the only building material really ever at hand: His own part-comic, part-tragic, part-cussed, but part-glorious nature. I, for one, would not count a global free society out. Coercion, after all, merely captures man. Freedom captivates him."

SUGGESTED READING

Despite the recency of the Kennedy administration, its impact on intellectuals and the country can be measured in the large number of books that have already appeared on the President and his few years in the White House. Undoubtedly the best book on the prepresidential years is James MacGregor Burns, *John Kennedy: A Political Profile** (1959). It is written by a skilled political scientist and draws upon Kennedy's private papers. Hugh Sidey, *John F. Kennedy, President* (1964), by a journalist, is less critical than Burns' study. Several people who were close to the President have written books, sometimes very lengthy ones, detailing the years in the White House. A dramatically written, but partisan one is by a trained historian, Arthur M. Schlesinger, Jr., *A Thousand Days* (1965); Kennedy's closest assistant and adviser has written a more straight-forward, though equally laudatory, account of the same White House years, Theodore Sorensen, *Kennedy** (1965). More personal and less weighty accounts of the President are Pierre Salinger, *With Kennedy** (1966), a memoir by his friend and Press Secretary, and Evelyn Lincoln, *My Twelve Years with John F. Kennedy* (1965) by the President's private secretary. Roger Hilsman, a close adviser on foreign affairs in the Kennedy administration, has provided his version of the several diplomatic crises in *To Move a Nation* (1967). The very dramatic and awesome confrontation with Russia over Cuba has been told in detail by a respected newspaperman, Elie Abel, *Missile Crisis* (1966). An expert on Communism has realistically dissected the Cuban revolution in two books, Theodore Draper, *Castro's Revolution: Myths and Realities** (1962) and *Castroism: Theory and Practice** (1965).

The official version of the assassination of the President is contained in the massive *Report of the Warren Commission** (1964). That report and the assassination have been the subject of a good bit of controversy. Perhaps the most temperate of the many critiques of the report is Edward Jay Epstein, *Inquest: The Warren Commission and the Establishment of Truth* (1966). The story of the events leading up to the assassination and its immediate aftermath is told in great detail in William Manchester, *The Death of a President* (1967).

The election of 1964 is reported in loving detail and analyzed incisively in Theodore H. White, *The Making of the President, 1964** (1965). The ideas of the losing candidate in that election, Barry M. Goldwater, can be examined in his book, *The Conscience of a Conservative** (1960). William S. White, *The Professional: Lyndon B. Johnson* (1964), by a personal friend of the President, is extremely laudatory. More critical and yet understanding is Rowland Evans and Robert D. Novak, *Lyndon B. Johnson: The Exercise of Power* (1966). The story of Johnson as Vice-President is told sympathetically in journalistic fashion in Leonard Baker, *The Johnson Eclipse* (1966).

No aspect of the Johnson administration has produced more books than the Vietnam war. Perhaps the most rewarding and balanced presentation of the war and its background is Bernard Fall. *The Two Vietnams: A Political and Military Analysis*

*Available in a paperback edition.

(revised edition, 1965). Ellen Hammer, *Vietnam Yesterday and Today** (1966) is a work by a historian of southeast Asia. The relationship between the United States and China in Vietnam is explored in a scholarly fashion in Melvin Gurtov, *The First Vietnam Crisis: Chinese Communist Strategy and the United States Involvement, 1953–1954* (1967). Jean Lacourtre, *Vietnam: Between Two Truces** (1966) is a penetrating study by a French authority on the region. John Mecklin, *Mission in Torment* (1965) is a report by a former United States aide in the region. David Halberstam, *Making of a Quagmire* (1965) is by a newspaper correspondent who served in Vietnam. His book was influential in arousing opposition to the administration's policy in Vietnam. A detailed history of Vietnam from colonial days down to 1963 is Joseph Buttinger, *Vietnam: A Dragon Embattled*, 2 vols. (1967).

The worldwide commitments of the United States, symbolized by the extensive involvement in Vietnam, have been criticized as being beyond its capacity or interest. Edmund Stillman and William Pfaff, *Power and Impotence: The Failure of America's Foreign Policy** (1966) contains the informed and closely reasoned views of two political scientists. J. William Fulbright, *The Arrogance of Power** (1967) and Eugene McCarthy, *The Limits of Power* (1967) are statements by liberal Democratic senators, strongly critical of administration policy. Among many, two studies of the problems of economic development deserve to be mentioned. Robert Heilbroner, *The Great Ascent** (1963), a short introduction to the subject, emphasizes the difficulties involved. Cyril E. Black, *The Dynamics of Modernization** (1966) shows the historical varieties of development among the industrial countries and, therefore, the problems facing the undeveloped countries.

After World War II, Americans faced a tremendous housing shortage. It is not surprising that the first solutions to this need were simple, direct, aggressive. The easiest way to house people was to build homes on cheap, vacant land at the edge of the city—a policy encouraged by the promise of fast profits for the developer, the eagerness and affluence of the home-buyer, the general suspicion of planning, and the mortgage policies of such government agencies as the Federal Housing Administration. The result of unplanned and uncontrolled housing led to a new form of residential monotony, like that shown at the right below. Where suitable flat land was not available, the new methods of development—erecting a house on a barren tract of level land—were applied to whatever land there was, without any attempt to preserve the natural environment. The picture at the right shows such methods.

A similar monotony and sterility were found in many of the new one-

Reston, Virginia, a new town. *Photo: William A. Graham*

Hills in southern California turned into flat "pads" for easy construction. *Photo: Spence Air Photos. Below:* Tract housing in California. *Photo: Joe Munroe—Photo Researchers*

class, and often one-race, inner-city housing developments. This was especially true of low-income housing. The simplest way to deal with urban blight was to bulldoze the slums away and erect huge, impersonal towers, like the ones pictured at the right. Only a small part of the slums cleared by this process, often resulting in greater overcrowding in other areas, as the new structures did not accommodate as many people as the old ones. The proliferation of governmental units—1000 in Chicago, for example—made comprehensive planning nearly impossible. Vital decisions were either made by single-function agencies with broad jurisdication, such as state highway departments, often on the basis of narrow interests, or else were not made at all. After a decade American cities were clearly in trouble and might literally be destroyed unless dramatic actions were taken.

By the mid-1960's hesitant efforts to find better solutions were underway. Several dozen new towns were either under construction or being planned. Reston, Virginia, pictured on p. 164, is a prominent example. Reston combines a variety of housing types with new commercial areas and even light industry in a completely new, and hopefully better, environment. Efforts were made to retain such features as streams, lakes, and wooded areas.

Integration of old and new in an urban renewal area. *Photo: James Ballard. Left:* Low-income housing in Tacoma, Washington. Public housing for low-income people can be a neighborhood asset. *Photo: Morley Baer*

Typical low-income urban "renewal": mass destruction followed by massive public housing projects isolated from the rest of the city by expressways or other barriers. *Photo: James Ballard*

At the same time, private industry and government began to work together to find new solutions to inner-city problems. Programs were initiated to preserve old neighborhoods. Old buildings of sound construction were restored, rather than destroyed. If new buildings were necessary, they were integrated architecturally with the existing structures. The buildings at the far left reflect such efforts. The structure next to it in Tacoma, Washington, demonstrates that low-income housing can be attractive. Two of the innovations that made such solutions possible were the application of mass production techniques to one-of-a-kind buildings and new, "uneconomic" financing methods, i.e., government subsidies, that enabled people of limited means to buy decent housing.

The question is still unanswered, however, as to whether these efforts to deal with the complex of physical and social problems will succeed—or whether they will prove to be too little and too late. The answer depends in part on whether we use our nearly unlimited technological capacity to destroy or to enhance our physical environment. But it also depends on another question which is not technical at all: will white America recognize that housing in the black ghettos needs to be replaced or made livable; if it does not, then the present inhabitants may burn the ghettos down.

CHAPTER FIVE

THE CULTURE OF AFFLUENCE AND ANXIETY

IN 1928 OBVIOUSLY impressed by the ability of a machine civilization to produce enormous quantities of goods, Herbert Hoover optimistically spoke of the possibility of abolishing poverty in the United States. After the crash of the next year and the ensuing Great Depression, his words became ashes in his mouth. Yet in the years that followed World War II, Hoover's prophecy seemed close to realization. For the first time Americans were living in a society of plenty.

The Shape of the Postwar Economy

In 1945 after four years of wartime prosperity, the per capita income of the country was $1350 (in 1960 dollars); by 1960 even that all-time high had been raised to $1824 or 35 per cent in 15 years. No people in the world, presently or historically, had achieved such a high level of consumption. That was the first big fact of the postwar economy.

The second was full employment. After the ordeal of the Depression, no industrial country, and certainly not the wealthy United States, would accept anything less than jobs for everyone who wanted to work. During the 1930's the realization of the goal of full employment, which the New Deal had courageously proclaimed, eluded Americans. Throughout that black decade, between 15 and 25 per cent of the civilian labor force was unemployed. After 1945, however, unemployment was reduced to almost minimal proportions; during the 1950's, for example, the average annual rate was 4.6 per cent. At the end of the 1950's and the beginning of the 1960's, the rate was above 5 per cent, but this proved to be temporary; in 1966 unemployment fell still lower, to levels reached heretofore only during the Korean War. Indeed, in some sections of the country and in some industries, there were acute labor shortages.

The third characteristic is really an aspect of the first two, but it was so important psychologically and historically that it deserves to be mentioned explicitly. For the 20 years after 1945, the United States did not experience a major depression. During no other span of 20 years in the history of the Republic had that statement been true. There were two recessions, to be sure—those in 1949 and 1958—but both were shallow and short lived. Moreover, the period from 1961 until 1967 constituted the longest period of uninterrupted prosperity in the history of the nation.

Finally, there was a fourth characteristic of the American economy that marked a new stage in the history of the United States. During the 1950's the United States became a major importer of industrial and consumer goods, thereby reversing a trend that had begun in the 1870's, when the country first moved into industrialization. In the 1950's the U.S. passed the United Kingdom as the country with the greatest amount of imports. The large increase in industrial imports was yet another measure of the high rate of consumption among Americans, for with new wealth they demanded more and more foreign

Mechanized agriculture. *Photo: Loomis Dean, LIFE Magazine © Time Inc.*

goods, as, for one example, the large number of foreign cars on the road testified.

In the years after 1945, in short, the great fact of American social life was the sustained growth of the economy. To the emerging countries of Africa and Asia, the economy of the United States appeared fabulous; to other industrial states like the U.S.S.R., Germany, and Japan, it provided a goal to be achieved sometime in the future. For Americans the burgeoning economy, despite some ups and downs in the business cycle, was the underlying pulse of their culture. As we shall see, abundance affected not only how Americans lived but also the values by which they lived. But before we examine some of the cultural consequences of prosperity, let us look more closely at the changing shape of the economy and the causes for its growth.

The Roots of Economic Growth. One of the underlying causes for the boom of the postwar years was the growth of population.* In the years after 1945, the birth rate climbed until it reached a high of 25.2 births per 1000 population in 1956–1957. At the same time the death rate fell and, owing to improvements in medicine, life expectancy at birth lengthened. One of the surprises for demographers was the increase in family size that took place during the 1950's, especially among the middle-income classes. Heretofore, rising income and increasing urbanization had been accompanied by a contraction in the size of the family. This baby boom and the longer lives of Americans lay at the root of the prosperity, for together they spelled a growing demand for housing, food, manufactured goods, and services. Demographers also recognized that the uninterrupted prosperity after the Depression years undoubtedly encouraged people to enlarge their families. In that fashion, it might be said, the new prosperity perpetuated itself.

This rapidly expanding economy was highly institutionalized. The individual entrepreneur or operator, so celebrated in national myth, was still in evidence, but he was no longer a significant figure in the functioning of the economy. In 1958 there were some five million individually owned businesses, outside of farming, mining, and fishing, but even when all of these are taken together, 85 per cent of all employed persons were working for someone else. In 1900, by way of comparison, 36 per cent of all members of the working force were self-employed.

The largest businesses were corporations, but even among them only a small fraction dominated the economy. In 1958, for instance, one tenth of the almost 600,000 corporations received over half of the net income of corporate

*It may seem confusing that in this context an expanding population is viewed as a source of economic growth while in the previous chapter the growth in population was discussed as a cause for concern. The explanation lies in the fact that population growth is a hazard when it threatens to outrun the food supply, as it tends to do in many underdeveloped countries in which agricultural productivity is low. In the United States, however, the rate of increase in the food supply far exceeds the rate of population growth. In advanced countries like the United States, a rising rate of population growth, therefore, provides new consumers for the highly productive industrial sector. It is in that sense that population growth is seen as one of the factors encouraging the postwar prosperity. (Seen from the perspective of world food production, however, the rising population of the United States is an undesirable development, for that increase in mouths to feed detracts just that much from the very limited *total* world food supply.)

enterprises. Indeed, the large corporation was one of the sources of the nation's economic growth. As we shall see a little later, one requirement for economic growth was the constant flow of new products and techniques which came primarily from scientific and technological research. Large corporations with the facilities and the large amounts of capital necessary for research were, therefore, an important impetus to that growth.

The large corporations, in turn, were encouraged by the boom. With the federal government now acknowledging its responsibility to prevent or at least to mitigate a depression, corporate businesses could afford to be less cautious in their operations and therefore to invest more in the economy. Moreover, the enormous military spending, which had reached 50 billion dollars annually by the early 1960's, acted as an incentive to corporate activities and profit accumulation. Business enterprises often enjoyed, also, the security of the long-term labor contract, which protected them from interruptions by labor stoppages. In view of these supportive circumstances, it is not surprising that few large manufacturing enterprises failed. Out of the 1001 largest manufacturing firms in 1951, all but 9 were in existence 9 years later.

The important role played by large-scale enterprises was one of the reasons for an intensified interest in antitrust activities after 1945. Perhaps the most notable antitrust action of the government after the war was its order to Du Pont, the giant chemical firm, to divest itself of its holdings of General Motors stock. The courts agreed with the contention of the Justice Department that such a connection between the two industrial giants was conducive to economic collusion and therefore harmful to competition. Also, in 1950 Congress passed an important piece of antitrust legislation—the Celler-Kefauver Anti-Merger Act—designed to plug some of the loopholes in the Clayton Anti-Trust Act of 1914 by giving the government new grounds for dissolving mergers that seemed to give the combined firms too large a share of the market or too dominant a position in the industry. The courts upheld the government in ordering the breakup of mergers, under the act, in milk, steel, paper, and sugar. Moreover, by invoking the act, the Justice Department in 1958 prevented the merger of Bethlehem Steel and Youngstown Steel. Yet antitrust policy remained complicated and even confused, since large-scale enterprises were obviously conducive to a high level of production, while they were at best only moderately competitive and, at worst, close to monopolies in some industries. In 1968, for example, the merger of the Pennsylvania and New York Central railroads was approved by the government.

Undoubtedly one of the most powerful forces stimulating economic growth was government. By the 1950's government was more than a regulator of the economy; it was also a very substantial and active participant in it. Indeed, the expenditures of the local, state, and federal governments after 1955 were so large that they dwarfed those of any other "industry," constituting about one fifth of all purchases made in the private sector. In fact, the federal government's role as purchaser, aside from any of its other economic roles, was so great that in 1965 and in 1966 the Johnson administration was able to prevent price increases in aluminum and then in copper simply by releasing large quantities of these strategic metals from its stockpiles.

In quite a direct fashion, the federal government was one of the principal forces sustaining the housing boom of the 1950's, which, in turn, was one of the important causes of the economic growth after 1945. Through agencies like the Federal Housing Administration and the Veterans Administration, the federal government helped to finance mortgages for the construction and purchase of millions of one-family homes. The federal government also poured money into the economy through its support of low-cost public housing during these same years. Many economists believe that the demand for housing, which had been building up all through the Depression, was the principal cause for the postwar prosperity. Certainly the backlog of demand was enormous. In 1945, one authority has calculated, all the housing in the country was actually worth 8 per cent less than in 1929, despite the wartime inflation. Very little construction had taken place during the depressed thirties, yet since 1929 the number of households had risen by eight million, or 26 per cent. When the defeat of the Axis powers released American savings from government restrictions, the housing boom began, lasting all through the 1950's. The importance of housing to economic growth can hardly be exaggerated, since residential construction usually makes up between 20 and 25 per cent of all private investment. During the 1950's, when the housing boom was at its height, over a million dwelling units were built each year, a number greater than the annual number of new families. Out of all the houses in existence in the country in 1960, perhaps as many as a quarter of them had been built in the preceding decade alone.

Population growth, increased government expenditures, a backlog of consumer savings, and the housing boom were not the only sources of economic growth, important as they were. The large increase in productivity must also be included in the list. Between 1890 and 1914 the advance in output per man-hour was 22 per cent; in the years from World War II to 1959 the increase was between 35 and 40 per cent, almost double the earlier rate.

Mechanization and Automation. What was it that enabled the American worker to increase his productivity? Primarily, it was an expanded use of machines and power. As machines became more sophisticated and versatile, the workers became only feeders, supervisors, and operators of mechanisms, with almost all the labor being done by the machine. Efficiency was further advanced by new integration processes, whereby interruptions in the manufacturing of goods were avoided and time saved, as in the so-called continuous-flow processes in many industries. In a good number of industries, it was now possible to combine a sequence of operations into a single one. For example in the automobile industry, one machine now drilled holes in automobile crankshafts, whereas before 29 different machines had been required.

Dramatic as were the new machines and processes in advancing productivity, they paled beside automation, which was the great contribution of the 1950's. All machines, even those of the 1950's, required men to stop and start them, to regulate and adjust them. Automation differs from ordinary machine production in that men no longer are necessary for the operation of the machines. With automation the machines are self-regulating through the use of electronic devices, which work much as a thermostat does when it turns the heat on or off in a room as the temperature changes. This process of adjustment is called feedback, because, in effect, the machine makes appropriate self-adjustments on the basis of information that is fed back to the controlling mechanism. In a way the machine makes choices or decisions. Perhaps the best-known and most sophisticated form in which electronic automation appears is the computer. Although a computer appears to have the capacity to think—that is, to make decisions—in reality it has already been instructed ("programmed" is the technical term) with all the possible answers to any question it may be asked, as well as the reasons why one answer should be preferred over another. Its alleged thinking, therefore, is actually an incredibly rapid electronic checking of all the alternatives, from which the most appropriate answer is selected.

Already the computer has become a part of virtually every form of enterprise, including colleges and universities. It is fast becoming indispensable for the processing of records that once were tediously and expensively handled by innumerable clerks. Medium-sized business firms, for example, can now handle orders and transactions that once would have been beyond the capacity of any but the largest firms. Hundreds of thousands of correlations among the products of a firm, their location in warehouses, and customers' orders can now be made by computer within a few seconds. A few industries, such as oil and chemicals, though not nearly so many as some people think, were introducing feedback techniques into their production processes in the 1960's.

An important consequence that flowed from these advances in mechanization and automation was the reduction in hours of labor needed to turn out goods. In 1947, for example, it took 310.5 man-hours to make an automobile; in 1962 the figure was 153.0; in 1947 it required 1300 man-hours to dig out 1000 tons of coal; in 1962 only 500 were needed. From the standpoint of the worker, increased productivity meant a higher standard of living. In 1947 an industrial worker, at average wage rates, needed to put in 180 hours to buy a refrigerator; in 1962 he could get one after 83 hours of work. In 1962 an industrial worker could buy a vacuum cleaner with the wages from 20 hours of labor; in 1947 he had to work almost twice as long.

Behind the drive for mechanization and automation lay the willingness of business and government to invest ever increasing amounts of money in scientific and technological research for the improvement of methods and techniques. During the 1950's outlays for research and development rose faster than the gross national product, reaching 12 billion dollars in 1959. About half of the total was contributed by the federal government. A new and fruitful relationship developed between business and government, on the one hand, and the universities and colleges, on the other. Recognizing that research was one of the sources of new products, techniques, and increased productivity, both business and government drew heavily upon the knowledge and skills of the intellectual community through research grants and consulting contracts. Never before had the university community been so heavily involved with and dependent upon government and private business; some far-sighted universities took elaborate precautions to prevent distortion of the commitment to free and untrammeled research and to lessen the dependence upon government and business funds. But no major institution of higher learning could function in the 1960's without some support from government or business.

Advertising as Symbol. Strictly speaking, advertising was not a cause of the increased productivity of the postwar years. Yet it also deserves to be mentioned here because it was so characteristic of the new economy of abundance. For one thing, it clearly reflected the consumer-oriented character of the economy; for another, it measured the increase in productivity. For as more and more goods poured into the market, advertising was necessary to stimulate consumers to buy, if a glut were to be avoided. In some industries like cosmetics, cigarettes, and soft drinks, advertising constituted the principal, if not the only difference between competing products. The importance of advertising is reflected in the fact that expenditures for advertising between 1950 and 1959 rose at a faster rate than did the gross national product.

The Social Consequences of Prosperity

Regional Transformations. One of the most striking changes that has followed upon the new prosperity after 1945 has been the improvement in the economy of the South, long the most depressed region of the nation. Although the South continued to report a high birth rate and inadequate out-migration to counterbalance it, personal income per capita during the 1950's rose faster than it did in the rest of the nation. Moreover, by 1961 the proportion of workers in the South engaged in manufacturing had risen from 18 per cent to almost 24 per cent, a proportion that put the region on a par, for the first time since the Civil War, with the Far West. The South is still, in the 1960's, the most rural region of the country, but its cities are growing at a faster rate than those of the rest of the nation. The beginnings of the change go back to the 1930's, with the improvement in cotton prices because of the AAA, and the building of the TVA, which not only brought electricity to the rural South, but, through its reclamation and conservation programs, helped to rehabilitate the region. During the war the many army training camps in the South injected large amounts of federal money into the southern economy, helping to raise per capita income, thereby providing a firmer and broader market for southern industry. After the war the weakness of organized labor in the South, as well as the mild climate, which cut heating costs, attracted much northern industry southward. The continuing migration of Negroes out of the South has also reduced the downward pressure on wages that the South's high birth rate has long exerted. Increased expenditures on education and a determined interest by white Southerners in economic growth have been instrumental as well in creating a truly New South in the years since 1945.

Among all the southern states, Texas was the most spectacular in its economic growth. Many of the new growth industries, like chemicals, instruments, and airplane construction, which were located there, doubled or tripled in output between 1947 and 1960. The proportion of the state's labor force engaged in agriculture fell from 16 per cent to 9 per cent during the 1950's alone. The new Texas millionaires and the burgeoning economy of the state became a source of humor and of envy throughout the rest of the country.

No region of the country, however, could equal California in growth and prosperity. In the 1960's it has become richer than many nations in the rest of the world. Indeed, it is bigger in area than all but four of the countries of Europe, and its population in 1961 was larger than that of all but three countries in Latin America. In short, California is a country in itself, boasting an informal and almost flamboyant style of life built around its mild, sunny climate, and possessing a remarkably productive economy. Among the states of the American union, California is first in both agricultural and industrial production. Almost half the vegetables marketed in the nation are grown in that one state. At the same time, the number of workers engaged in manufacturing increased 82 per cent between 1950 and 1960 alone. In the early 1960's Los Angeles surpassed Chicago as a manufacturing center, having gained a quarter of a million operatives, craftsmen, and foremen in the preceding decade, while Chicago showed a net loss of 66,000. Aside from its climate, which minimizes both heating costs and absenteeism resulting from illness, one of the principal reasons for the state's fabulous growth has been the large number of federal defense contracts it has received for airplane and missile construction. In 1960–1961 California received more government contracts than Texas and New York combined, though both those states were leaders in defense work. Soon after the census of 1960, California proudly announced that it had surpassed New York as the wealthiest and most populous state.

The New Agriculture. One of the minor miracles of the postwar economy was the revolution in agriculture. During the nineteenth century the expansion of agricultural production had been one of the bases that supported the nation's successful take-off into economic maturity. But between the First World War and the Second, agriculture stood almost still, blighted and depressed. Since 1945, however, farmers have once again made a major contribution to the affluent society. Their efforts on the land have made the

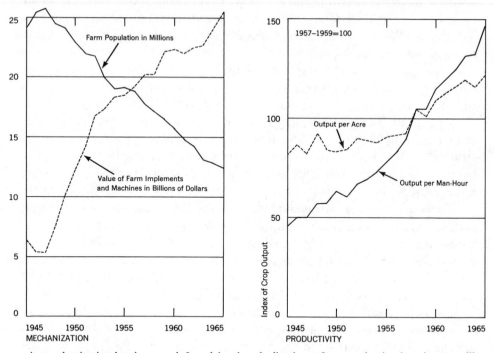

As mechanization has increased, farm labor has declined, yet farm production has risen steadily. The index of total farm output (1957–1959=100) has increased from 70 in 1940 to 113 in 1966. As a result each farmer now works less time to produce more from each acre of his land. *Source:* Department of Agriculture, Economic Research Service.

cost of food in the United States cheaper for American city dwellers than for any other people in the world. In western Europe, for instance, a worker typically spends 30 to 40 per cent of his income for food; in the Soviet Union the proportion is 55 per cent. In underdeveloped countries in Latin America and Asia, almost all of a worker's income goes for food. In the United States about 20 per cent of an average family's income is taken up by food purchases. Moreover, relative to the rise in the American worker's income since the 1930's, the prices of farm products have fallen. In 1966, for example, an hour of industrial employment would buy on the average 2.5 pounds of round steak; in 1929 only 1.2 pounds. In 1966 the same amount of labor bought almost 11 quarts of milk; in 1929 less than 4. Today an hour's work purchases 2.5 times as many oranges as it did in 1929. Although quality of food is not as easily measured, a general impression of much higher quality in chicken, turkey, meat, fruits, and vegetables is evident to any person who is old enough to have lived through the twenties and thirties.

To cite such changes is but to call attention to the high level of productivity in agriculture. But this high productivity was only reached through a social transformation of farming. For if agriculture is efficient, competitive, and scientific, as the above facts testify, it is at the same time inefficient, backward, and a source of poverty for millions of Americans who depend upon it for their livelihood. During the 1950's agriculture entered upon that lengthy transition through which industrial labor had passed during the middle years of the nineteenth century—that is, from the small individual enterprise to the highly capitalized corporate enterprise. In the course of the nineteenth century, industrial workers gradually recognized that they could not compete with highly capitalized corporations and so became reconciled to working for others. (It will be recalled that the Knights of Labor, as recently as the 1880's, was still setting as its goal the self-employment of industrial workers through cooperatives.) Today farmers are being required to make the same adjustment.

It is true that ever since 1935 the number of farm units in the United States has been declining, and that in 1961 there were only 3.7 million farms as against 6.8 million in 1935. But even with this steady decline, there are still 1.6 million farm families, or 44 per cent of the total, who receive most of their income not from agriculture, but from second jobs in nearby towns and cities. These people—Negro sharecroppers in the South, migrant farm laborers in California and elsewhere, and farmers on marginal lands in Appalachia and the Middle West—actually live more meanly than welfare recipients in the great cities. They are the inefficient producers as contrasted with highly efficient farmers, who make up only a tiny fraction of the whole. In fact in 1959, 1200 highly efficient farmers marketed commodities worth almost as much as the production of the whole 1.6 million farm units at the bottom end of the scale; in 1960 1.4 million farms produced 87 per cent of all agricultural commodities. The other 2.2 million farms could have lain fallow and not have been missed.

The large, efficient units that are doing most of the producing are really highly organized and highly capitalized factories in the field. Since the 1930's agricultural acreage has been gravitating into larger and larger units, from an average of 157 acres in 1930 to 336 acres in 1962. A mere 800,000 farms in 1962 encompassed three quarters of all the land under cultivation. The average amount of capital invested per worker on American farms in 1960 was $21,000, or $5000 more than the amount per worker in non-agricultural enterprises. It is this amazingly high level of capitalization that explains the tremendous productivity of American agriculture, which in the 1950's was almost double that of the average for all other industries in the economy.

This great investment of capital is used in a number of ways to increase productivity. One is the liberal use of machines, such as the five million tractors on American farms in 1960, or the thousands of mechanical cotton pickers, combines, and corn pickers, or the airplanes used for spraying pesticides and fertilizer, and even for planting seeds. Advances in chemicals, implied in the wide use of pesticides, are undoubtedly one of the major causes of the enormous increase in agricultural productivity since 1945. Chemicals are used not only to kill harmful insects, but to hasten crop maturity, to kill weeds, to remove leaves in order to facilitate harvesting or to inhibit unwanted growth, as in tobacco, where only the main leaves are desired. Newly developed chemical fertilizers used in conjunction with new types of seeds have doubled wheat and corn yields. The chemical industry has also developed new feeds for chickens, which speed up growth and make it possible to raise broiling hens from egg to maturity in eight or nine weeks. The large broiler houses, which are three stories high and 600 feet long, containing as many as 50,000 birds, all under the control of one man, are a far cry from the make-shift hen houses of the old farm. In the early 1960's Georgia chicken farmers were able to undersell German chicken producers in Germany, despite the added cost of transportation across the Atlantic.

The principal incentive for using the new chemicals, seeds, and equipment has been the government agricultural support policies, which began with the New Deal. Once again the role of government in bringing about the postwar prosperity is illustrated. Since the support prices have been set at the level necessary to sustain inefficient producers, the policy offers incentives to efficient producers to invest increasing amounts of capital in production and to adopt ever greater efficiencies. For, with a floor on prices, every reduction in the cost of production becomes an increase in profits. In 1961, for instance, support prices were about double the cost of an efficient farmer's production in the best growing areas. The difference, of course, was gross profit. Although at first it might seem desirable to encourage the inefficient farmers to leave the land, a closer look indicates that removal would not help them much unless new and better-paying jobs could be found for them. That will not be easy to do in an economy that increasingly demands well-educated and highly skilled industrial workers, rather than old style farmers who have few skills to bring to industrial and urban employment.

One further consequence of the continuing presence of inefficient farmers was an attempt in 1962 by the newly formed National Farmers Organization in the plains states to keep up beef prices by holding their cattle off the market. A survey showed that the bulk of the farmers in the organization were not the efficient producers, who had little to fear from a drop in meat prices, but the small or middling farmers who were finding it difficult to compete with the highly capitalized, efficient producers. The attempt of the NFO to control prices attracted nationwide publicity, but it did not succeed in raising prices. Instead, it simply aroused alarm in the cities, where the higher prices would have to be paid.

Perhaps the most important consequence of the changes in agriculture since 1945 is the gradual disappearance of the family farm as it has been known throughout most of United States history. It is true that the number of "adequate" family farms, as the Department of Agriculture defined efficient producers, jumped from 334,000 in 1949 to 680,000 in 1959. But during the same period the number of inadequate farms dropped from 3.1 million to 1.6 million. In short, in ten years 1.2 million farm families simply left farming entirely. By 1960 less than 8 per cent of the American population lived on farms; by 1970 the proportion would be even smaller. Yet all signs point to the conclusion that the output of American agriculture will be greater than ever. As the agricultural revolution of the late nineteenth century had made the farmer a businessman, the governmental policies of the 1950's have either made him a big businessman or forced him off the farm altogether.

Stagnation in Organized Labor. Prior to the 1920's the pattern of labor organization had been that unions gained members in times of prosperity and lost them in times of depression. But this pattern has been reversed since World War I. During the twenties, for example, organized labor lost members, despite the general prosperity; in the Depression years that followed, trade unions more than doubled their membership, thanks to the encouragement of the National Labor Relations Act and the friendly attitude of the Roosevelt administration. The prosperity of the years after 1945 also seems to contradict the nineteenth-century pattern. Membership, it is true, did not significantly decline in the 1950's, as it had in the prosperous 1920's, but neither did it keep pace with the growth of the labor force. In 1956 about a third of nonagricultural workers were organized into labor unions; in 1965 the proportion was down to 29 per cent. (Actually, numbers also fell slightly, from 17.5 million in 1956 to 16.8 million in 1965.)

This stagnation in labor organization can be attributed to several factors. One is undoubtedly the stodginess of the labor movement itself. Once militant, enthusiastic, and convinced of its mission, it had become fat and satisfied by the 1950's, resting on the successes it had achieved during the turbulent thirties. Most of its leaders were old men, veterans, to be sure, of the great organizing drives of earlier years, but now tired and lacking in imagination. There were few dynamic young men to take their places. Moreover, despite the energy and idealism still evident in a leader like Walter Reuther of the automobile workers, some of the more energetic new leaders like James Hoffa, president of the Teamsters Union, by their use of strong-arm tactics and their narrow conception of labor's responsibility to the community made organized labor unattractive to outsiders. Furthermore, by the 1950's many large corporations had learned well the lessons of the 1920's. They gained a favorable public reputation and simultaneously undercut union organizing drives by anticipating some of the demands of their workers for fringe benefits and higher wages. The chemical industry, for example, has been able to prevent national unions from organizing its workers by simply accepting independent, unaffiliated unions. But undoubtedly the principal reason for the stagnation in trade union membership is the changing shape of the employment structure.

The Dominance of White Collar. In *The Conditions of Economic Progress* (1940), the economist Colin Clark pointed out that in a mature industrial society the labor force can be divided into three categories: primary (farming, fishing, and forestry), secondary (manufacturing, constructing, and mining), and tertiary (services, trade, and government). One sign of the increasing maturity of an economy, he observed, is the growth of the tertiary category, since such growth is dependent upon the efficiency of the first two. In 1940 about a third of the labor force in the United States fell into the third category; by 1956 half did. Hence, today most employed workers in the United States are engaged in rendering services or in handling the hard goods which a minority of workers produce. The greatest proportion of the members of this majority are white-collar workers—as distinguished from so-called blue-collar workers who mine the coal, till the soil, and fabricate the goods.

On the one hand, the dominance of the white-collar class testifies to the high level of productivity in an economy that can dispense with its labor in fields and factories. On the other hand, this dominance also emphasizes the consumer nature of the modern American economy, for the white-collar class is either distributing the food and goods produced by the blue collars, or it is providing personal consumer services, as physicians, barbers, teachers, TV repairmen, investment counselors, bank tellers, and the like.

Early in the period one observer, David Riesman, in his widely read *The Lonely Crowd* (1950), called attention to the way in which this emphasis upon consumption was affecting American habits. In a society of consumers, he pointed out, the idea of self-denial, the need for steady and hard work, and for frugal habits of life would no longer command their old allegiance. Indeed, just the opposite is demanded if the great outpouring of goods is to be consumed. Furthermore, in a society of consumers and service workers the emphasis is on personal relations, for instead of things being the object of work, people are. Sometimes this emphasis results in the outright manipulation of people, as in certain types of selling and advertising. Even when manipulation is not involved, the thrust of a consumer-oriented economy is to reinforce a long-standing tendency of Americans to conform to their neighbors' tastes and opinions—an attitude that Alexis de Tocqueville had discerned as early as the age of Jackson.

As far as the labor movement is concerned, the importance of the dominance of the white collar is the traditional resistance of that class to unionization. Although white-collar workers generally are less well paid than blue-collar workers, they do not join unions, principally because they tend to see themselves as having a higher social status than blue-collar workers. Since it is the latter who are largely unionized, many white-collar workers shy away from the institutions and practices associated with blue-collar status. For example, teachers and bank employees, highly organized in Europe, are almost entirely unorganized in the United States. In fact, many white-collar workers in America are quite hostile to labor organization; there is good evidence, for instance, for believing that many white-collar workers supported legislation like the Taft-Hartley and Griffin-Landrum Acts which labor unions strenuously opposed. If in the advanced American economy the proportion of

THE CHANGING LABOR FORCE

One important change is the increase in the numbers of working women. Now, two out of every five women are in the labor force. Between the ages of forty-five and fifty-four, after children have been raised, one out of two women work outside the home. On the other hand, fewer men and women eighteen and nineteen years old are in the work force, reflecting the fact that for the first time, half of all high school graduates go on to institutions of higher learning. Another important aspect is the increase in the number of white-collar workers, who after 1955 surpassed the number of blue-collar workers. This is one reason why the proportion of union members has not risen above the level of the 1940's. Note, also, that the number of farm workers continues to fall.
Source: Manpower Administration, *Statistical Tables on Manpower.*

COMPOSITION OF THE LABOR FORCE

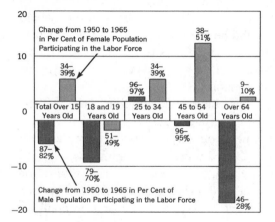

OCCUPATIONS OF EMPLOYED PERSONS

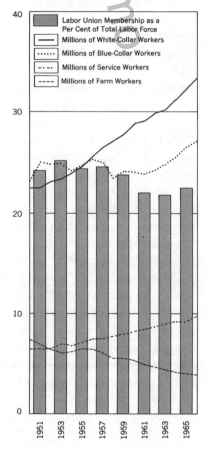

UNEMPLOYMENT RATES

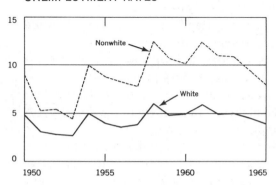

white-collar workers seems destined to grow, the proportion of workers in unions seems equally destined to shrink, unless some breakthrough in organizing workers in the tertiary category of the labor force is made.

Organized labor, like labor in general, was also hit hard by automation. For a while the new, automatic processes of the 1950's threw many workmen into a panic. A public opinion poll in Detroit in 1955, for example, revealed that only the threat from Communist Russia outranked automation as a cause for concern among American workers. Most of them were convinced that automation would lead only to unemployment, and that in the long run its evils would outweigh any advantages to be gained from it.

Soon, however, most unions and workers came to recognize that the truth was just the reverse. In the short run, automation would undoubtedly be painful, but with planning and cooperation among management, labor, and government, it could be prevented from permanently harming the workers. Increasingly, in situations where automation threatened to destroy jobs, the unions began to work out arrangements with management whereby dismissals would be spread over a period of time, and the dismissed workers would receive generous severance payments and be retrained for a new line of work. Management as well as labor contributed to the funds to provide such opportunities. The federal government also helped in the transition with programs for retraining workers displaced by automation.

Not all unions, however, accepted this enlightened solution. The Brotherhood of Locomotive Firemen, for example, fought desperately from 1959 to 1963 to prevent the elimination of firemen from diesel engines, even though it was evident that without coal to be shoveled a fireman was unnecessary. At one point in August 1963, Congress, by a large majority, imposed arbitration on the firemen in order to prevent a railroad strike over the issue. This act, which applied only to that particular controversy, was the first compulsory arbitration law passed by Congress in peacetime. The growing complexity and interdependence of the economy, which meant that large strikes could cause a national crisis, promised that it would not be the last.

The Paradox of Labor's Power. It was certainly ironic that, as organized labor's proportion of the work force declined, its power in the economy mounted. The explanation lay not with labor, but with the changes in the structure of the economy. As all parts of the country became closely linked and dependent upon each other, any disruption of service or production hurt large numbers of people and threatened the overall growth of the economy. A steel or automobile strike, for example, would not only severely reduce the income of hundreds of thousands of workers, but would also, by that fact, weaken the economy as a whole. Moreover, strikes by certain classes of workers like longshoremen, transport workers, or railroad employees, simply because they constitute vital links in the complex economic chain, could bring the economy to a halt, even though the number of workers involved in any such strike might be relatively small.

It was the recognition of this high degree of interdependence among the various sectors of the economy that accounts for the federal government's intervention in recent years to prevent or to end nationwide strikes. Although Congressional action was unusual, presidential pressure to prevent a strike or to end one was not. This is as true in the 1960's as it was in the 1940's under Truman. For instance, President Kennedy's strong reaction to a price increase by U.S. Steel in 1962 grew out of his administration's earlier success in preventing a strike by the steelworkers union. Having cajoled the union into not striking for higher wages, the President felt he could not permit the company to gain an advantage while the workers sacrificed theirs. Both Kennedy and Johnson worked to head off nationwide railroad strikes in 1963 and 1964, and in 1966 Johnson used the influence of his office to end a strike of airplane machinists that had closed down all but one major airline.

The Changing Place of Women. A large part of the white-collar class was made up of women who after 1940 entered the labor force in ever increasing numbers. Between 1940 and 1960, for example, some 9.4 million women joined the ranks of the gainfully employed as compared with 7.5 million men. In the 1960's two out of every five adult women were gainfully employed, constituting a third of the work force in the economy.

For a variety of reasons, the new prosperity makes it possible for married women to work. Employers accept married women more readily than ever before, if only because they need the skills and labor of these women. Women have been finding jobs in fields like finance and computer programing open to them for the first time as a result of the boom. By the close of the 1950's, about one third of all married women were working outside the home, as compared with 17 per cent in 1940. Only rarely did one now hear the complaint of the Depression years that a working wife deprived a man with a family of a job. It has become increasingly commonplace in the prosperous 1960's for young women to continue to work when they marry. Indeed, young people take it for granted that if the husband's pursuit of higher education precludes his taking a job, his wife will support him. In affluent America marriage no longer waits on a man's having a good job and a steady income. Moreover, in this consumer-oriented economy, married women work in order to buy more goods and services for their families.

Generally the married working woman is a mother. (In 1962 out of 13.5 million married working women, 8.8 were mothers.) Simply because women are marrying earlier (the median age in 1960 was 20) and having their children earlier, they have been able to enter, or return to, the work force after the children have gone off to school. The combination of marriage and work for women, however, has not been easy nor highly remunerative. Women continue to be paid less than men; discrimination against them in promotion and responsibility make up one third of the charges laid before the Equal Employment Opportunity Commission, which has been created under the Civil Rights Act of 1964. Failure to obtain jobs commensurate with their training has been a problem especially for college women, who work outside the home in greater proportion than do noncollege women.

Although the growing rate of employment of women indicates that their labor is needed, women are still not using their talents to the fullest. In the 1950's women constituted a smaller proportion of all college students than they had in the 1920's, and their percentage of the recipients of advanced degrees was smaller than earlier in the century. In short, in an age when brain power is said to be at a premium, the brains of women are being underused.

The Limits of Affluence

The Dimensions of Prosperity. The prosperity of the postwar years was so spectacular that it could be measured only in astronomical terms. Between 1945 and the middle 1960's, the gross national product more than doubled, even after price changes were taken into account. In 1966 the GNP was over $700 billion, though as recently as 1960 it had been only $500 billion. Other periods in American history, to be sure, like the 1920's, had been notable for their prosperity, but the significance of the years after 1945 was that the lower-income groups, as well as the upper, farmers as well as businessmen, workers as well as employers, have shared in the wealth. Income distribution, it is true, has remained unequal—in 1962, for example, 5 per cent of all families received almost 20 per cent of all personal income—yet there was a tendency in the direction of greater equality. During the 1930's the top 5 per cent of income receivers took almost 27 per cent of all personal income.

There could be no doubt that the lower-income groups were sharing in the prosperity. Weekly wages of workers in manufacturing, for example, increased 16 per cent between 1947 and 1957 even after one takes into account changes in prices. During the same period the lowest-income group shrank in size; in 1947 over a quarter of all American families fell below an income level of $2500 per year (in 1957 dollars), which authorities denominated as the minimum level for a family of four. In 1957 this low-income group constituted only 19 per cent of American families. Moreover, between 1945 and 1960 public welfare payments rose six times in amount, thereby helping to improve the income of the lowest group. Another measure of the improved standard of living was the increase in home ownership. In 1940 fewer than 44 per cent of American families, including farmers, lived in homes they had bought; in 1960 amost 62 per cent owned their own homes. However, as we shall see a little later, the urge to home ownership, indicative as it may have been of prosperity, brought problems, too.

The New Face of Poverty. Despite the abundant evidence of an improving standard of living and the reduction in the numbers of poor people, by the close of the 1950's large dark spots still remained in the society. Two influential books pointed up the limits of the new prosperity. The first, John Kenneth Galbraith's *The Affluent Society,* appeared in 1958; the second, Michael Harrington's *The Other America,* was published in 1962.

Galbraith's thesis was that, despite the acknowledged prosperity, the public sector of the economy was shamefully neglected. Hospitals, prisons, mental institutions, and clinics were inadequate, understaffed, and crowded; schools were overflowing with students, teachers underpaid, recreational facilities overtaxed, and other social services neglected. So long as the society depended upon the profit motive to energize investment, he pointed out, these public services, which brought no profit, would continue to be inadequate even as the private sector of the economy bounded from one peak to other still higher ones. It was up to government, he counseled, to increase taxes and improve the public sector of the society. Galbraith's book became the intellectual justification for the legislation of the Kennedy and Johnson administrations to improve schools, provide medical care for the aged, and mount the war on poverty. (Galbraith himself was an adviser to John F. Kennedy before and after 1960.)

Galbraith pointed out that poverty in the United States was no longer an economic, but a social problem; the poor remained so because they could not participate in the economy. He divided them into two classes: those who were unable to earn an adequate living because of lack of education, illness, or old age, and those who were geographically isolated in economic backwaters like Appalachia or rural New England.

Michael Harrington's *The Other America* carried Galbraith's contention much further, emphasizing the social neglect of the poor. "The millions who are poor in the United States," he wrote, "tend to become increasingly invisible." It takes "an effort of the intellect and will even to see them." Yet, he contended, they are all around, not only in the back country of the Appalachian Mountains, but in the Negro slums of the big cities, among migrant workers in the West, among those everywhere who lack a high school education, and among the millions of people over sixty-five who live on incomes of less than $1000 a year. Like Galbraith, Harrington recognized that a generally advancing economy would not improve the condition of these poor. They could be helped only by specific programs for their rehabilitation and inclusion in the general economy, since almost all of them were disadvantaged in some fashion, by lack of education, by illness, old age, or racial discrimination.

Unlike the poor of earlier times, Harrington pointed out, these people were dispirited and without hope because they knew they were ignored by the prosperous majority and unable to secure good jobs in an advanced economy. Doomed to live out their days in poverty and misery in a society that seemed to worship material well-being, they passed on to their children their hopelessness and sense of defeat, evolving what Harrington called "the culture of poverty." Their world was quite a different one from that of the prosperous middle class. The children of the very poor even talked differently because their speech lacked the control of the printed word; hence they found school difficult and a place of failure rather than an avenue to success. The poor experienced not only higher illness and death rates, but were also more likely to be mentally ill than the better-off members of society. Whereas to the middle class the police were friends and protectors of life and property, to the poor they were menaces, for the police represented the landlord, the propertied, and the established order that ignored the poor. And since the poor ran afoul of the law more often than the middle class, the police were suspicious of them.

Harrington placed the number of poor at 50 million, or about 30 per cent of the population. A more objective figure is about 30 million, or 20 per cent. But even the lower figure constituted a distressingly large figure for a nation that was undoubtedly the richest in the history of the world. It was the recognition of this contrast that brought about the antipoverty legislation of the Kennedy and Johnson administrations.

The Blight of the Cities

The Suburban Explosion. Although many of the poor lived on small, impoverished farms or in the migratory labor camps, much of the new poverty was concentrated in the cities. Since 1920 a majority of Americans have been living in cities of 2500 population or more. By 1965 almost 70 per cent lived there, and the urban tide seemed irreversible; each census reported a decline in the number of people living on farms. After the Second World War, however, Americans began to change the kind of cities in which they lived. The movement to the suburbs, which began in the 1920's, grew into a mass exodus in the 1950's. The editors of *Fortune* compared it in 1953 to the great immigration into the United States in the early twentieth century. About as many people—1.2 million—moved to the suburbs that year as entered the United States in 1907, the high-water mark of European immigration. The suburbs to which these restless apartment and tenement dwellers moved were most often sprawling developments, composed of thousands of houses, often of the same design and price class. But these bulldozer-created suburbs did provide more space for the children and the air was cleaner.

The census of 1960 revealed the dimensions of the flight to the suburbs. Of 212 cities of 50,000 or more, 60 actually lost population between 1950 and 1960, though urban population as a whole increased by 26 per cent. This absolute decline in population for such a large number of big cities was unprecedented in American urban history. Especially striking was the exodus from the six great cities of a million or more, all of them, with the exception of Los Angeles, lost population in the decade before 1960. Meanwhile, the suburban communities that ringed the central cities grew nearly 50 per cent during the same ten years.

An Automobile-Created World. It was primarily the automobile that encouraged and stimulated the flight to the suburbs and the consequent decline of the central cities. Between 1940 and 1955 the number of cars in use doubled; it was estimated that by 1976 the number would double again. The new prosperity of the postwar years provided almost every family with an

THE IMPACT OF THE AUTOMOBILE

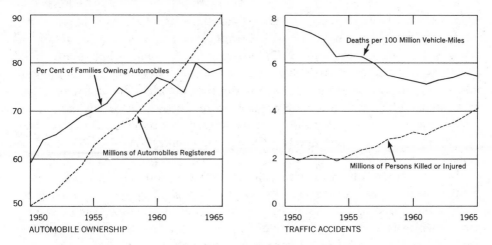

After cancer, heart disease, and pneumonia, automobiles killed more people in 1966 than any other single cause. For one reason, the number of automobiles almost doubled between 1950 and 1965. Yet, improved roads and auto safety features contributed to a decline in the number of deaths in proportion to the amount of travel. The popular appeal of the automobile is reflected by the fact that only 20 per cent of American families do not own cars, although a quarter to a third of the population is conservatively defined as poor. *Sources:* Bureau of Public Roads. National Safety Council. The Travelers Insurance Company. The University of Michigan, Survey Research Center.

automobile, and by the end of the 1950's, the movement to the suburbs required many families to have two. With three quarters of the adult population licensed drivers, the United States was truly a nation behind wheels. Thus the automobile, which was welcomed because it enabled urban dwellers to free themselves from the tyranny of commuter trains and trolley car lines, became a tyrant itself, threatening to choke the cities to death in a glut of traffic.

In the central cities the large number of automobiles impeded the movement of goods and people to such a degree that the *New York Times* estimated that, because of the delays, $5 billion was added each year to the cost of doing business. Milwaukee bus companies put on 45 more buses than were actually needed in order to compensate for delays occasioned by the heavy traffic in the city's streets.

The fact, of course, is that the automobile is an inefficient means of moving large numbers of people into and out of the cities, where most suburbanites work. (An automobile with a single driver takes up nine times the space required to move a single person in a public conveyance.) Yet the convenience of the individual car easily overrode the social efficiency of the commuter train. Since World War II over 150 public transit systems have been put out of business by the automobile. Although by the middle sixties it was evident to almost everyone that the traffic congestion problem called for heroic measures, including a return to public transportation systems, the changes brought about by the automobile are difficult to reverse. As more and more workers have used cars to get to their jobs, factories have begun to be built outside the city limits and without reference to public transportation. A study of Spokane in the mid-1950's, for example, revealed that almost three quarters of the workers arrived by automobile. By spreading the population into suburban developments and scattering the factories, the automobile has prevented the concentration of population that alone financially justifies a public transit system. Only government subsidy can now provide fares low enough to meet the social need and to compete with the undeniable convenience of the automobile.

In a desperate effort to reduce traffic congestion, cities and states have built massive freeways and highways to speed up traffic, and large parking lots to hold the horde of cars once they arrive at their destination. Two thirds of downtown Los Angeles is given over to the auto, for roads, parking facilities, and garages. It is estimated that in 1980 that city will have 34 square miles devoted to freeways alone. But each such concession to the automobile removes valuable land from productive use and from the tax rolls just when the needs of cities for increased revenue are mounting sharply. In Cleveland, for example, a three-mile stretch of freeway removed $20 million worth of assessed property from taxation.

New roads are obviously not the final answer to urban sprawl and traffic congestion. In the middle 1960's some cities were planning new rapid transit systems, like that in the San Francisco Bay area, which promises to compete successfully with the automobile by reducing commuters' traveling time by 75 per cent. The federal government is also giving financial support to the development of exceptionally rapid inter-city rail transportation that would cut down on both air and auto traffic in the megalopolis of the northeast. In 1966 Congress created a new Cabinet-rank Department of Transportation, in recognition of the urgency of the problem.

A Multiplicity of Problems

It was the great size of the cities that rendered their problems so difficult to grapple with. The Athens of Pericles was only the size of Yonkers, N.Y.; renaissance Florence was smaller than New Haven; Chicago is three times as large as imperial Rome. With two thirds of the nation's population concentrated in cities, the number of people to govern, the amount of wastes to remove, food to distribute, water to supply, crimes to prevent, fires to fight, and air to clean have reached astronomical proportions. To take but one example: all over the nation cities were building incinerators or desperately seeking new dump sites as the "production" of wastes almost tripled between 1940 and 1961. A Boston official in charge of sanitation said in 1961 that his city was running out of dump sites, though already 60 per cent of its wastes were being burned in a recently built incinerator. Meanwhile, some cities continued to grow like runaway cancers. Washington, D.C., for example, jumped 40 per cent in population between the census of 1950 and 1960.

The Need for Water. As population increased, especially in the cities, the search for potable water became almost frantic. Los Angeles had already run its tentacle-like aqueducts some 200 miles to the east, to tap the Colorado River; in the late 1960's California's Feather River Project would bring water 550 miles from the northern to the southern part of the state, at a construction cost of $2 billion. New York City, not so farsighted, found itself with a severe water shortage in 1964–1965, even though its reservoirs and pipes extended over 100 miles into the Catskill Mountains, tapping the headwaters of the Delaware, upon which the city of Philadelphia also depended. Denver spent six years and $50 million drilling a 23-mile tunnel beneath the Rockies to secure sufficient water for its growing population. Throughout the country the millions of cesspools for the new housing developments threatened the purity of the water in the wells newly sunk in the same developments. The large number of wells in housing developments along the seacoast often drew off such large amounts of ground water that sea water began to seep into the water table.

Much as men needed clean water for life, they often contaminated whole rivers with their wastes. Fifty million pounds of solid wastes, it has been calculated, pour into the nation's waterways daily. Municipal sewage systems in 1961 were dumping twice as much wastes into waterways as had been considered the maximum permissible in 1955. About a quarter of all sewage emptying into rivers was completely untreated. Moreover, man not only polluted the water but did so in such a manner as to make cleansing it more costly and difficult than if the water had been contaminated by organic wastes. Modern detergents used in home washing machines, for instance, did not break down under bacterial attack as did organic compounds; instead, they seeped into the water table and then gushed forth as suds from water taps in thousands of homes.

As the country became aware of the mounting need for water, eyes naturally turned toward the inexhaustible supply in the oceans. Unfortunately, known processes for removing salt from sea water are still not competitive in cost with natural fresh water or even with cleansed water. In 1961, for example, the cost of converted sea water was ten times the price per gallon of cleansed water. Mindful of the world's as well as the United States' growing requirements for clean water, President Kennedy said in May 1962 that the nation which developed an economical way of converting salt water to fresh "could do more for mankind than the nation that is first in space."

Fouling the Air. Despite the widespread use of electricity, a clean power source, modern cities and factories still poured millions of pounds of contaminants into the air. Once again, however, the biggest culprit was the automobile, the exhausts of which were noxious, and unknown in the nineteenth century. Los Angeles was no longer alone in having smog that brought tears to the eyes and pain to the lungs of its citizens. Authorities reported, for instance, that breathing air in Birmingham, Alabama, was equivalent to smoking two packs of cigarettes a day, insofar as cancer producing substances were concerned. As the automobile population of California leaped up between 1950 and 1960, the mortality rate from emphysema, a respiratory disease, quadrupled. Significantly, the increases were twice as great in urban as in rural areas. Some states began to require automobile manufacturers to provide filters on the exhaust systems of automobiles to remove the pollutants before they got into the air. And in 1965 a federal law required that all new cars be equipped by 1968 with "afterburners" capable of absorbing at least 75 per cent of the contaminants from exhausts.

Problems of Social Order. Basically, the physical problems of urban life mounted because numbers of people increased. But mere gain in numbers could not by itself account for the marked increase in social disorganization in the cities. Crime, which had always been higher in the city than in the country, shot upward in the postwar years. Between 1950 and 1960 population increased 12 per cent, but the crime rate, according to FBI figures, increased 14 per cent between 1959 and 1960 alone. Violence against persons, burglary, and grand larceny became so common in some of the big cities that citizens feared to walk the streets at night or to use the public parks.

As the Negro revolution gained momentum, it ignited the highly combustible Negro ghettos of the great cities of the North, causing sporadic, but massive outbursts of violence, burning, and looting. In the summers of 1964, 1965, 1966, and especially 1967, large scale riots erupted in the Negro sections of more than a score of the principal cities of the North. The most shocking incidents occurred in the Watts section of Los Angeles in 1965, where over 34 deaths and $40 million in property damage were reported, and in Detroit and Newark in the riot-filled summer of 1967. In the Detroit upheaval 40 people died, 2000 were injured and some 5000 left homeless by the fires that swept large sections of the city, in what was the bloodiest and most extensive eruption of urban violence since the nineteenth century. Only the introduction of several thousand federal troops brought order to the stunned and gutted city. For the nation the impact was magnified by the fact that only six days before, Newark's Negro ghetto had risen in violence and destruction that were dwarfed only by the events in Watts and Detroit. Although the causes of the riots were undoubtedly complex and even different from city to city, it is evident that in general they stemmed from the two most pressing domestic problems facing Americans in the 1960's: the rising demand of Negroes for equality of opportunity and the rapidly deteriorating environment of the great cities.

City Governments Unprepared for the Task. For any government, the problems confronting the burgeoning cities were formidable, but for American municipal institutions, with limited powers and resources, they were night-

THE URBAN CRISIS

THE COST OF CITY GOVERNMENT

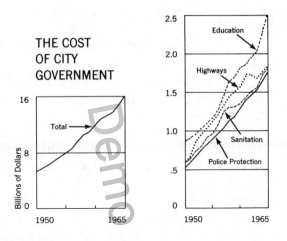

As these graphs dramatically show, during the 1950's the suburbs grew much faster than the central cities. More striking—and unprecedented in the history of American cities—was the actual fall in the population of several of the largest cities. Since only the more prosperous (usually white) people could move out, the flight to the suburbs left the poor (mainly Negroes) in the central cities. In that way, the growth of the suburbs was more than simply a measure of the failure of the big city as a place to live. It was also a dangerous example of the continuation of racial segregation and racial antipathy in America.

Despite the loss of people to the suburbs, the cities faced mounting costs, especially for education. One reason was that poor families tended to have more children than middle-class families, thereby placing a larger financial burden on the cities while providing less tax income. Rising crime rates, one reason for the flight to the suburbs, not only made the cities less safe places to live in, but also increased the cost of police protection. *Source:* Bureau of the Census. Federal Bureau of Investigation.

CRIME RATES PER 100,000 POPULATION, 1965

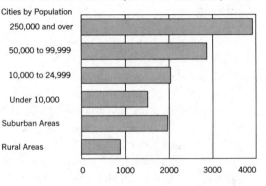

SUBURBANIZATION IN THE 1950's

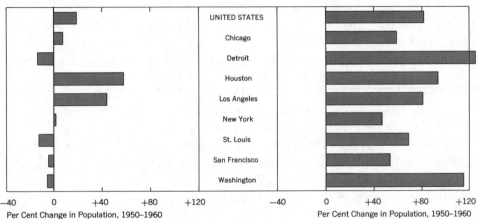

mares. For one thing, many of the problems, like air and water pollution, crime and migration of people into the city, originated or were exacerbated by circumstances outside the city's legal jurisdiction. Police and fire departments were often "balkanized," though neither crime nor fires stopped at invisible municipal boundaries. Even within the city limits, jurisdiction was often fragmented, dissipating responsibility for meeting problems or resulting in confusion or duplication of efforts. The metropolitan area around New York City, which was the natural region in which to grapple with the city's myriad social and economic ills, was actually divided into some 550 different cities, towns, and villages, each with its own government. Los Angeles County in 1960 contained over 600 different taxing bodies, which needed to be coordinated if planning was to take place.

Perhaps the most common barrier to the solution of urban ills was the separation between the central city, where suburbanites worked, and the surrounding suburbs where they lived. By residing outside the city's jurisdiction, suburbanites made no contribution to meeting the costs of the various social services they depended upon as employees. On the other hand, the suburbs, lacking industrial and large commercial enterprises, were often without substantial sources of revenue for the schools and other social services they needed. The high property taxes that necessarily resulted often discouraged new tax-paying commercial enterprises from coming in.

Since local governments secured about four fifths of their revenues from taxes on real estate, the adequacy of schools and other social services in the suburbs was endangered by the refusal of small home owners to accept the higher tax rates necessitated by the rocketing costs of education, health, and recreation. Between 1952 and 1959 expenditures by local governments rose almost twice as fast as the gross national product.

One result of the rising cost of municipal government was that the public debt of localities rose 40 times as fast in the 1950's as did the federal debt. In 1960 alone, expenditures by local governments exceeded their total income by $18 billion. As a result, in 1961 municipalities were spending more on interest payments than they were on fire departments. To help ease the burden on local government, state and federal governments more than doubled their contributions, but obviously more, rather than less, would be needed in the future as the cities continued to grow. One sign of the recognition of the need for broader supervision over the problems posed by cities was the effort by President Kennedy to establish a Cabinet-level Department of Urban Affairs. Congressional resistance to the suggestion, however, was not overcome until 1965, when the Department of Housing and Urban Development was established. In view of the great numbers of Negroes among the poor in the cities, it was appropriate that the first secretary of the department should be a Negro, Robert Weaver.

Urban Renewal. The most obvious way of dealing with the major urban problem of housing had begun in the early years of the postwar prosperity.

Most of the large cities began to tear down antiquated, or unsafe housing and crowded business districts, replacing them with modern, multi-storied housing projects and convenient shopping malls, designed to accommodate the automobile. Results were uneven. Many cities still lost business enterprises to the mushrooming suburban shopping plazas. Moreover, the new housing structures, simply because they were less closely spaced than the old, could not accommodate as many people; the result was greater congestion elsewhere in the city. Furthermore, the new, aseptic, concrete-construction housing projects bred crime and violence because the myriad activities of a busy city street were absent. In mixed residential and commercial districts, no one was alone and unprotected, as they often were on the isolated and impersonal housing project grounds. So telling was this last criticism, which was emphasized by Jane Jacobs in her widely read *The Death and Life of Great American Cities* (1961), that by the middle 1960's some urban renewal funds were being put into renovating old tenements and dwellings in mixed residential and commercial districts rather than bulldozing them down and replacing them with the stark, cold concrete towers so characteristic of public housing.

In addition to dissatisfactions with the methods of urban renewal, there were also complaints about its progress. In 1961, for instance, 3000 acres of urban land were acquired for purposes of renovation, yet the nation's cities were growing by a million acres each year. Although New York City has long been a leader in slum clearance, in 1962 it was reported that less than three square miles of inadequate housing had been cleared out of a total of 250 square miles in the city.

By the 1960's American cities are, as they were at the end of the nineteenth century, the primary frontier of reform. The poor, immigrants, and Negroes are increasingly concentrated in the big cities, while the largely native, white middle class flees to the suburbs. By 1960 half the population of Washington, D.C., was Negro; about 40 per cent of the population of Newark, New Jersey, is black; many other large cities count Negroes as making up from a quarter to a third of their populations. The slums and ghettos of these cities are often as dilapidated and unhealthy as those against which Jacob Riis protested in 1890. Instead of being places where the races and the classes meet and mingle to form a cosmopolitan society, the cities are places where race and class division are fostered. Over half of the 700 public schools surveyed in New York City in the mid-1960's were either 90 per cent Negro and Puerto Rican or 90 per cent white in composition. Instead of being centers of civilization as the common root of the two words implies, cities are more often places of fear, violence, and crime—dirty and unwholesome.

Heroic measures are needed if the big city is not to become the home of the poor exclusively, abandoned by the middle class. In truth, the testing of the quality of American civilization will take place in the city where two thirds of Americans now live. Unless the cities can be made both safe and liveable, there will be no American civilization worth talking about.

The Culture of Affluence in a Nuclear Age

During the 1930's the Depression set the tone and supplied the focus for the culture of the decade. Not surprisingly, therefore, a reversal in the economic circumstances of Americans during the postwar years brought about a marked alteration in their cultural patterns. Because widespread prosperity provided the masses of people with both the money and the time to participate in many of the cultural activities of the times, the postwar years witnessed the rise of mass culture.

Mass Leisure. At the heart of this mass culture lay the increased amount of leisure available at the lower levels of society. The average work week for the entire labor force, including farmers, was down in 1956 to 41.5 hours as compared with 44 hours in 1940. By 1960 virtually no manufacturing employees worked more than 40 hours regularly, and some highly skilled and therefore powerful unions actually reduced the hours of their members to 35. Paid vacations, which had been enjoyed by only about 40 per cent of production workers in 1940, had been extended by the 1960's to almost all employees; moreover, in the 1960's the typical vacation was at least two weeks in length, as compared with one week in 1940. Furthermore, paid holidays and paid sick leave, which were widely enjoyed benefits by 1960, further extended the amount of leisure, while at the same time maintaining income. Even working hours had begun to become more leisurely in the 1950's. The coffee break, which in 1940 was viewed by most employers as boondoggling, was not only accepted, but institutionalized in most offices and factories in the 1950's. Even outdoor construction workers took time off for coffee and doughnuts at a caterer's truck that arrived punctually at the work site each morning.

As might be expected of a people increasingly suburban and property owning and with more time free from the job, the average American by the 1950's was spending less money on certain kinds of spectator leisure activities and more on participation pastimes. Attendance at movies, for example, reached its height in 1948 and, despite an increase in population, has not reached that level again, even in the 1960's. Part of the decline can be explained by increased television viewing, for expenditures for radio and television sets rose sharply during the fifties. But the upsurge in spending for active pastimes suggests that a change of habits was taking place. In 1953 Americans spent six times as much money on power tools as they had only six years before; they paid out $800 million for boats of all kinds as compared with $500 million in 1947. (By 1960 there were about seven million motorboats in use. That same year Americans spent $1.5 billion on books and maps, or more than they did on movies.) Another sign of the new leisure activities of Americans was the variety of special purpose clothes for camping, fishing, boating, skiing, or just relaxing, to be found in the wardrobes of many average citizens. Travel and sightseeing became small industries in themselves. Visitors to the national parks tripled in number between 1950 and

1963, reaching a total of 102 million a year. Two million Americans found time and money to travel outside the United States (not counting Mexico and Canada) in 1963 as compared with less than half a million in 1947.

Although they enjoyed more free time than ever, Americans acted to increase their leisure time still further. A great variety of mechanical and electronic contrivances, such as power mowers and cultivators, and electric mixers, can openers, toothbrushes, and shoeshiners, were bought to lighten the chores of the home. Prepared foods, which in the 1930's had meant little more than vegetables in a can, now included a whole range of elaborately processed and packaged foods, from pastry and cake mixes, frozen fruit juices, and prebaked biscuits to frozen bread, fruits, and whole dinners. Even cocktails could be purchased already mixed. Although such prepared foods were more expensive, Americans preferred to exchange their increased income for still more free time.

There was also a deeper significance to the trend. The use of processed foods, along with the increased use of refrigerators, washing machines, dishwashers, and clothes driers, mirrored the steady movement of the wife out of the home and into the paid labor force. Even the drudgery and distasteful tasks connected with baby care were eliminated when possible. Diaper services and the sales of commercially prepared baby food boomed during the 1950's and 1960's.

Mass Culture. Literature, the arts, and culture in general, in the years after 1945, became increasingly oriented toward the many. In a society characterized by high productivity, expanding leisure time, and widely distributed wealth, mass culture has flourished. The highly productive economy brings to millions of people new opportunities for cultural and intellectual enrichment. Books, records, phonographs, tape recorders, televisions, and reproductions of art works are cheap enough to be within the financial reach of nearly everyone. Critics of American culture speak of a mass culture, in which the intellectual and artistic activities of the society cater to or are affected by the tastes and interests of the mass of people, rather than by those of the few highly educated or wealthy. During the 1950's some 7000 magazines turned out a total of 3.5 billion copies each year. More than 40 of these magazines reached an audience of a million or more. Individual television programs count their viewers in the millions, for more Americans have television sets than have telephones. With the same movies, books, magazines, and television and radio programs deluging millions of people daily, American popular culture has achieved a degree of intellectual homogeneity never dreamed of before. A man from a small town in Oregon meeting a man from upstate New York in St. Louis can discuss a television program or an issue of *Time,* which each had seen or read in his own town only a day before. Not without reason do critics of American society decry the homogenizing of the culture. The diversities of speech, dress, manner, and style of life that once set off the South and the West from the East are rapidly disappearing.

But if there is a dreary sameness to popular culture, there is also a new availability for serious artistic and intellectual productions. It is true that many millions of adult Americans spend their augmented income and free time reading comic books and cheap, sensational novels, but many others use their new wealth and leisure to read serious novels and scholarly nonfiction in the paperback editions that have flooded from the presses. Before 1939 the paperback book was unknown in the average American bookshop, much less in the drugstore or supermarket. That year Pocketbooks, Inc. issued its first 25 titles; in 1966 there were 38,500 titles in print in paperback.

A similar revolution in the availability of high culture has occurred in music, where serious music of excellent quality is readily available to the ordinary citizen in low-priced recordings. Many small communities now boasted of good symphony orchestras that could not have been supported in earlier decades. More tickets were being sold to concerts and operas throughout the country than to baseball games. At the same time millions of copies of effusions by crooners or by raucous quartets like "The Beatles" passed across the counters, too.

The explanation for such cultural diversity—some called it chaos—lay not with the vulgarity of editors and television producers, but with the exigencies of mass production. The great social benefit of mass-produced goods of any kind is their cheapness, but they remain cheap only as long as they can be sold by the millions. To dictate taste or even to stress quality unduly is to court consumer disapproval and commercial extinction. The safest course is to give a little of something for everybody. In a democratic society no other course is really possible. Even in those democratic countries, like Great Britain, in which the television is government owned and therefore not dependent upon commercial advertisers, educational and high-culture programs take up only a small fraction of the air time. Not surprisingly, incidentally, as the standard of living in European countries has improved, many of the same signs of mass culture that had appeared earlier in the United States began to show up. "The Beatles," after all, are British, and the western is almost as popular on European TV as it is on American.

Of all the artistic forms, the theater has been most obviously affected by the economics of an affluent society. High wages and high costs have meant that theatrical productions are very expensive to put on; in order to make sure that plays will attract a sufficient audience to meet these costs, producers steer away from controversial or experimental drama. As a result the musical comedy has become the staple item on Broadway. In protest, some producers have opened off-Broadway houses, with lower costs and simpler productions, where more experimental and serious plays can be put on. Nevertheless, the theater in the 1950's and 1960's, though heavily patronized by an affluent public, has lost the power and social bite with which O'Neill electrified it in the 1920's, and with which Odets excited it in the 1930's.

If in many ways mass culture tends to a sameness and a level of approach that are oppressive, it has at least not insisted upon the prudishness or opposition to controversy that had characterized earlier periods in American cultural history. The movies and, to a lesser extent, television, in the 1950's and 1960's have found it possible to discuss heretofore explosive questions like the race issue (*Pinky*), religious fanaticism (*Elmer Gantry*), and sexual deviation (*Tea and Sympathy*). In 1966 when Edward Albee's violent play *Who's Afraid of Virginia Woolf?* appeared as a movie, it marked a new high in freedom of expression in language and ideas, yet it suffered no bans. Even television in the early 1960's felt bold and free enough to discuss candidly and maturely heretofore forbidden issues such as abortion and contraception. Two novels long banned from the United States because of their alleged pornographic content, D. H. Lawrence's *Lady Chatterley's Lover* and Henry Miller's *Tropic of Cancer,* were both permitted to be published in 1959–1960. Perhaps the most shocking novel of artistic quality written in the 1950's, Vladimir Nabokov's best-selling *Lolita* (1959), which was later made into a movie, was subjected to no federal ban at all.

A Literature of Prosperity and Individuality. Two broad influences shaped the literature of post-1945 America. One was the boom, which removed from the center of the stage the social themes of the literature of the 1930's. Writers now felt free to indulge their interest in and concern for more individual matters. And in a society increasingly affluent, many artists felt a strong desire to examine critically individual character and values.

Furthermore, the unsettled state of the post-1945 world encouraged individualistic introspection and analysis. Until the death of Stalin in 1953, the threat of nuclear war in Europe was ever present; after that date the rising power of China in Asia offered new causes for anxiety. And following 1960 the increasing American involvement in the war in Vietnam exacerbated fears of war with China, possibly leading to World War III, and the nuclear destruction of the world. Affluence and anxiety became central themes. The irony of the 1950's and 1960's was that as nations became more powerful with their rockets, hydrogen bombs, and supersonic jets, individual men seemed to shrink in power. It was almost as if with each scientific gain in the ability to destroy, men felt less and less able to effect changes either in their own highly organized and complex society or in the world at large. Man may have been gaining ever greater mastery over nature, but individual men felt more helpless than ever.

This awareness of the alienation of man from himself and from the mass production society that he has created runs through much of the literature of the time. Indeed, alienation—the feeling that man is a stranger to himself—is a central theme in European as well as American culture. Existentialist philosophy, emphasizing the individual's total responsibility for his own acts, even in a universe viewed as absurd, became almost a fad in intellectual circles in

Europe and America soon after 1945. Albert Camus, the great French novelist of the period, became the high priest of cultural existentialism after the publication of *The Stranger* (1946) and *The Plague* (1948). Camus' novels were widely read on college campuses, and for a while in the 1950's, he was an intellectual hero of many American college students.

The most noticeable effect of the new prosperity on American writing was the abandonment of social concern and criticism. There was still, to be sure, rebellion against society in postwar novels, but the dissatisfaction was not directed against specific injustices as in Steinbeck's *Grapes of Wrath* or the proletarian writings of the 1930's. In fact, few of the novels of the 1950's and 1960's were problem novels, as Sinclair Lewis' *Main Street* or John Dos Passos' *U.S.A.* were, though the naturalism of these earlier works is still clearly in evidence. Norman Mailer's *The Naked and the Dead* (1948), one of the best of the novels about World War II, and Saul Bellow's *The Adventures of Augie March* (1953), for example, are cast in the naturalistic mold that had begun to be in evidence in the 1890's and which had shaped the fiction of the 1920's and 1930's. The focus of the naturalistic novel after the war, however, is not society itself, but the place of the individual within society. For that reason, some critics see the inspiration of these postwar writers as coming from the giants of the nineteenth century—Melville and Twain, for example—rather than from the more recent and strictly naturalistic writers like Dreiser, Dos Passos, and Sinclair Lewis.

Because many writers feel acutely the loss of identity in a highly organized, gigantic mass society that threatens to overwhelm them, they emphasize the individual. Critic Ihab Hassan, writing on the literature of the 1950's, characterizes the hero of the novels of the period as being both rebel and victim. The hero typically rebels against organization and society while at the same time he is also a victim of the state and technology. Simply because the protagonists (they are drawn on too small a scale to be called heroes) in these novels are aware of their slightness, the emphasis is placed upon their identity or their search for identity. The purpose in many of these novels is to find existential fulfillment—that is, freedom and self-definition. The important thing is action, for in doing something the individual defines himself by differentiating himself from the mass. Resistance against authority or rebellion is the surest way of asserting one's humanity. As Albert Camus summed it up, "I rebel—therefore we exist." Only in the assertion of self against society can a man's humanity be recognized. Another critic, R. W. B. Lewis, saw the principal novelists of the period as being united on "the subject of self—of acquiring a clear sense of the self or of charging on against fearful odds to an integral self already in being." Manifestations of this same philosophy will be seen later in this chapter in the action painting of Jackson Pollock and Willem de Kooning and in the commitment of many college students to civil rights action and protests against the Vietnam war.

The concern with individual identity can be observed in a number of the major novels of the period. In James Jones' *From Here to Eternity* (1951), Private Prewitt seeks to maintain his individuality in the prewar army. He likes the army life, even though he cannot express himself freely. Yet he will not meekly accept his place either. Hence he is both a rebel and a victim. He rebels against the organization itself, but he does not rebel against the system that created it, unlike what so often happened in the social novels of the 1930's. He stands as a symbol of antipower in an organization (the Army) and in a society, the powers of which are overwhelmingly stronger than that of any individual. Even in a relatively minor novel like Mary McCarthy's *The Group* (1963), the concern for individuality is clear. Although the novel ostensibly takes place in the socially concerned thirties, it is striking that the book itself deals with the struggles of eight young women for self-hood and individual identification.

William Styron's powerful *Lie Down in Darkness* (1951) depicts the deteriorating relationship between a girl and her father in the stifling atmosphere of a small southern town. Each is searching for his own identity as well as for an enduring relationship with the other. The failure of the search ends in suicide for one and chronic alcoholism for the other. Even more clearly manifest is the search for identity in two novels by Saul Bellow, one of the most significant writers of the postwar years. In *Henderson the Rain King* (1959) the question of identity is only lightly disguised by fantasy and in *Herzog* (1964) it is not hidden at all. Bernard Malamud's *A New Life* (1961), though comic in form, is clearly pursuing the theme of identity, both in the title and in the story of the inadequate college instructor who seeks his identity by changing his environment.

J. D. Salinger is one of the most popular and highly regarded writers of the period. His first book, *Catcher in the Rye* (1951) portrays the inner rebellion of the adolescent youth in his own language by chronicling the struggle of Holden Caulfield for identification and self-awareness. Salinger continues his exploration of the youthful search for self in his later work about college age youths, *Franny and Zooey* (1961).

An Exception. It is true that generally the period after 1945 witnessed the rapid decline of the socially conscious novel, but novels by Negro writers, it needs to be added, constitute an important exception to this generalization. In a way, Negro writers only came into their own after the Depression, and even then, as a people, Negroes were still dominated by the discrimination and poverty, which they experienced even in the prosperous fifties. Hence it is not surprising that there continues to be a deep social anger in the writings of James Baldwin and Ralph Ellison. (One of the reasons for the wider appreciation of Negro writers since the Depression was that prosperity brought forth a new and growing Negro book-reading public.) Probably the most highly regarded novel by a Negro is Ralph Ellison's *The Invisible Man*

(1952), which convincingly and relentlessly portrays the frustrations and dangers of being a black man in white America. Undoubtedly the best-known Negro writer of the 1950's and 1960's is James Baldwin, an erstwhile protégé of the outstanding Negro novelist of the 1930's, Richard Wright, and, like Wright, for a time an expatriate in Paris. In his first novel, *Go Tell It on the Mountain* (1953), Baldwin wrote about the great Negro migration from the South to the urban slums of the North, but the book's point of view is essentially devoid of social criticism. As the Negro revolution boiled up, however, Baldwin, in his nonfiction writings, notably *Notes of a Native Son* (1955), *Nobody Knows My Name* (1961), and *The Fire Next Time* (1963), was revealed as an unusually articulate and powerful spokesman for the militant Negro in his drive for equality. Not surprisingly, Baldwin's fiction became increasingly imbued with his social concerns. Thus his ambitious, but only moderately successful, novel *Another Country* (1962) is given over almost entirely to a frontal assault on both sexual and racial conventions.

Although as a Negro, Baldwin was especially aware of social hypocrisy, and ruthlessly exposed it in fiction and nonfiction alike, other writers of the period also put a premium upon honesty and ruthless candor. In 1962, for example, Baldwin wrote, "It is, alas, the truth that to be an American writer today means mounting an unending attack on all that Americans themselves hold sacred. . . . One must be willing, indeed, one must be anxious to locate, precisely, that American morality of which we boast." The obligation of the writer, Baldwin contended, and most of his fellow writers would echo his remarks, is "to tell as much of the truth as one can bear and then a little more." Edward Albee, in his play *Who's Afraid of Virginia Woolf?* (1962), mercilessly exposed the illusions that most people use to make life tolerable.

Youthful Restlessness.   The rejection of hypocrisy in favor of individual integrity, which characterized much of the writing of the period, was also very evident in the restlessness among many young people of college age. In the first decade after the war, it is true, the Cold War and the Great Fear impelled youth, inside and outside of colleges, to maintain a quiet that earned them the title "The Silent Generation." But with the moderating of the Cold War in the middle 1950's and the continuation of prosperity, an unwonted social awareness and unrest began to stir among people under twenty-five. One catalyst was undoubtedly the Negro upheaval in the South, which, with the Montgomery bus boycott in 1955, reached a new level of moral persuasiveness and national attention. With the sit-ins that began in 1960, led by young Negro college students, many white students for the first time became involved in the Negro revolution. Scores of them, for example, went to the South in the summers of 1963 and 1964 to work on voter registration and education projects among Negroes in the Black Belt, drawn there by the contrast between the national promise of equality for the Negro and his actual oppressed condition.

But the dissatisfaction of many young people with a society of plenty and gigantic institutions that dwarfed the individual found its most dramatic expression in the upheaval among the 21,000 students on the Berkeley campus of the University of California in 1963. Student resistance to the administration culminated in a demonstration during which the police were mobbed and the university's operations brought to a standstill for several days. When the immediate agitation died down, it seemed clear that behind the dramatic events lay a broadly based student dissatisfaction with being merely unrecognized cogs in a complex, overpowering educational machine. Students at Berkeley, and at other universities and colleges in which similar revolts and protests erupted, complained that they were little more than numbers in an IBM machine. They protested that professors did not even know their names, that the operation of the university was impersonal and mechanical, that courses were often completely irrelevant to their lives. Scornfully, young radicals on campus began to talk of the "Establishment" — which the civil rights movement called "the power structure" and an earlier generation had called "the powers that be." Whatever the name, the enemy was the same — the large, impersonal institutions of a highly organized society that seemed to have no place for the unusual, different, or individual. The radical social critic Paul Goodman gave voice to youth's disenchantment with the prosperous Establishment in his *Growing Up Absurd* (1960), which bitingly portrayed the estrangement of many youths from a society they had not made and did not like.

The alienation of many college students also manifested itself in their opposition to the United States involvement in Vietnam. During 1964 and 1965 scores of colleges and universities were the scene of marathon "teach-ins" designed to evoke opposition to the policy of the American government in Southeast Asia. Many of the protesters rejected the government's position for political reasons. But it was manifest from the arguments and rhetoric of most that their opposition stemmed primarily from what they considered the immorality of the administration's position. Sometimes the moral stance was essentially pacifistic, emphasizing the slaughter of the war; at other times it pointed to the failure of the United States to insist on elections in South Vietnam in 1956. Whatever the instance, however, the argument was essentially a moral one, stressing the need in international affairs for a morality by government which was similar to the morality that was expected in an individual. These youthful critics were carrying out to the last period the counsel of James Baldwin quoted earlier. Writers, too, found the war in Vietnam a rallying cause. Many of them were to be found supporting the protest meetings sponsored by professors and college students. One of the largest protest demonstrations (100,000 persons) was held in Washington in 1967. A march by some 50,000 of them on the Pentagon resulted in an ugly encounter between soldiers and demonstrators, in which 50 people were injured.

It would be misleading, however, to leave the impression that the opposition to American participation in the Vietnam war was representative of either student or national sentiment. Despite the growing unpopularity of the war in 1966–1967, most Americans supported the administration. But the large number of college students active in opposition to the war was without equal in the history of American youth. Although the protests stemmed from many sources, such as pacificism and objections to the purpose of the war or the ways of waging it, they also drew support from the feeling among many students that the war was a large, impersonal, overpowering operation that engulfed the individual and submerged his identity. Though the view of admittedly only a tiny minority, the protests were yet another straw in the wind, signifying the assertion of individuality against bigness. There were other, more significant straws as well, notably the decisions of the Supreme Court of the United States.

The Activist Supreme Court

The New Freedom of the Court. Prior to 1945 the Supreme Court was best known as the guardian of the established order. But in the 1950's it assumed a new position as the defender of individual rights, even when the accused were Communists. In the case of *Yates* v. *United States* (1957), for example, the Court seriously modified the decision in *Dennis* (1951), which had upheld the conviction of eleven Communist leaders for conspiring to advocate the overthrow of the government by force in violation of the Smith act (1940). In the *Dennis* decision Chief Justice Vinson had written that the mere existence of "a highly organized conspiracy" to overthrow the government gave the government the right to act. In the *Yates* decision in 1957, however, the Court found that a purely abstract belief in the advocacy of force, which the Smith act proscribed, was, in fact, protected by the First Amendment, and could not be the basis for a criminal proceeding. Moreover, the Court continued, "mere membership or holding of office in the Communist party" was not sufficient proof of specific intent to "incite" persons to overthrow the government.

That same year, in *Watkins* v. *United States,* which upheld a defendant who had admitted past Communist activities but had refused to disclose names of Communist associates, the Court, in effect, warned Congressional investigating committees that not every kind of question asked of a witness was constitutionally permissible. A citizen possessed the right to be fully informed of the purpose of the inquiry before he answered questions; Congress, the Court asserted, cannot "expose the private affairs of individuals without justification." The constitutional rights of citizens under Congressional investigation, the Court further declared, included freedom of speech, of political belief, and of association, and protection against self-incrimination. Boldly the Warren Court was defending the rights of the individual citizen against one of the most treasured powers of Congress: the right of the legislature to secure facts for the writing of legislation. In a decision in 1964 that declared unconstitutional an act of Congress denying passports to members of the American Communist party, the Court continued to protect the rights of all individuals, even if they happened to be Communists.

More important as a measure of the extent of the Court's defense of individual rights is the series of decisions in the 1960's protecting the rights of persons accused of crimes. In *Gideon* v. *Wainwright* (1962), the Court not only overturned a 20-year-old precedent, but took an important step in providing equal justice for the poor. Clarence Earl Gideon, a fifty-two-year-old, four-times-convicted ne'er-do-well, at his trial for burglary had asked for a court-appointed lawyer because he could not pay for one himself. The refusal of the trial court to provide a lawyer caused the Supreme Court to order a new trial on the ground that without a lawyer Gideon could not receive a fair hearing, as required by the Fourteenth Amendment. Interestingly enough, at his second trial, with a lawyer, Gideon was found innocent. After the Gideon decision, a number of states began to provide for public defenders or to appoint lawyers for all defendants too poor to hire their own.

The Court pushed its defense of the individual still further in a series of cases between 1963 and 1966, laying down the rule that the police must not in any way jeopardize the individual's right to the presumption of his innocence, even when in pursuit of a known criminal. The decisions promised to have long-range and profound effects upon police methods, since the most recent one, *Miranda* v. *Arizona* (1966), required that no suspect could be questioned by the police without having his lawyer present. Although many law enforcement officials and others vehemently disagreed with the Court's approach, arguing that it would seriously handicap the work of the police, it was clear that the Court was striving to protect individual rights even in a highly organized and complex society with a rising crime rate. Like those who probed to the realities of the Negro's social position rather than stopping merely with his formal rights, the Court was insisting that justice must be as nearly equal for the poor and the weak as for the well-to-do and the powerful. Like the protesting students and the novelists of the period, the Court sought to make real the morality to which most Americans too often gave mere lip service.

The Court continued its concern for individual freedom by overturning in 1965 a Connecticut statute prohibiting the sale of contraceptives. The decision of the Court, written by Justice William O. Douglas, rested its conclusion on "a right of privacy older than the Bill of Rights—older than our political parties, older than our school system." It was the right of married couples to be secure in their privacy to practice contraception without fear of intervention by the state. In 1967 the Court carried still further the protection of individual rights in marriage. In a case concerning a Virginia law prohibiting marriage between Negroes and whites, a unanimous Court held that "freedom to marry" cannot be restricted on grounds of race alone. The decision was broad enough to strike down the antimiscegenation laws of the 15 other states with restrictions on freedom of individual choice in marriage.

Recognition by the Court of a new basis for individual belief was forthcoming in the case of *U.S.* v. *Seeger* (1965). The Court held that Daniel Seeger could claim exemption from military service as a conscientious objector even though he was not a member of a recognized religious group advocating pacifism. Heretofore the Court had interpreted the law as exempting only those individuals who professed pacifism because of a belief in God. The Court interpreted Seeger's vaguer belief in moral principles as a religious conviction within the protection of the law.

The Court on the Side of the Cities.   If the Court's decisions reflected the prevailing concern for the individual in a mass society, its decisions on legislative apportionment reflected the dominance of the city in American life. Although population had been concentrating in cities for a generation, that social fact had not been mirrored in the distribution of seats in the state legislatures. The principal reason was that these legislatures were controlled by rural representatives, who refused to make any changes that would diminish their power. Protests by urban representatives were to no avail. Recognizing the impasse, the Supreme Court intervened in the case of *Baker* v. *Carr,* which is as significant in the urban history of the United States as *Brown* v. *Board of Education* is in social history. The *Baker* case derived from Tennessee's refusal to reapportion its legislative seats in accordance with changes in the distribution of population since 1900, when the last redistricting had been made. Until *Baker* the Court had held that such an inequity was "a political" question beyond its jurisdiction. But in the *Baker* case the Court ordered that markedly unequal districts constituted an inequity for which the courts could rightly be expected to provide a remedy.

The Court did not stop there, however. In an almost equally revolutionary decision, *Reynolds* v. *Sims* (1964), the Court applied to the upper houses of the state legislatures the same principle it had asserted for the lower houses, that is, that districts in a given state must be of roughly equal population. In pithy justification of his position, Chief Justice Warren wrote, "Legislators represent people, not trees or acres." The implication was that even if the voters wished to give special representation to rural regions, the Constitution, as interpreted by the Supreme Court, prevented them from doing so. Since the *Sims* decision destroyed the last bastion of the declining rural interests in the states, it aroused great opposition. But a Congressional attempt to pass a constitutional amendment which would overturn the decision of the Court failed to pass in August 1965. The urban majority was well represented in Congress, even if its power was not yet effective in the individual states. Yet already in a state like Georgia, where malapportionment had long given the rural interests predominance, the big city of Atlanta played a new and powerful role in the legislative and gubernatorial elections of 1963 and 1964. A similar flow of power to urban districts was discernible in a number of other states, as they began to reapportion their districts in accordance with the Supreme Court's principles. In view of the needs of the cities the more equitable representation had not come a moment too soon.

The Individual Artist in a Mass Society

Painting.   As in literature, social concerns became muted in painting as prosperity replaced depression. A few well-known, socially committed artists like Ben Shahn continued to concern themselves in the 1950's with social themes, representationally presented. As Shahn said in connection with his "Miners' Wives," he assumed, "that most people are interested in the hopes, fears, and dreams and tragedies of other people, for those are the things that life is made of." But Shahn's social interests, like his representational style, were clearly a minority approach in the 1950's and after. Abstractionism has held the center of the artistic stage. Simply because abstract works deny to themselves the traditional symbols of visual communication, they fitted into the new individualism and freedom of the 1950's. Painting became individually expressive rather than socially communicative.

Two of the best representatives of the new American school of abstract expressionism are Jackson Pollock and Willem de Kooning. Both men consciously broke with the social concerns of the 1930's, picking up where the great European abstractionists had left off when the war began. As De Kooning later said, "Jackson Pollock broke the ice." Even in the 1940's Pollock shunned representation in his paintings. This complete rejection of representational art admirably represents the dominant trend in modern art. For today, more than at any other period, art is a means of self-release and self-discovery, almost a substitute for religion. It is keyed to the individual artist, not to society. The absence of the traditional symbols of visual communication make it unavoidably individualistic. Each painting is a distinctly individual statement by the artist, removing any need even for titles and, in fact, there often are none. At a time when men fear being lost in a mass society, or being destroyed by nuclear war, the artistic accent is upon originality and uniqueness.

When Pollock talked about his method of painting, the emphasis upon individuality was clear in his deliberate departure from convention and in his desire to be *in* the painting, thereby making it fully his. "My painting does not come from the easel," he said. "I hardly ever stretch my canvas before painting. I prefer to tack the unstretched canvas to the hard wall or the floor. I need the resistance of hard surface. On the floor I am more at ease. I feel nearer, more a part of the painting, since this way I can walk around it, work from the four sides and literally be *in* the painting. . . .

"I continued to get further away from the usual painter's tools such as easel, palette, brushes, etc. I prefer sticks, trowels, knives, and dripping fluid paint or a heavy impasto [thickly laid paint] with sand, broken glass and other foreign matter added.

"When I am *in* my painting, I'm not aware of what I'm doing. It is only after a sort of 'get acquainted' period that I see what I have been about. I have no fears about making changes, destroying the image, etc., because the painting has a life of its own. I try to let it come through. It is only when I lose contact with the painting that the result is a mess. Otherwise there is pure harmony, and easy give and take and the painting comes out well.''

Typical of Pollock's many paintings is ''Blue Poles'' (1953), which makes only a vague concession to representation in the eight slanting lines (poles?) that dominate the canvas. Using silvery aluminum paint along with brilliant red, yellow, and orange as well as cool blue, the huge painting overwhelms the viewer. To some critics the purpose of this and other works of abstract expressionism is to convey the intensity of the artist's personal reaction to an affluent and complex society composed of big organizations, where he is constantly oppressed by the anxiety resulting from the ever present threat of nuclear destruction. Pollock conveys the force of his feeling largely through brilliant color; in De Kooning's works after 1954, the same feeling is often portrayed in bold and powerful strokes in broad slashes of paint. The assertion of individuality is also symbolized in the enormous size of the canvases. (''Blue Poles,'' for example, is 7 feet by 16 feet, or about the size of a wall of a large room.) The very size of the pictures fairly shouts for attention. In fact, the size of the giant canvases, often as large as a traditional mural, has become the hallmark of the new American abstract expressionism.

Willem de Kooning made his entrance into the front rank of international, as well as American, modern art with a remarkable series of six paintings, collectively entitled ''The Women.'' The story of the creation of ''Woman I'' (1953) exemplifies the extremely individualistic attitude of contemporary art. De Kooning worked for years on ''Woman I,'' changing it, scraping off pounds of paint, hurling more pounds upon the canvas with almost demonic energy, all the while anxiously scrutinizing it by day and by night. Then, in a fit of despair over getting it right, he hurled the paint-laden canvas into a corner, disgusted. Later, after reconsideration, he attacked the job once again, bringing it to completion and public view. The word ''attack'' is accurate, for the painting is a battleground of his own emotions; the result is the carnage left by the struggle to express himself fully. In the end the vaguely hateful woman who emerged on the canvas symbolizes art itself, still triumphant in the age of the machine. It is clear that the justification of the painting is De Kooning's own individual expression and nothing else. As he himself said, ''Painting is a way of living. . . . That is where the form of it lies.''

De Kooning's work fits into this age of alienation in still another fashion. His paintings depict what one critic has called ''no-environment''—that is, they are made up of anything at hand, a scrap of this, a piece of that. The resulting paintings are thus nothing and yet everything. They are all pieces of the real world, but jumbled together in such a way that no single place and yet every place is suggested. And perhaps that is how it feels to be an alienated man; he has no place and is therefore at home everywhere; he is no one and yet is everyone.

At one time during the long years of his early obscurity, De Kooning concluded that the artist has no place in the modern world, especially in

America. But the subsequent recognition accorded him as an important artist has belied that view. By realizing himself in his paintings, without compromise, without truckling to popular tastes, he has triumphed both as a person and as an artist. For him, as for modern art in general, this achievement signals the triumph of the individual.

The New Architecture. The prosperity of the postwar years had an immediate and direct effect upon architecture, for it made possible much new construction, thereby providing numerous opportunities for experimentation by new and enterprising architects. The direction taken by the experimenters would be dictated, it appeared at the outset, by the austerity of the dominant architectural style of the prewar years. In 1945 American architectural design was dominated by the plain, boxlike structures of the so-called international style which, in America, was best represented by the work of Ludwig Mies van der Rohe. The Lever Building (1952) and the United Nations Secretariat, both in New York City, well exemplified the Miesian style, though he did not design either of them. Perhaps the most striking example of his own efforts are the buildings on the campus of the Illinois Institute of Technology, completed in 1950. One architectural critic has called it "An astonishing exhibit of meticulous craftsmanship in brick, steel, and glass; the campus might almost pass for a series of factory buildings built by and for a crew of automatons."

As one of the consequences of the new prosperity, architects began to turn away from the plain, rectangular lines of the Miesian style, seeking instead variety, texture, and decoration. "The mid-fifties mark an interim attempt to explore a richer vocabulary of form for certain kinds of buildings," is the way one critic described the shift. In a sense, individuality was manifesting itself in architecture as it was in the painting of men like Pollock and De Kooning. Eero Saarinen in architecture, like Pollock in painting, was the bellwether of the change. Early in the 1950's Saarinen began to experiment with radical changes in roof design, which expressed themselves in the great whalelike structure of the Yale Hockey Rink and the massive wings that he used for the roof of the TWA Terminal at John F. Kennedy Airport in New York. Saarinen's distinctive innovations in roof design were paralleled by Edward Stone's characteristically personal use of decoration. Abandoning the slick, shining walls of the upward-thrusting Miesian style, Stone favored broad, horizontal, even low-lying structures, decorated with filigree work, tiles, hanging plants, concrete sun screens, and lily ponds. He designed the American embassy at New Delhi and the Legislative House of North Carolina, at Raleigh.

The work of the young Nisei, Minoru Yamasaki, has combined Saarinen's experimentation in roof design with Stone's interest in horizontal shape and decoration, while not completely abandoning the clean lines of the Miesian style. One of his earliest designs, though not his most typical, is the St. Louis Airport Terminal, with its three giant barrel vaults in the main waiting room, to provide, as he said, an appropriate entrance to a great city. He sprang into prominence as one of the rising new architects of the time with the light,

Library at Illinois Institute of Technology. *Photo: James Ballard*

Above left: Yale Hockey Rink. *Photo: Courtesy of Yale University. Above right:* Community Center. *Photo: Courtesy Wayne State University. Below:* American Embassy, New Delhi. *Photo: Edward Durell Stone, architect*

airy-looking, yet very sturdy Science Building at the Seattle World's Fair in 1962. He used high, graceful arches that were reminiscent of medieval Gothic, with curves and textured surfaces. He resolutely rejected Mies van der Rohe's celebrated dictum, so inimical to architectural decoration, "Less is more." Instead, after a visit to the Taj Mahal, he concluded that "the need for ornamentation and texture in our times was deeply impressed on me." Though severely criticized by the more orthodox Miesians, Yamasaki scathingly denounced "glass and porcelain-enamel rectangles," as he called the great glass sheathed towers that dominated many American skylines. Two of his most recent and typical buildings are the Community Center on the Wayne State University campus and the Woodrow Wilson School of Public Affairs at Princeton University.

The individualistic, attractive, and sensitive buildings of Yamasaki are only one example of the effect of an age of affluence on architecture. For it is affluence that permits such lavish use of glass, ornamentation, air conditioning, and special materials. It is in literature and art, as we have seen, however, that the age of anxiety can be most readily observed. It was anxiety that plunged men into introspection and individuality, but it was affluence that made it possible for them to express it.

Yet, as one looks over the 20 years since 1945, it would be a mistake to see anxiety and affluence as leading only to individualism and introspection. The responses of men to the world they live in are always varied. In this age of the threat of nuclear war, Americans have also become more sensitive about moral values and social responsibility than at any time in their history. The widespread dissatisfaction with the cruel and even brutal war in Vietnam, justified as it may be in the language of international politics, is only one measure of the heightened moral sensitivity of the time. The great crusade to right the historic injustice to the Negro in America is yet another instance of the new concern for morality and decency. The emphasis upon education for all and the seriousness with which young people approach their education in the 1960's also attest to the more constructive side of affluence and anxiety. Like man himself, the years since 1945 have been a mixture of gains, frustrations, and outright failures.

They have also been years of upheaval. How different are the sixties to an American who, in 1945, contemplated his country and the world. Who then would have predicted the Cold War, its shattering of American isolation and its propelling of the United States into heavier commitments around the world than any nation has ever assumed? Who would have foreseen the rise and threat of China, the rapid dissolution of once great colonial empires and the quickening of nationalism in Africa? What prophet would have foretold the conquest of space, the computer, the eradication of poliomyelitis or the Negro revolution? And who was there to warn Americans that man's power over nature would reach the ultimate in his ability to destroy civilization itself. But after two decades of affluence and anxiety it required no prophet for Americans to recognize that in the next 20 years the prospect was for even greater and more profound change; now the central question was man himself. Could he survive at all when his scientific achievements so easily outran his social wisdom?

SUGGESTED READING

The great social changes and innovations of the quarter century since 1945 have brought forth a myriad of books. One recent attempt to chart the domestic changes is John Brooks, *Great Leap: The Past 25 Years in America* (1966). Something of the variety inherent in American culture is discernible in the massive, but eminently readable, Max Lerner, *America As a Civilization* (1957). Less favorably disposed toward American society is C. Wright Mills, *The Power Elite** (1956), a book of social criticism, not always based on fact. Perhaps the most influential study of the changes in postwar America is David Riesman, *et al., The Lonely Crowd** (1950).

Already some important studies of the economy have appeared. An excellent introduction and analysis is Harold G. Vatter, *The United States Economy in the 1950's** (1963). Agricultural change is handled forthrightly and uncompromisingly in Edward Higbee, *Farms and Farmers in an Urban Age** (1963), which was written for the Twentieth Century Fund. An informative study of the technological revolution in agriculture is R. W. Hecht and E. G. McKibben, "Efficiency of Labor," in *Power to Produce, Yearbook of Agriculture* (1960). The position of organized labor is looked at pessimistically in Paul Jacobs, *The State of the Unions* (1963). A little more optimistic regarding the possibilities of growth in union membership and the organization of white-collar workers is Irving Bernstein, "The Growth of American Unions, 1945 – 1960," *Labor History,* II (Spring, 1961), 131 – 157.

The question of automation and the explosion of technology in general are central to an understanding of the economic history since World War II. Frederick Pollock, *Automation: A Study of Its Economic and Social Consequences* (1957), though written by a German, draws almost entirely, significantly enough, upon the United States experience. Charles Silberman, *Myths of Automation** (1966), written by a staff member of *Fortune* magazine, minimizes the exaggerated and unwarranted fears associated with automation. The more conventional attitude of concern is vigorously set forth in Ben B. Seligman, *Most Notorious Victory* (1966). Social philosopher Robert Theobald in *The Challenge of Abundance** (1961) points to the economic, social, and political changes that will be called for in a society capable of producing at high levels. Jacques Ellul, *The Technological Society** (1964) is a powerful study by a French political scientist calling attention to the irreversible dangers threatening a society increasingly dependent on technology and organization. Less apocalyptic, but still concerned with the actual functioning of the economy are A. A. Berle, *Power Without Property** (1959) and John K. Galbraith, *The New Industrial State* (1967).

*Available in a paperback edition.

Perhaps the two most influential books on the nature of poverty are J. K. Galbraith, *The Affluent Society** (1958), which emphasizes the hard-core character of poverty, and Michael Harrington, *The Other America* (1962), which calls for national action in behalf of the poor. Gabriel Kolko, *Wealth and Power in America** (revised edition, 1964) is a highly statistical and critical study of the distribution of wealth in the United States. A good survey of the problems confronting the cities is Mitchell Gordon, *Sick Cities** (1963); Jane Jacobs, *The Death and Life of Great American Cities** (1961) is a provocative answer to those who think that cities should be redesigned to resemble parks.

A fine study of the improvement in civil liberties gained through court decisions in the past quarter century is the authoritative Milton R. Konvitz, *Expanding Liberties: Freedom's Gains in Post-War America** (1966). Anthony Lewis, *Gideon's Trumpet** (1964) is an exciting account of one of the central civil liberties cases of the period by a knowing legal correspondent of *The New York Times*. The Supreme Court's decisions on legislative apportionment are authoritatively discussed in C. Herman Pritchett, "Equal Protection and the Urban Majority," *American Political Science Review*, LVIII (December 1964), 869–875.

Important books on the Negro revolution, in addition to those cited in the Suggested Readings for Chapter Three, are the following. Robert Penn Warren, *Who Speaks for the Negro?** (1965) is the work of a well-known southern writer who interviewed Negroes in the South to ascertain their goals and aspirations. E. U. Essien-Udom, *Black Nationalism** (1962) is a first-hand, scholarly study by a visiting Nigerian of the movement for separation among American Negroes. Malcolm Little, *The Autobiography of Malcolm X* (1965) is the story of the best known of the Negro leaders of the early 1960's who advocated separation as the solution to the Negro's plight in the United States. His book also offers insight into the life of poverty-stricken Negroes. John Griffin, *Black Like Me** (1961) is a remarkable story of what it is like to be a Negro written by a white man who temporarily posed as a Negro and lived in the South. Jerry Cohen and William S. Murphy, *Burn, Baby, Burn!** (1966) is a journalistic account of the great riot in the Negro ghetto of Los Angeles in 1964.

The popular culture of the United States has generally been appraised unfavorably. Dwight MacDonald, *Against the American Grain** (1962) is a collection of that caustic critic's views. Bernard Rosenberg and David M. White, editors, *Mass Culture: The Popular Arts in America** (1957) is similarly jaundiced. One of the best studies of the postwar novels is Ihab Hassan, *Radical Innocence: The Contemporary American Novel** (1961). Robert Bone, *The Negro Novel in America** (revised ed., 1965) deals with an important new development in American literature since the War. The developments in painting and sculpture are examined in an interesting manner in Sam Hunter, *Modern American Painting and Sculpture** (1959). Two informative studies of the controversial artist, Jackson Pollock, are Frank O'Hara, *Jackson Pollock* (1959) and Bryan Robertson, ed., *Jackson Pollock* (1960). The work of another major painter of these years is well discussed in Harriet Janis and Rudi Blesh, *De Kooning* (1960) and Thomas B. Hess, *Willem de Kooning* (1959).

INDEX